Anonymus

Agricultural statistics of Ireland 1893

Anonymus

Agricultural statistics of Ireland 1893

ISBN/EAN: 9783742810496

Manufactured in Europe, USA, Canada, Australia, Japa

Cover: Foto ©Suzi / pixelio.de

Manufactured and distributed by brebook publishing software
(www.brebook.com)

Anonymus

Agricultural statistics of Ireland 1893

AGRICULTURAL STATISTICS

OF

IRELAND,

WITH

DETAILED REPORT ON AGRICULTURE,

FOR THE YEAR

1893.

DIVISION OF LAND; ACREAGE UNDER CROPS; NUMBER AND SIZE OF HOLDINGS; NUMBER OF OCCUPIERS OF LAND; WOODS AND PLANTATIONS; RATES OF PRODUCE; AVERAGE PRICES OF AGRICULTURAL PRODUCE; NOXIOUS INSECTS; NUMBER, AGES, &c., OF LIVE STOCK; DISEASES OF CATTLE; EXPORTS AND IMPORTS OF LIVE STOCK; DAIRY INDUSTRIES; HONEY PRODUCED; NUMBER OF SCUTCHING MILLS; NUMBER OF CORN MILLS; SILOS AND ENSILAGE; FORESTRY OPERATIONS; AGRICULTURAL SCHOOLS; WAGES OF AGRICULTURAL LABOURERS; LOANS FOR LABOURERS' DWELLINGS; OBSERVATIONS ON THE PRODUCE OF THE CROPS BY SUPERINTENDENTS OF ENUMERATION; THE WEATHER.

Presented to both Houses of Parliament by Command of Her Majesty.

DUBLIN:

PRINTED FOR HER MAJESTY'S STATIONERY OFFICE,
BY ALEXANDER THOM & CO. (LIMITED).

And to be purchased, either directly or through any Bookseller, from
Hodges, Figgis, and Co. (Limited), 104, Grafton-street, Dublin; or
Eyre and Spottiswoode, East Harding-street, Fleet-street, E.C.; or
John Menzies and Co., 12, Hanover-street, Edinburgh, and 90, West Nile-street, Glasgow.

1894.

[C.—7531.] *Price 1s. 3d.*

CONTENTS.

CONTENTS.

SUMMARY TABLES.

Tillage; Meadow and Clover; &c.:

Live Stock:

APPENDIX.

AGRICULTURAL STATISTICS OF IRELAND,

FOR THE YEAR 1893.

TO HIS EXCELLENCY ROBERT OFFLEY ASHBURTON, BARON HOUGHTON,

&c., &c., &c.,

LORD LIEUTENANT-GENERAL AND GENERAL GOVERNOR OF IRELAND.

MAY IT PLEASE YOUR EXCELLENCY,

I have the honour to submit to your Excellency the following Report and detailed Tables concerning Agriculture in Ireland for the year 1893.

A review of the detailed Tables confirms the observations I made when presenting the General Abstracts in August, 1893, and the Produce Returns in January last.

DIVISION OF LAND, TILLAGE, &c.

The acreage under Crops, Grass, Fallow, Woods and Plantations, and Bog, Waste, Water, &c., in 1892 and 1893, was as follows:— Division of land, 1892 and 1893.

—	1892.	1893.	Increase or Decrease between 1892 and 1893.	
			Increase.	Decrease.
	Acres.	Acres.	Acres.	Acres.
Under Crops, including Meadow and Clover,	4,883,108	4,878,041	—	5,067
" Grass, or Pasture,	[illegible]	10,321,107	87,283	—
" Fallow,	34,096	31,676	—	2,420
" Woods and Plantations,	[illegible]	[illegible]	—	2,200
" Bog, Waste, Water, &c.,*	4,642,518	4,604,985	—	37,533
Total,†	[illegible]	[illegible]	—	—

The area under Crops in 1893, compared with 1892, shows a net decrease of 5,067 acres—there being a decrease of 29,730 acres in tillage, an increase of 6,194 acres in the area under hay on permanent pasture or grass not broken up in rotation, and an increase of 18,469 acres under hay on clover, sainfoin, and grasses under rotation. There is an increase of 87,283 acres under Grass, and a decrease of 2,420 acres of Fallow land; a decrease of 2,200 acres under Woods and Plantations; and a decrease of 37,533 acres under Bog, Waste, Water, &c.

Of the 4,604,985 acres given as under "Bog, Waste, Water, &c.," in 1893, 1,191,086 acres were enumerated as "Turf Bog," 455,178 acres as "Marsh," 2,041,365 acres as "Barren Mountain Land," and 917,356 acres as "Water, Roads, Fences, &c." Compared with 1892 "Bog and Marsh" appears to have decreased by 55,318 acres, while "Barren Mountain Land" increased by 17,937 acres.

* Including 120,[illegible] Acres under Water. † Exclusive of [illegible] acres under the larger rivers, lakes, and tideways.

Acreage under crops 1892 and 1893.

The area and proportionate extent of each crop in 1892 and 1893, with the increase or decrease in the latter year, are given in the following Table (I.), from which it appears that, compared with 1892, there was last year a net decrease of 5,415 acres, or 0·4 per cent. in cereals, as wheat decreased by 20,410 acres, barley by 6,402 acres, and beans and pease by 828 acres, while oats increased by 22,094 acres, and bere and rye by 131 acres.

In green crops there was a net decrease of 21,155 acres, or 1·8 per cent., potatoes having decreased by 16,290 acres, mangel wurzel and beet root by 4,320 acres, vetches and rape by 697 acres, and carrots, parsnips, and other green crops by 1,827 acres, while turnips increased by 2,677 acres, and cabbage by 32 acres.

Flax shows a decrease of 3,160 acres, or 4·5 per cent., and meadow and clover an increase of 24,663 acres, or 1·2 per cent.

In 1893, 30·5 acres in every 100 under crops were under cereals, 23·7 under green crops, 1·4 under flax, and 44·4 under meadow and clover.

Varieties of Potatoes.

POTATOES.—The tables relating to the potato crop point to several important conclusions. It will be observed (see Table 14, page 74) that of the 723,735 acres planted with potatoes, 79·1 per cent. belonged to one variety, namely, "Champions," showing no appreciable difference in the percentage of this variety as compared with the previous year. Of the total number of acres under potatoes 7·4 per cent. were under Flounders, 3·6 per cent. under Magnum Bonums, 2·2 per cent. under Irish Whites, 2·1 per cent. under Skerry Blues, 1·1 per cent. under White Rocks, 0·9 per cent. under Kemps, 0·7 per cent. under Scotch Downs, and 3·6 per cent. under all other varieties exclusive of Champions. It will be seen by a reference to Table 16 that not only was the Champion variety the one planted in greatest quantity, but that it was generally the most prolific in its yield.

Table 16 also points out the best potato-growing districts in Ireland, and the varieties which appear to thrive best in particular counties.

Extent under Crops.

Of the total extent under crops in 1893, 84·7 per cent., or over five-sixths, were under three crops—oats (25·5), potatoes (14·6), and meadow and clover (44·4).

(TABLE I.)—The Acreage under Crops in 1892 and 1893, and the Increase or Decrease in the latter year:—

Crops.	1892.	1893.	Increase in 1893.		Decrease in 1893.	
			Extent.	Per Centage.	Extent.	Per Centage.
	Acres.	Acres.	Acres.		Acres.	
Wheat,	75,408	54,998	—	—	20,410	27·1
Oats,	1,223,244	1,245,338	22,094	1·8	—	—
Barley,	175,178	168,776	—	—	6,402	3·7
Bere and Rye,	13,525	13,656	131	1·0	—	—
Beans and Pease,	4,433	3,605	—	—	828	1·9
TOTAL EXTENT under CEREAL CROPS,	1,464,788	1,458,373	—	—	5,415	0·4
Potatoes,	740,025	723,735	—	—	16,290	2·2
Turnips,	300,167	302,774	2,677	0·9	—	—
Mangel Wurzel and Beet Root,	51,354	47,034	—	—	4,320	8·4
Cabbage,	41,184	41,216	32	0·1	—	—
Vetches and Rape,	11,948	11,251	—	—	697	5·8
Carrots, Parsnips, and other Green Crops,	29,705	27,878	—	—	1,827	6·2
TOTAL EXTENT under GREEN CROPS,	1,174,843	1,153,708	—	—	21,155	1·8
Flax,	70,647	67,487	—	—	3,160	4·5
TOTAL under TILLAGE,	2,740,398	2,710,668	—	—	29,730	1·1
Meadow and Clover:—						
Clover, Sainfoin, and Grasses under Rotation,	628,335	643,335	15,460	3·0	—	—
Permanent Pasture or Grass not broken up in Rotation,	1,318,934	1,325,118	6,184	0·4	—	—
TOTAL EXTENT under CROPS,	4,583,108	4,578,041	—	—	5,067	0·1

The Proportionate Area under each Crop in 1892 and 1893 :—

Crops.	Proportion per cent. 1892.	Proportion per cent. 1893.	Crops.	Proportion per cent. 1892.	Proportion per cent. 1893.
Wheat, ...	1·3	1·1	Cabbage, . . .	0·6	0·9
Oats, ...	25·1	25·5	Vetches and Rape, . .	0·3	0·3
Barley, ...	3·9	3·5	Carrots, Parsnips, and other Green Crops, .	0·6	0·4
Bere and Rye, . .	0·3	0·4			
Beans and Pease, .	0·1	0·1			
TOTAL CEREAL CROPS, .	30·4	30·6	TOTAL GREEN CROPS, .	24·1	23·7
			Flax, ...	1·4	1·4
Potatoes, ...	15·3	14·6	Meadow and Clover, .	43·9	44·4
Turnips, ...	5·3	6·1			
Mangel Wurzel and Beet Root, . . .	1·1	1·0	TOTAL, . .	100·0	100·0

Tables showing the extent of land under crops in 1893 by Counties and Provinces, and by Poor Law Unions, and from 1884 to 1893 by Counties and Provinces, are given at pages 42, 46, and 54, respectively.

The extent of land under grass in 1893 (*exclusive of that under meadow and clover*) was 10,331,107 acres, or 30·8 in every 100 of the entire country, against 10,258,824 acres or 50·4 per cent. in 1892. The relative proportions under grass in each Province were —in Munster 54·3 per cent. in 1893, and 54·3 per cent. in 1892; Leinster 55·8 per cent. in 1893, and 55·0 per cent. in 1892; Connaught 49·7 per cent. in 1893, and 48·9 per cent. in 1892; and Ulster 43·5 per cent. in 1893, and 43·1 per cent. in 1892. Grazing Land, 1893 and 1892.

There appears to have been an increase of pasture land in 1893 in Leinster of 0·8 per cent. of the total area of the province, in Ulster of 0·4 per cent., and in Connaught of 0·8 per cent. There was no appreciable variation in Munster.

Of the counties—Clare, Limerick, Meath, Roscommon, and Westmeath had each 60 acres or upwards in every 100 of their entire area under grass in 1893; Fermanagh, Kildare, Kilkenny, Leitrim, Tipperary, and Wexford had above 55 and under 60 acres; Carlow, Cavan, Cork, Dublin, Longford, Monaghan, Queen's, Sligo, and Waterford had from 50 to 55 acres; Antrim, Armagh, Galway, Kerry, King's, Louth, Mayo, Tyrone, and Wicklow had above 40 and under 50 acres; and Donegal, Down, and Londonderry had over 30 and under 40 acres in every 100 acres under grass in 1893. Only 35·0 per cent. of the total area of Donegal was enumerated in 1893 as under grass. Meath shows the highest percentage, 69·8. Grazing Land in 1893.

The area of each County and Province, and the extent and percentage under grass in 1893, are given at page 38.

As already stated, the land under grass in 1893 formed a little more than half of the total area (20,333,344 statute acres) of the country. And it will be observed from the succeeding Table (Table II.) that the area under grass in 1893 was somewhat in excess of the average for the preceding ten years, and was also slightly in excess of the extent for the year 1892. Division of Land, 1884–1893.

In Cereal Crops a continuous decrease is shown for all the years covered by the Table, except 1885 and 1892, in each of which there was a slight increase as compared with the extent for the year immediately preceding. The average area under cereals in the ten years 1883–92 was 1,563,470 acres, and the extent in 1893 was 1,489,373 acres, being a decline of 74,097 acres or 4·7 per cent.

The average area under Green Crops in the ten years was 1,215,605 acres, and in 1893 the area was 1,153,708 acres, being 61,897 acres or 5·1 per cent. under the average. The extent under Green Crops in 1892 was 1,174,863 acres.

The area under Flax fell from 70,617 acres in 1892 to 67,487 acres in 1893, and the latter extent shows a decrease of 34,609 acres or 33·9 per cent. as compared with the average for the ten years 1883–92.

There were 2,142,810 acres under Meadow and Clover in 1892, and 2,167,473 acres in 1893; the average extent for the ten years 1883–92 was 2,087,254 acres, the yearly average varying from 1,931,784 acres in 1883 to 2,231,960 acres in 1888.

The extent of Fallow or uncropped arable land in 1893 was 21,875 acres, being a decline of 2,428 acres as compared with the preceding year, but 3,253 acres over the average extent for the ten years 1883–92.

The area returned under "Bog, Waste, Barren Mountain, Water, &c." in 1893 was 4,804,935 acres, being 57,593 acres below the corresponding extent for the preceding year, and 44,754 acres under the average for the ten years 1883–92.

Division of Land.

TABLE II.—The Extent of Land in Statute Acres, and the proportional Area, under Cereal Crops, Green Crops, Flax, Meadow and Clover, Grass, Woods and Plantations, Fallow, Bog, Waste, Water, &c., in each Year from 1883 to 1893, with averages for the ten years, 1883-92, also the Number of Holdings exceeding 1 acre.

Years.	Number of Holdings exceeding 1 Acre.	Cereal Crops.	Green Crops.	Flax.	Meadow and Clover.	Grass.	All Land in use for Agriculture.	Woods and Plantations.	Fallow.	Bog, Waste, Mountain, Roads, &c.	Total.*
		Extent of Land in Statute Acres under									
		Acres.	Acres.	Acres.	Acres.	Acres.	Acres.	Acres.	Acres.	Acres.	
1883, .	[illegible]	[illegible]	[illegible]	[illegible]	[illegible]	[illegible]	[illegible]	[illegible]	[illegible]	[illegible]	20,3[illegible] Statute Acres.
1884, .	[illegible]	[illegible]	[illegible]	[illegible]	[illegible]	[illegible]	[illegible]	[illegible]	[illegible]	[illegible]	
1885, .	[illegible]	[illegible]	[illegible]	[illegible]	[illegible]	[illegible]	[illegible]	[illegible]	[illegible]	[illegible]	
1886, .	[illegible]	[illegible]	[illegible]	[illegible]	[illegible]	[illegible]	[illegible]	[illegible]	[illegible]	[illegible]	
1887, .	[illegible]	[illegible]	[illegible]	[illegible]	[illegible]	[illegible]	[illegible]	[illegible]	[illegible]	[illegible]	
1888, .	[illegible]	[illegible]	[illegible]	[illegible]	[illegible]	[illegible]	[illegible]	[illegible]	[illegible]	[illegible]	
1889, .	[illegible]	[illegible]	[illegible]	[illegible]	[illegible]	[illegible]	[illegible]	[illegible]	[illegible]	[illegible]	
1890, .	[illegible]	[illegible]	[illegible]	[illegible]	[illegible]	[illegible]	[illegible]	[illegible]	[illegible]	[illegible]	
1891, .	[illegible]	[illegible]	[illegible]	[illegible]	[illegible]	[illegible]	[illegible]	[illegible]	[illegible]	[illegible]	
1892, .	[illegible]	[illegible]	[illegible]	[illegible]	[illegible]	[illegible]	[illegible]	[illegible]	[illegible]	[illegible]	
Average 1883-92,	[illegible]	[illegible]	[illegible]	[illegible]	[illegible]	[illegible]	[illegible]	[illegible]	[illegible]	[illegible]	
1893, .	[illegible]	[illegible]	[illegible]	[illegible]	[illegible]	[illegible]	[illegible]	[illegible]	[illegible]	[illegible]	
		Proportion per Cent. under									
Years.	—	Cereal Crops.	Green Crops.	Flax.	Meadow and Clover.	Grass.	All Land in use for Agriculture.	Woods and Plantations.	Fallow.	Bog, Waste, Mountain, Roads, &c.	Total.
1883, .	—	[illegible]	[illegible]	[illegible]	[illegible]	[illegible]	[illegible]	[illegible]	[illegible]	[illegible]	100·0
1884, .	—	[illegible]	[illegible]	[illegible]	[illegible]	[illegible]	[illegible]	[illegible]	[illegible]	[illegible]	
1885, .	—	[illegible]	[illegible]	[illegible]	[illegible]	[illegible]	[illegible]	[illegible]	[illegible]	[illegible]	
1886, .	—	[illegible]	[illegible]	[illegible]	[illegible]	[illegible]	[illegible]	[illegible]	[illegible]	[illegible]	
1887, .	—	[illegible]	[illegible]	[illegible]	[illegible]	[illegible]	[illegible]	[illegible]	[illegible]	[illegible]	
1888, .	—	[illegible]	[illegible]	[illegible]	[illegible]	[illegible]	[illegible]	[illegible]	[illegible]	[illegible]	
1889, .	—	[illegible]	[illegible]	[illegible]	[illegible]	[illegible]	[illegible]	[illegible]	[illegible]	[illegible]	
1890, .	—	[illegible]	[illegible]	[illegible]	[illegible]	[illegible]	[illegible]	[illegible]	[illegible]	[illegible]	
1891, .	—	[illegible]	[illegible]	[illegible]	[illegible]	[illegible]	[illegible]	[illegible]	[illegible]	[illegible]	
1892, .	—	[illegible]	[illegible]	[illegible]	[illegible]	[illegible]	[illegible]	[illegible]	[illegible]	[illegible]	
Average 1883-92,	—	7·7	[illegible]	[illegible]	[illegible]	[illegible]	[illegible]	[illegible]	[illegible]	[illegible]	
1893, .	—	[illegible]	[illegible]	[illegible]	[illegible]	[illegible]	[illegible]	[illegible]	[illegible]	[illegible]	

Turf Bog.

Tables showing the extent and the proportionate area under Crops, Grass, Fallow, Woods and Plantations, Turf Bog, Marsh, Barren Mountain Land, and Water, Roads, Fences, &c., in 1893, by counties and provinces, will be found at page 38. From these it appears that there are three counties with upwards of 100,000 acres under "Turf Bog," viz.:—Mayo, with 243,610 acres, or 18·5 per cent. of its entire area; Galway, 151,183 acres, or 10·3 per cent., and Donegal, 116,810 acres, or 9·8 per cent. The following counties contain the smallest areas under "Turf Bog" viz.:—Louth, 1,109 acres, or 0·5 per cent. of its entire area; Wexford, 1,239 acres, or 0·2 per cent.; Carlow, 1,315 acres, or 0·6 per cent.; Down, 2,321 acres, or 0·4 per cent.; and Kilkenny, 2,921 acres, or 0·6 per cent. There is no Turf Bog returned for Dublin. In the province of Connaught 521,395 acres, being 12·3 per cent. of its entire area, are returned as under "Turf Bog," including 67,340 acres, or 11·5 per cent. of the County of Roscommon, in addition to the large extent in Mayo and Galway as before mentioned.

Marsh.

In Galway, 69,074 acres, or 4·6 per cent. of the area of the county are under Marsh; in Cork, 64,725 acres, or 3·5 per cent.; in Mayo, 57,057 acres, or 4·4 per cent.; in Kerry, 46,258 acres, or 4·0 per cent., and in Donegal, 37,187 acres, or 3·1 per cent. The counties with the smallest area under "Marsh" are, Dublin with 174 acres, or 0·1 per cent. of its entire area; Monaghan, 1,425, or 0·4 per cent.; Louth, 1,574, or 0·8 per cent.; Meath, 2,687, or 0·5 per cent.; and Down, 2,845 acres, or 0·4 per cent.

* The total area adopted for 1891, 1892, and 1893, is 20,333,344 acres.

The following statement shows in a concise manner the extent of Meadow and Clover and Pasture respectively in Ireland during the 11 years, 1883–93, and the average extents for the 10 years, 1883–92:— Meadow and Clover and Pasture.

Years.	Meadow and Clover.	Pasture.	Total Grass Land.
	Acres.	Acres.	Acres.
1883,	1,931,784	10,192,447	12,124,231
1884,	1,962,487	10,346,876	12,309,363
1885,	2,034,768	10,621,180	12,6[illegible]
1886,	2,095,309	10,162,707	12,[illegible]
1887,	2,143,818	10,048,307	12,1[illegible]
1888,	2,231,960	9,925,087	12,157,077
1889,	2,187,523	9,998,297	12,185,819
1890,	2,073,634	10,318,536	12,[illegible]
1891,	2,059,529	10,398,654	12,[illegible]
1892,	2,142,810	10,[illegible]	12,[illegible]
Average, 1883–92,	2,081,304	10,167,078	12,[illegible]
1893,	2,167,413	10,321,167	12,488,580

It will be observed that the total area of grass lands has increased from 12,124,231 acres in 1883 to 12,488,580 acres in 1893, being an increase of 364,349 acres or 3·0 per cent. The cattle and sheep, however, have increased in a greater proportion than the area of pasture lands, so that these are more fully stocked than they were 11 years ago.

"Barren Mountain Land" covers an area of 100,000 acres and upwards in each of the following seven counties, viz.:—Donegal, 336,182 acres, or 27·4 per cent. of its entire area; Kerry, 288,978 acres, or 24·9 per cent.; Galway, 261,488 acres, or 17·4 per cent.; Cork, 256,768 acres, or 14·0 per cent.; Mayo, 199,660 acres, or 15·1 per cent.; Wicklow, 117,719 acres, or 23·6 per cent., and Tyrone 104,894 acres, or 13·4 per cent. Barren Mountain Land, 1893.

13·3 per cent., or 60,867 acres of Sligo, 8·7 per cent., or 70,570 acres of Tipperary, 14·6 per cent., or 75,074 acres of Londonderry, 17·3 per cent., or 81,018 acres of Waterford, and 11·0 per cent., or 84,666 acres of Clare are under "Barren Mountain Land." The counties containing the smallest areas under "Barren Mountain Land" are Westmeath with 657 acres, or 0·2 per cent. of its entire area; Meath, 760 acres, or 0·1 per cent.; Longford, 988 acres, or 0·4 per cent.; Monaghan, 1,452 acres, or 0·5 per cent.; and Kildare, 2,036 acres, or 0·5 per cent. Only 230,286 acres, or 4·6 per cent. of Leinster are returned as being under "Barren Mountain Land," while 904,330 acres, or 15·6 per cent. of Munster; 633,302 acres, or 11·3 per cent. of Ulster; and 363,117 acres or 13·3 per cent. of Connaught are so returned.*

917,868 acres (including 129,681 acres under water), or 4·5 per cent. of the entire area of the country, were returned in 1893 as "Water, Roads, Fences, &c." In the counties the highest percentage is 7·6 in Dublin, and the lowest 3·4 in Kildare and Wicklow. These figures do not include the acreage under the larger rivers, lakes, and tideways. See note (†), page 5. Water, Roads, Fences, &c., 1893.

A table showing the division of land by Poor Law Unions is given at pages 39 and 40.

* With reference to the question whether waste land is increasing or decreasing in Ireland, the following from Part I. of Dr. Grimshaw's "Facts and Figures about Ireland" (Hodges, Figgis & Co., Limited, Dublin, 1893), may be of interest: it shows that an enormous amount of waste land has been reclaimed during the past fifty years.

* DIVISION OF LAND IN 1841, '51, '61, '71, '81, AND 1891.

Division of Land.	1841.	1851.	1861.	1871.	1881.	1891.
	Statute Acres.	Statute Acres.	Statute Acres.	Statute Acres.	Statute Acres.	Statute Acres.
Under Crops (including Meadow and Clover),	[illegible]	[illegible]	[illegible]	[illegible]	[illegible]	[illegible]
Grass,		[illegible]	[illegible]	[illegible]	[illegible]	[illegible]
Woods and Plantations,	[illegible]	[illegible]	[illegible]	[illegible]	[illegible]	[illegible]
Barren Mountain Land,	[illegible]	[illegible]	[illegible]	[illegible]	[illegible]	[illegible]
Bog and Marsh,					[illegible]	[illegible]
Waste Land, &c.,					[illegible]	[illegible]
Total,			[illegible]			[illegible]†

NOTE.—The information for 1841 and 1851, respectively, has been obtained from the Census Reports for those years; and that for the subsequent periods from the Agricultural Statistics.

† The difference between the total area returned for 1841 and that given for the other years is owing to [illegible] in the County of [illegible].

The subject of the apparent increase of waste land in recent years is referred to at some length in the Agricultural Statistics Reports for 1884 and 1885.

NUMBER OF HOLDINGS AND NUMBER OF OCCUPIERS.

Number and size of holdings, 1892 and 1893.

According to the returns for 1893, the number of separate holdings was 571,442, being 1,788 more than in the previous year. The holdings which *decreased* in number were—those above 5 and "not exceeding 15 acres" by 100; those "above 15 and not exceeding 30 acres" by 172; those "above 50 and not exceeding 100 acres" by 44; and those "above 200 and not exceeding 500 acres" by 22. The holdings which increased in number were those not exceeding 1 acre by 1,696; "above 1 and not exceeding 5 acres" by 57; those "above 30 and not exceeding 50 acres" by 311; those "above 100 and not exceeding 200 acres" by 48; and those above 500 acres, by 20.

Size of Holdings.	Number in 1892.	Number in 1893.	Increase or Decrease in 1893.	
			Increase.	Decrease.
Not exceeding 1 Acre,	54,201	55,897	1,696	–
Above 1 and not exceeding 5 Acres,	62,8[illegible]	62,8[illegible]	57	–
" 5 " 15 "	160,025	159,925	–	100
" 15 " 30 "	135,614	135,438	–	177
" 30 " 50 "	78,532	78,843	311	–
" 50 " 100 "	54,673	54,629	–	44
" 100 " 200 "	22,920	22,968	43	–
" 200 " 500 "	8,792	8,770	–	22
Above 500 Acres,	1,645	1,665	20	–
Total,	569,654	571,442	1,788	–

A table showing the number of holdings, by classes, for each Poor Law Union, in 1893, will be found on pp. 39 and 40.

The number of separate holdings in each county and province, in 1892 and 1893, is given by classes in Table III. at page 11.

Number of separate Holdings and of Occupiers, 1892 and 1893.

As in many instances landholders occupy more than one farm, and as, in other cases, farms extend into two or more townlands—*the portion in each townland being enumerated and classified as a separate holding*—it has been considered desirable, with the view of ascertaining the number of *Occupiers*, and of classifying them according to the total extent of land held by each, to obtain a Return of the number of persons having more than one farm or holding. Each Enumerator is, therefore, required to furnish the name of every landholder residing in his district who has two or more farms, or whose farm extends into two or more townlands, together with the area of each portion, and the locality in which it is situated. The number of actual occupiers in 1893 thus arrived at is given in Table IV., page 12, by counties and provinces. On comparing the results in this Table with the figures given in Table III., it appears that in 1893 there were 571,442 holdings in the hands of 527,364 occupiers.

The number of separate holdings and the number of occupiers in each Province in 1892 and 1893 respectively were:—

Provinces.	Number of Separate Holdings.		Number of Occupiers.	
	1892.	1893.	1892.	1893.
Leinster,	131,781	132,019	108,678	109,216
Munster,	1[illegible]	1[illegible]	114,306	115,180
Ulster,	200,[illegible]	198,810	188,020	187,416
Connaught,	121,777	121,584	114,314	111,489
Total,	569,654	571,442	525,372	527,364

The number of occupiers of land returned in 1893 was 527,364, being 2,089 more than in the previous year. Excluding those holding land "not exceeding one acre," who are to a great extent merely occupiers of small gardens, they numbered 472,918 in 1893, or 398 more than in 1892. There was a increase in Leinster of 72—from 91,926 in 1892 to 91,998 in 1893; in Connaught of 43—from 108,753 in 1892 to 108,796 in 1893; and in Munster of 309—from 99,617 in 1892 to 99,926 in 1893; while in Ulster there was a decrease of 26—from 171,524 in 1892 to 171,498 in 1893. The increase in occupiers holding land above 1 and not exceeding 50 acres was 379, and the number holding land exceeding that acreage increased by 19.

Table III.—The number of Holdings, by classes, for each County and Province, in 1893 and 1892, and the increase or decrease in the latter year:—

Number and size of holdings, 1893 and 1892.

Counties.	Year	Not exceeding 1 Acre.	Above 1 and not exceeding 5 Acres.	Above 5 and not exceeding 15 Acres.	Above 15 and not exceeding 30 Acres.	Above 30 and not exceeding 50 Acres.	Above 50 and not exceeding 100 Acres.	Above 100 and not exceeding 200 Acres.	Above 200 and not exceeding 500 Acres.	Above 500 Acres.	Total.
Antrim,	[illegible]	[illegible]	[illegible]	[illegible]	[illegible]	[illegible]	[illegible]	[illegible]	[illegible]	[illegible]	[illegible]
Armagh,	[illegible]	[illegible]	[illegible]	[illegible]	[illegible]	[illegible]	[illegible]	[illegible]	[illegible]	[illegible]	[illegible]
Carlow,	[illegible]	[illegible]	[illegible]	[illegible]	[illegible]	[illegible]	[illegible]	[illegible]	[illegible]	[illegible]	[illegible]
Cavan,	[illegible]	[illegible]	[illegible]	[illegible]	[illegible]	[illegible]	[illegible]	[illegible]	[illegible]	[illegible]	[illegible]
Clare,	[illegible]	[illegible]	[illegible]	[illegible]	[illegible]	[illegible]	[illegible]	[illegible]	[illegible]	[illegible]	[illegible]
Cork,	[illegible]	[illegible]	[illegible]	[illegible]	[illegible]	[illegible]	[illegible]	[illegible]	[illegible]	[illegible]	[illegible]
Donegal,	[illegible]	[illegible]	[illegible]	[illegible]	[illegible]	[illegible]	[illegible]	[illegible]	[illegible]	[illegible]	[illegible]
Down,	[illegible]	[illegible]	[illegible]	[illegible]	[illegible]	[illegible]	[illegible]	[illegible]	[illegible]	[illegible]	[illegible]
Dublin,	[illegible]	[illegible]	[illegible]	[illegible]	[illegible]	[illegible]	[illegible]	[illegible]	[illegible]	[illegible]	[illegible]
Fermanagh,	[illegible]	[illegible]	[illegible]	[illegible]	[illegible]	[illegible]	[illegible]	[illegible]	[illegible]	[illegible]	[illegible]
Galway,	[illegible]	[illegible]	[illegible]	[illegible]	[illegible]	[illegible]	[illegible]	[illegible]	[illegible]	[illegible]	[illegible]
Kerry,	[illegible]	[illegible]	[illegible]	[illegible]	[illegible]	[illegible]	[illegible]	[illegible]	[illegible]	[illegible]	[illegible]
Kildare,	[illegible]	[illegible]	[illegible]	[illegible]	[illegible]	[illegible]	[illegible]	[illegible]	[illegible]	[illegible]	[illegible]
Kilkenny,	[illegible]	[illegible]	[illegible]	[illegible]	[illegible]	[illegible]	[illegible]	[illegible]	[illegible]	[illegible]	[illegible]
King's,	[illegible]	[illegible]	[illegible]	[illegible]	[illegible]	[illegible]	[illegible]	[illegible]	[illegible]	[illegible]	[illegible]
Leitrim,	[illegible]	[illegible]	[illegible]	[illegible]	[illegible]	[illegible]	[illegible]	[illegible]	[illegible]	[illegible]	[illegible]
Limerick,	[illegible]	[illegible]	[illegible]	[illegible]	[illegible]	[illegible]	[illegible]	[illegible]	[illegible]	[illegible]	[illegible]
Londonderry,	[illegible]	[illegible]	[illegible]	[illegible]	[illegible]	[illegible]	[illegible]	[illegible]	[illegible]	[illegible]	[illegible]
Longford,	[illegible]	[illegible]	[illegible]	[illegible]	[illegible]	[illegible]	[illegible]	[illegible]	[illegible]	[illegible]	[illegible]
Louth & Drogheda Co. of Town,	[illegible]	[illegible]	[illegible]	[illegible]	[illegible]	[illegible]	[illegible]	[illegible]	[illegible]	[illegible]	[illegible]
Mayo,	[illegible]	[illegible]	[illegible]	[illegible]	[illegible]	[illegible]	[illegible]	[illegible]	[illegible]	[illegible]	[illegible]
Meath,	[illegible]	[illegible]	[illegible]	[illegible]	[illegible]	[illegible]	[illegible]	[illegible]	[illegible]	[illegible]	[illegible]
Monaghan,	[illegible]	[illegible]	[illegible]	[illegible]	[illegible]	[illegible]	[illegible]	[illegible]	[illegible]	[illegible]	[illegible]
Queen's,	[illegible]	[illegible]	[illegible]	[illegible]	[illegible]	[illegible]	[illegible]	[illegible]	[illegible]	[illegible]	[illegible]
Roscommon,	[illegible]	[illegible]	[illegible]	[illegible]	[illegible]	[illegible]	[illegible]	[illegible]	[illegible]	[illegible]	[illegible]
Sligo,	[illegible]	[illegible]	[illegible]	[illegible]	[illegible]	[illegible]	[illegible]	[illegible]	[illegible]	[illegible]	[illegible]
Tipperary,	[illegible]	[illegible]	[illegible]	[illegible]	[illegible]	[illegible]	[illegible]	[illegible]	[illegible]	[illegible]	[illegible]
Tyrone,	[illegible]	[illegible]	[illegible]	[illegible]	[illegible]	[illegible]	[illegible]	[illegible]	[illegible]	[illegible]	[illegible]
Waterford,	[illegible]	[illegible]	[illegible]	[illegible]	[illegible]	[illegible]	[illegible]	[illegible]	[illegible]	[illegible]	[illegible]
Westmeath,	[illegible]	[illegible]	[illegible]	[illegible]	[illegible]	[illegible]	[illegible]	[illegible]	[illegible]	[illegible]	[illegible]
Wexford,	[illegible]	[illegible]	[illegible]	[illegible]	[illegible]	[illegible]	[illegible]	[illegible]	[illegible]	[illegible]	[illegible]
Wicklow,	[illegible]	[illegible]	[illegible]	[illegible]	[illegible]	[illegible]	[illegible]	[illegible]	[illegible]	[illegible]	[illegible]
SUMMARY OF IRELAND.											
Provinces.											
Leinster,	[illegible]	[illegible]	[illegible]	[illegible]	[illegible]	[illegible]	[illegible]	[illegible]	[illegible]	[illegible]	[illegible]
Munster,	[illegible]	[illegible]	[illegible]	[illegible]	[illegible]	[illegible]	[illegible]	[illegible]	[illegible]	[illegible]	[illegible]
Ulster,	[illegible]	[illegible]	[illegible]	[illegible]	[illegible]	[illegible]	[illegible]	[illegible]	[illegible]	[illegible]	[illegible]
Connaught,	[illegible]	[illegible]	[illegible]	[illegible]	[illegible]	[illegible]	[illegible]	[illegible]	[illegible]	[illegible]	[illegible]
Total of Ireland,	[illegible]	[illegible]	[illegible]	[illegible]	[illegible]	[illegible]	[illegible]	[illegible]	[illegible]	[illegible]	[illegible]
Increase or Decrease in 1893,		Increase, [illegible]	Increase, [illegible]	Decrease, [illegible]	Decrease, [illegible]	Increase, [illegible]	Decrease, [illegible]	Increase, [illegible]	Decrease, [illegible]	Increase, [illegible]	Increase, [illegible]

[illegible]

TABLE IV.—Return of the number of Occupiers resident in each County and Province in 1893, classified according to the *total extent* of land held, without reference to the Townland, Poor Law Union, County, or Province in which the portions of land are situated:—

COUNTIES.	Number of Occupiers holding Land									
	Not exceeding 1 acre.	Above 1 and not exceeding 5 acres.	Above 5 and not exceeding 15 Acres.	Above 15 and not exceeding 30 Acres.	Above 30 and not exceeding 50 Acres.	Above 50 and not exceeding 100 Acres.	Above 100 and not exceeding 200 Acres.	Above 200 and not exceeding 500 Acres.	Above 500 Acres.	Total.
Antrim,	[illegible]	[illegible]	[illegible]	[illegible]	[illegible]	[illegible]	[illegible]	[illegible]	[illegible]	[illegible]
Armagh,	[illegible]	[illegible]	[illegible]	[illegible]	[illegible]	[illegible]	[illegible]	[illegible]	[illegible]	[illegible]
Carlow,	[illegible]	[illegible]	[illegible]	[illegible]	[illegible]	[illegible]	[illegible]	[illegible]	[illegible]	[illegible]
Cavan,	[illegible]	[illegible]	[illegible]	[illegible]	[illegible]	[illegible]	[illegible]	[illegible]	[illegible]	[illegible]
Clare,	[illegible]	[illegible]	[illegible]	[illegible]	[illegible]	[illegible]	[illegible]	[illegible]	[illegible]	[illegible]
Cork,	[illegible]	[illegible]	[illegible]	[illegible]	[illegible]	[illegible]	[illegible]	[illegible]	[illegible]	[illegible]
Donegal,	[illegible]	[illegible]	[illegible]	[illegible]	[illegible]	[illegible]	[illegible]	[illegible]	[illegible]	[illegible]
Down,	[illegible]	[illegible]	[illegible]	[illegible]	[illegible]	[illegible]	[illegible]	[illegible]	[illegible]	[illegible]
Dublin,	[illegible]	[illegible]	[illegible]	[illegible]	[illegible]	[illegible]	[illegible]	[illegible]	[illegible]	[illegible]
Fermanagh,	[illegible]	[illegible]	[illegible]	[illegible]	[illegible]	[illegible]	[illegible]	[illegible]	[illegible]	[illegible]
Galway,	[illegible]	[illegible]	[illegible]	[illegible]	[illegible]	[illegible]	[illegible]	[illegible]	[illegible]	[illegible]
Kerry,	[illegible]	[illegible]	[illegible]	[illegible]	[illegible]	[illegible]	[illegible]	[illegible]	[illegible]	[illegible]
Kildare,	[illegible]	[illegible]	[illegible]	[illegible]	[illegible]	[illegible]	[illegible]	[illegible]	[illegible]	[illegible]
Kilkenny,	[illegible]	[illegible]	[illegible]	[illegible]	[illegible]	[illegible]	[illegible]	[illegible]	[illegible]	[illegible]
King's,	[illegible]	[illegible]	[illegible]	[illegible]	[illegible]	[illegible]	[illegible]	[illegible]	[illegible]	[illegible]
Leitrim,	[illegible]	[illegible]	[illegible]	[illegible]	[illegible]	[illegible]	[illegible]	[illegible]	[illegible]	[illegible]
Limerick,	[illegible]	[illegible]	[illegible]	[illegible]	[illegible]	[illegible]	[illegible]	[illegible]	[illegible]	[illegible]
Londonderry,	[illegible]	[illegible]	[illegible]	[illegible]	[illegible]	[illegible]	[illegible]	[illegible]	[illegible]	[illegible]
Longford,	[illegible]	[illegible]	[illegible]	[illegible]	[illegible]	[illegible]	[illegible]	[illegible]	[illegible]	[illegible]
Louth and Drogheda, Co. of Town,	[illegible]	[illegible]	[illegible]	[illegible]	[illegible]	[illegible]	[illegible]	[illegible]	[illegible]	[illegible]
Mayo,	[illegible]	[illegible]	[illegible]	[illegible]	[illegible]	[illegible]	[illegible]	[illegible]	[illegible]	[illegible]
Meath,	[illegible]	[illegible]	[illegible]	[illegible]	[illegible]	[illegible]	[illegible]	[illegible]	[illegible]	[illegible]
Monaghan,	[illegible]	[illegible]	[illegible]	[illegible]	[illegible]	[illegible]	[illegible]	[illegible]	[illegible]	[illegible]
Queen's,	[illegible]	[illegible]	[illegible]	[illegible]	[illegible]	[illegible]	[illegible]	[illegible]	[illegible]	[illegible]
Roscommon,	[illegible]	[illegible]	[illegible]	[illegible]	[illegible]	[illegible]	[illegible]	[illegible]	[illegible]	[illegible]
Sligo,	[illegible]	[illegible]	[illegible]	[illegible]	[illegible]	[illegible]	[illegible]	[illegible]	[illegible]	[illegible]
Tipperary,	[illegible]	[illegible]	[illegible]	[illegible]	[illegible]	[illegible]	[illegible]	[illegible]	[illegible]	[illegible]
Tyrone,	[illegible]	[illegible]	[illegible]	[illegible]	[illegible]	[illegible]	[illegible]	[illegible]	[illegible]	[illegible]
Waterford,	[illegible]	[illegible]	[illegible]	[illegible]	[illegible]	[illegible]	[illegible]	[illegible]	[illegible]	[illegible]
Westmeath,	[illegible]	[illegible]	[illegible]	[illegible]	[illegible]	[illegible]	[illegible]	[illegible]	[illegible]	[illegible]
Wexford,	[illegible]	[illegible]	[illegible]	[illegible]	[illegible]	[illegible]	[illegible]	[illegible]	[illegible]	[illegible]
Wicklow,	[illegible]	[illegible]	[illegible]	[illegible]	[illegible]	[illegible]	[illegible]	[illegible]	[illegible]	[illegible]
SUMMARY OF IRELAND.										
Provinces.										
Leinster,	[illegible]	[illegible]	[illegible]	[illegible]	[illegible]	[illegible]	[illegible]	[illegible]	[illegible]	[illegible]
Munster,	[illegible]	[illegible]	[illegible]	[illegible]	[illegible]	[illegible]	[illegible]	[illegible]	[illegible]	[illegible]
Ulster,	[illegible]	[illegible]	[illegible]	[illegible]	[illegible]	[illegible]	[illegible]	[illegible]	[illegible]	[illegible]
Connaught,	[illegible]	[illegible]	[illegible]	[illegible]	[illegible]	[illegible]	[illegible]	[illegible]	[illegible]	[illegible]
Total of Ireland,	[illegible]	[illegible]	[illegible]	[illegible]	[illegible]	[illegible]	[illegible]	[illegible]	[illegible]	[illegible]

Number of Occupiers of Land, 1887 to 1893.

The following statement shows the number of occupiers of land in each year from 1887 to 1893, by Provinces:—

PROVINCES.	Number of Occupiers in the Year.						
	1887.	1888.	1889.	1890.	1891.	1892.	1893.
Leinster,	106,848	105,384	103,731	103,631	103,468	103,573	103,915
Munster,	111,712	111,198	112,334	113,849	114,396	114,806	115,159
Ulster,	187,884	187,646	189,618	188,540	188,185	188,030	187,515
Connaught,	116,392	114,422	114,969	113,661	111,867	114,274	114,880
IRELAND,	522,151	521,656	525,152	524,310	526,679	524,275	527,664

Increase or decrease in Holdings by Classes between 1841 and 1893.

As will be seen from Table V. on the opposite page, the number of holdings "above 1 and not exceeding 5 acres" diminished greatly between 1841 and 1893. In Leinster the decrease was 84·3 per cent.; in Munster 80·7; in Ulster 79·3; in Connaught 67·2; and in all Ireland 75·7 per cent.

In the same period holdings "above 5 and not exceeding 15 acres" also diminished in number; the decrease in all Ireland was 35·8 per cent.; it was—in Leinster 44·2 per cent.; in Munster 65·9; and in Ulster 35·3; while in Connaught these holdings increased 2·6 per cent.

Holdings "above 15 and not exceeding 30 acres" increased 7·1 per cent. in Leinster; 113·3 per cent. in Ulster; and 470·6 per cent. in Connaught: they decreased 19·1 per cent. in Munster. In all Ireland they increased 63·2 per cent.

Holdings "above 30 acres" increased 116·3 per cent. in Leinster; 341·5 in Munster; 355·0 in Ulster; 433·6 in Connaught; and 235·3 per cent. in all Ireland.

The total number of holdings "above 1 acre" decreased between 1841 and 1893 by 22·2 per cent. in Leinster; 31·9 per cent. in Munster; 22·0 in Ulster; and 29·6 in Connaught.

The total number of holdings in Ireland "above 1 acre" was 691,202 in 1841; 570,338 in 1851; 568,484 in 1861; 544,143 in 1871; 528,743 in 1881; 517,012 in 1891; 515,463 in 1892, and 515,545 in 1893, showing a decrease of 175,657 or 25·4 per cent. in the period between 1841 and 1893.

Table V.—The number of Holdings above 1 acre in each Province in 1841, 1851, 1861, 1871, 1881, 1891, and 1893, according to the classification used by the Census Commissioners of 1841 (in which "above 30 acres" was the maximum); the increase or decrease in the numbers in each class, and the difference per cent., between 1841 and 1893:— Number of Holdings in 1841, 1851, 1861, 1871, 1881, 1891, and 1893.

Size or Extent.		Leinster.	Munster.	Ulster.	Connaught.	Total.
		Number.	Number.	Number.	Number.	Number.
Above 1 and not exceeding 5 Acres,	1841,	50,110	57,827	101,918	100,254	310,436
	1851,	25,711	14,980	27,709	18,663	88,083
	1861,	22,845	13,738	28,458	19,157	86,489
	1871,	21,189	10,292	24,939	16,666	74,089
	1881,	18,604	11,096	21,771	16,290	67,671
	1891,	18,034	11,307	21,287	18,224	66,664
	1893,	17,766	11,128	21,185	12,830	62,892
		Decrease.	Decrease.	Decrease.	Decrease.	Decrease.
Decrease in number between 1841 and 1893,		32,874	46,719	81,097	87,454	247,534
Rate per cent.,		64·5	80·7	79·8	87·2	79·7
Above 5 and not exceeding 15 Acres,	1841,	46,032	61,753	99,826	46,407	253,799
	1851,	33,018	34,383	83,170	49,985	191,854
	1861,	29,513	31,039	82,083	60,434	183,031
	1871,	27,776	28,409	73,047	48,094	171,383
	1881,	26,045	19,767	68,383	49,853	164,048
	1891,	26,351	19,844	64,760	46,764	158,982
	1893,	25,711	19,334	64,686	46,884	146,529
		Decrease.	Decrease.	Decrease.	Increase.	Decrease.
Increase or Decrease in number between 1841 and 1893,		20,321	42,419	35,320	1,181	93,276
Rate per cent.,		44·2	68·9	35·6	2·5	36·5
Above 15 and not exceeding 30 Acres,	1841,	20,638	27,411	25,919	5,596	79,342
	1851,	24,096	38,856	37,651	25,799	141,311
	1861,	24,785	36,806	47,860	32,880	141,331
	1871,	23,648	35,674	48,978	32,701	138,647
	1881,	22,833	30,260	48,537	33,310	134,785
	1891,	22,958	34,348	53,855	33,690	143,947
	1893,	22,161	34,565	53,733	33,231	133,443
		Increase.	Increase.	Increase.	Increase.	Increase.
Increase or Decrease in number between 1841 and 1893,		1,473	8,945	28,864	27,497	64,760
Rate per cent.,		7·1	19·?	111·6	470·8	69·?
Above 30 Acres,	1841,	17,893	12,656	9,633	4,988	48,623
	1851,	28,026	43,074	17,613	20,100	108,990
	1861,	29,294	43,033	33,464	22,169	127,922
	1871,	30,051	46,455	41,031	23,073	140,383
	1881,	30,475	54,161	42,110	21,708	149,534
	1891,	39,163	56,518	44,057	23,597	162,940
	1893,	39,176	55,814	43,863	23,877	163,836
		Increase.	Increase.	Increase.	Increase.	Increase.
Increase in number between 1841 and 1893,		21,333	43,159	34,273	18,919	114,671
Rate per cent.,		116·3	341·5	355·0	433·6	235·3
Total above 1 Acre,	1841,	134,780	162,968	236,694	155,042	691,202
	1851,	109,671	120,494	210,849	114,624	570,338
	1861,	114,972	114,823	207,435	122,348	568,484
	1871,	111,676	114,763	193,073	121,563	544,143
	1881,	104,930	118,014	188,770	118,709	528,743
	1891,	105,311	111,647	183,939	116,626	517,012
	1893,	104,834	111,631	183,236	116,092	515,545
		Decrease.	Decrease.	Decrease.	Decrease.	Decrease.
Decrease in number between 1841 and 1893,		29,946	52,336	53,458	38,950	175,657
Rate per cent.,		22·2	31·9	22·6	25·6	25·4

WOODS AND PLANTATIONS.

Woods and Plantations.

In addition to the information regarding the total area under Woods and Plantations, returns were obtained in 1893, showing the proportion of the area entered under this heading occupied by each of the various kinds of trees. From these Returns it appears that of the total area (307,386 statute acres) under Woods and Plantations last year, 49,887 acres were under Larch, 36,185 under Fir, 15,411 under Spruce, 9,385 under Pine, 29,836 under Oak, 9,205 under Ash, 11,308 under Beech, 5,188 under Sycamore, 9,537 under Elm, 4,010 under Other Trees, and 140,381 were returned as under Mixed Trees. The area under Woods and Plantations in Leinster was 94,709 acres, in Munster 102,283 acres, in Ulster 56,098 acres, and in Connaught 52,806 acres.

PRODUCE OF THE CROPS.

Mode of collecting the Returns of Produce.

The Tables relating to the produce of the crops have been carefully compiled from information obtained by members of the Royal Irish Constabulary and of the Metropolitan Police from practical farmers and other persons qualified to form an opinion as to the yield in that *Poor Law Electoral Division* for which they were requested to afford the information. The names and residences of the parties so co-operating and assisting are stated by the Enumerators on the Returns.

Notes of Superintendents of Enumeration.

On pp. 78 to 88 will be found the Observations of the District Inspectors of the Royal Irish Constabulary and of the Sergeants of the Metropolitan Police, who acted as Superintendents of Enumeration, in reply to a circular requesting their opinion on the probable cause to which the good or bad yield of the various crops, in each of their districts, may be attributed.

CONDITIONS INFLUENCING THE PRODUCE OF THE CROPS.

The Weather.

The Weather.

The Weather being a potent factor in influencing the produce of the crops, both as to quantity and quality, the following particulars, and those given on pages 131–45, are inserted by the kind permission of the Editor of the Dublin Journal of Medical Science: they have been derived from Returns of Meteorological Observations taken in Dublin City during the years 1876–93, by J. W. Moore, Esq., M.D., F.R.C.P.I., F.R. MET. SOC.; and published in the Journal during the years 1893–94. The Tables on pages 146–8 also, are founded on Dr. Moore's observations:—

The mean Atmospherical Pressure has been obtained from daily readings of the barometer at 9 A.M. and 9 P.M. corrected and reduced to 32° Fahrenheit at the mean sea level. The Mean Temperature values have been deduced from the maximal and minimal readings of the thermometer in the shade. The Rainfall is that measured daily at 9 A.M. A rainy day is one on which at least one-hundredth (·01) of an inch of rain falls within the twenty-four hours from 9 A.M. to 9 A.M.

The *Mean Height of the Barometer* during the year 1893 was 29·964 inches. The highest observed reading was 30·705 inches at 9 A.M. on December 30th. The lowest observed reading was 28·530 inches, at noon on December 10th. The extreme range of atmospherical pressure was 2·175 inches compared with 1·804 inches in 1892.

The *Mean Temperature* of the year, deduced from the arithmetical mean of the maximal and minimal readings of the thermometer in the shade was 51·5°. The highest reading was 79·8° on August 18th; the lowest reading was 20·2° on January 3rd. The average mean temperature for the years 1873–92 calculated in the same way was 49·4°. The mean temperature deduced from the daily readings of the dry bulb thermometer at 9 A.M. and 9 P.M. was 50·5°.

Rain fell on 174 days, including snow or sleet on 17 days, and hail on 21 days. The average number of rainy days in the years 1873–92 was 197·1. The total rainfall measured 20·493 inches compared with an average of 27·929 inches in the twenty years 1873–92. During the first half of 1893 (January to June, inclusive) the rainfall was 9·824 inches on 78 days; during the second half (July to December, inclusive) 10·669 inches fell on 96 days.

As regards the *Direction of the Wind*, 730 observations were made during the year, with this result—N., 40; N.E., 50; E., 86; S.E., 47; S. 50; S.W., 99; W., 216; N.W., 86; Calm, 57.

The season of 1893 was exceptionally dry, and having regard to the importance of the subject in connection with Agriculture, I have had the following Tables (VI. and VII.) compiled. They show by quarterly periods the rainfall of the City of Dublin—a low level station—for the 29 years, 1865–93, and at Fassaroe, Bray, County Wicklow—a hilly district—for the 41 years, 1853–93, with decennial and other averages, and have been prepared from data specially supplied to me; for Dublin by Dr. J. W. Moore, and for Fassaroe by Mr. R. M. Barrington, LL.B.

TABLE VI.—RAINFALL at 40, Fitzwilliam-square, West,* Dublin, during each Quarter of the 29 years 1865–93, with AVERAGES for the 6 years, 1865–70, and the Decennial Periods, 1871–80, 1881–90 and 1883–92.

YEAR.	RAINFALL IN INCHES.					
	1st Quarter.	2nd Quarter.	3rd Quarter.	Nine Months.	4th Quarter.	Whole Year.
1865, . .	5·690	5·440	7·084	18·214	9·245	27·459
1866, . .	7·381	7·497	5·919	20·797	4·[illegible]	25·879
1867, . .	9·647	6·103	6·594	22·344	4·877	27·241
1868, . .	5·616	3·498	8·170	17·184	7·751	24·945
1869, . .	7·952	7·495	5·258	21·920	5·637	27·559
1870, . .	5·675	2·791	3·897	13·064	8·[illegible]	20·[illegible]
Average 6 years, 1865–70, . .	7·060	5·604	6·[illegible]	18·738	6·670	25·[illegible]
1871, . .	5·087	5·605	9·604	20·[illegible]	4·979	25·[illegible]
1872, . .	7·640	8·025	7·[illegible]	23·799	11·747	35·[illegible]
1873, . .	5·956	2·944	9·730	18·030	5·790	23·820
1874, . .	5·656	3·461	9·170	18·[illegible]	8·894	27·186
1875, . .	5·658	5·[illegible]	7·614	18·640	11·410	29·[illegible]
1876, . .	5·576	4·459	6·743	16·978	15·[illegible]	32·[illegible]
1877, . .	5·635	7·971	6·[illegible]	20·[illegible]	8·911	29·148
1878, . .	4·290	11·948	6·975	23·213	5·049	28·[illegible]
1879, . .	7·247	8·091	9·437	25·775	3·[illegible]	28·[illegible]
1880, . .	6·275	4·645	9·549	20·[illegible]	13·645	34·[illegible]
Average 10 years, 1871–80, .	6·[illegible]	6·[illegible]	8·491	21·043	8·791	29·[illegible]
1881, . .	6·1[illegible]	5·397	8·201	19·[illegible]	7·179	27·[illegible]
1882, . .	5·596	7·445	8·215	21·254	9·[illegible]	31·181
1883, . .	7·467	6·162	9·186	22·815	6·636	29·[illegible]
1884, . .	7·734	4·138	4·641	16·513	4·[illegible]	20·[illegible]
1885, . .	5·939	6·249	7·064	19·974	6·440	26·414
1886, . .	7·290	6·[illegible]	5·896	21·375	11·461	32·[illegible]
1887, . .	3·643	2·[illegible]	4·237	10·[illegible]	5·433	16·401
1888, . .	6·097	6·016	5·[illegible]	17·[illegible]	10·[illegible]	28·[illegible]
1889, . .	3·763	4·[illegible]	9·[illegible]	18·[illegible]	7·[illegible]	25·[illegible]
1890, . .	7·470	5·943	7·448	20·[illegible]	6·707	27·[illegible]
Average 10 years, 1881–90, .	6·335	5·[illegible]	6·[illegible]	19·114	7·[illegible]	26·[illegible]
1891, . .	1·650	7·098	9·272	18·[illegible]	9·[illegible]	27·[illegible]
1892, . .	4·608	6·963	8·140	19·910	5·734	25·[illegible]
Average 10 years, 1883–92, .	5·606	5·[illegible]	7·059	18·796	7·[illegible]	26·[illegible]
1893, . .	5·196	4·425	5·484	15·108	5·[illegible]	20·[illegible]

* The Rain Gauge was at [illegible] Dublin, until October [illegible]

TABLE VII.—RAINFALL at Fassaroe, Bray, Co. Wicklow, during each Quarter of the 41 Years, 1853–93, with AVERAGES for the 8 Years, 1853–60; for each Decennial Period in the 30 Years, 1861–90; and for the 10 Years, 1883–92.

YEARS.	Rainfall in Inches.					
	1st Quarter.	2nd Quarter.	3rd Quarter.	First 9 Months.	4th Quarter.	Whole Year.
1853, .	8·49	8·80	7·28	24·05	10·18	34·23
1854, .	9·20	6·27	8·76	18·20	9·06	27·26
1855, .	3·94	5·08	6·78	15·78	10·23	26·01
1856, .	8·98	10·45	10·45	29·88	9·00	38·88
1857, .	7·44	11·34	5·92	24·70	7·08	31·78
1858, .	6·66	13·73	9·53	29·92	10·76	40·68
1859, .	9·15	9·07	9·14	27·36	12·20	39·56
1860, .	14·87	13·96	11·47	40·30	16·73	57·03
Average 8 years, 1853–60,	8·48	9·65	7·93	26·27	10·43	36·91
1861, .	10·23	6·32	11·50	28·05	11·04	40·09
1862, .	14·18	10·35	8·77	33·30	12·49	45·79
1863, .	9·60	4·14	6·04	19·78	15·93	35·71
1864, .	8·43	3·47	3·79	15·69	15·99	31·68
1865, .	10·15	7·46	6·97	24·58	16·63	41·21
1866, .	13·20	9·67	7·63	30·50	6·41	36·91
1867, .	14·05	8·61	6·43	29·09	6·18	35·27
1868, .	9·13	5·47	12·53	27·13	14·58	41·71
1869, .	13·31	11·15	8·24	29·67	9·09	38·96
1870, .	10·71	8·40	5·29	19·40	13·73	33·13
Average 10 years, 1861–70,	12·16	6·93	8·07	27·16	12·69	39·85
1871, .	9·69	6·87	8·61	25·17	7·08	32·25
1872, .	16·62	6·98	6·51	30·11	10·39	40·50
1873, .	9·86	2·61	9·77	22·24	5·50	27·74
1874, .	7·46	4·17	7·97	19·60	11·88	31·48
1875, .	9·64	5·35	10·11	25·10	16·23	41·33
1876, .	8·41	6·35	9·04	23·80	23·40	[illegible]
1877, .	14·80	10·60	10·90	36·30	10·90	[illegible]
1878, .	5·79	14·64	8·23	28·66	8·01	36·67
1879, .	12·63	12·34	10·97	35·94	6·66	42·60
1880, .	10·32	6·66	10·96	27·94	16·73	44·67
Average 10 years, 1871–80,	9·79	7·73	9·57	27·09	12·71	39·80
1881, .	11·62	6·48	9·67	27·77	16·77	44·54
1882, .	9·64	11·11	10·79	31·54	17·04	48·58
1883, .	18·64	10·39	13·16	42·19	9·66	51·85
1884, .	18·97	5·90	8·25	33·12	6·69	39·81
1885, .	13·37	10·35	9·48	33·20	9·97	43·17
1886, .	11·95	11·27	6·90	30·12	19·07	49·19
1887, .	7·67	3·37	7·60	18·64	10·73	29·37
1888, .	10·27	9·18	8·27	27·72	16·61	44·33
1889, .	9·89	8·10	9·97	27·96	12·88	40·84
1890, .	11·78	8·37	8·43	28·58	11·48	40·06
Average 10 years, 1881–90,	12·40	8·63	8·93	29·96	15·55	45·51
1891, .	3·96	11·08	9·75	24·79	20·62	45·41
1892, .	7·64	9·94	10·89	28·47	10·01	38·48
Average 10 years, 1883–92,	11·38	8·78	8·96	29·11	12·78	41·89
1893, .	9·10	2·66	6·84	18·60	7·64	26·24

Noxious Insects.

Several references to the injuries caused to crops by noxious insects, &c., are contained in the Observations of the Superintendents of Enumeration, on pages 78 to 83. Noxious Insects.

The following may be quoted :—

In Clontarf District, Dublin County.—"I have heard some complaints from farmers in the neighbourhood of Raheny, complaining of their potatoes being injured by wire-worm."

In Chancery Lane District (Suburban portion of), Dublin Metropolitan Police.—"The carrot yield was not quite as good as last year, owing to the damage done to the young sprouts by the 'blue-fly,' on account of the summer being so warm."

In Ballynacarrigy District, Westmeath County.—"The turnip crop suffered much in its early growth from the ravages of the 'fly.'"

In Kildysart District, Clare County.—"The turnip and mangold crops seem to have suffered by wire-worm to a noticeable extent, and the oat crop in some places appears also to have been affected when coming over the ground. The cabbage crop was also injured by caterpillars, of which there were great numbers this year."

In Millstreet District, Cork County, W.R.—"The oat crop suffered in the early part of the season from 'wire-worm,' which cut the young blades of the oats."

In Adare District, Limerick County.—"The cabbage crop was a good deal ravaged by the caterpillar."

In Nenagh District, Tipperary County, N.R.—"A worm called the 'red-worm' appears to have done damage to the oat crop."

In Cappawhite District, Tipperary County, S.R.—"In a few cases the oat crop was injured by being attacked in the early spring by the 'red-worm,' or wire-worm."

In Portlaw District, Waterford County.—"The first sowing of turnips failed in many places, in consequence of the fly."

In Downpatrick District, Down County.—"Turnips suffered a good deal from the fly, in the early part of the season."

In Westport District, Mayo County.—"Cabbage suffered very much from the caterpillar, especially in close kitchen gardens."

Total produce in 1892 and 1893.

Comparing the produce of the Cereal Crops in 1893 with 1892 we find a decrease in wheat of 293,960 cwts., or 24s. 8d. per cent.; in barley of 105,560 cwts., or 8·7 per cent.; in bere of 3,834 cwts., or 56·0 per cent.; in beans of 16,791 cwts., or 21·0 per cent.; and in pease of 2,757 cwts., or 44·8 per cent.; while there was an increase in oats of 1,838,275 cwts., or 7·4 per cent.; and in rye of 13,661 cwts., or 8·3 per cent.

In Green Crops, potatoes show an increase of 472,044 tons, or 18·5 per cent.; turnips, an increase of 777,385 tons, or 19·1 per cent.; mangel wurzel and beet root, an increase of 21,658 tons, or 2·9 per cent.; and cabbage, an increase of 68,356 tons, or 17·3 per cent.

Flax shows an increase of 910,522 stones of 14 lbs., or 58·7 per cent. (following an increase of 651,415 stones or 29·6 per cent. in 1892, as compared with 1891); hay on clover, sainfoin, and grasses under rotation, a decrease of 41,153 tons, or 3·2 per cent.; and hay on permanent pasture or grass not broken up in rotation, an increase of 23,212 tons, or 0·7 per cent.; the entire hay crop showing a decrease of 17,941 tons, or 0·4 per cent.

Estimated average produce per acre in 1892 and 1893.

The yield per acre of Cereal Crops in 1893 compared with that of 1892 shows an increase in wheat from 15·7 cwt. to 16·2 cwt.; in oats from 14·7 cwt. to 15·6 cwt.; and in rye from 12·5 cwt. to 13·2 cwt.; while there was a decrease in bere from 14·6 cwt. to 13·4 cwt.; in beans from 20·1 to 19·2 cwt.; and in pease from 18·4 cwt. to 10·5 cwt. Barley shows the same yield as in 1892. In other crops—potatoes show an increase from 3·5 tons to 4·9 tons; turnips from 13·5 tons to 16·0 tons; mangel wurzel and beet-root from 14·3 tons to 16·3 tons; and cabbage from 9·3 tons to 10·9 tons. Hay on clover, sainfoin, and grasses under rotation shows a decrease from 2·1 tons to 1·9 tons; and hay on permanent pasture or grass not broken up in rotation shows the same rate (2·1 tons) in both years. Flax gave a higher yield than in any previous year since 1853, and, compared with 1892, shows an increase from 21·9 stones to 36·5 stones per acre.

The total produce of the principal crops in 1892 and 1893, and the increase or decrease in the latter year, are given in Table VIII.; the *average produce* per statute acre in Table IX.; and in Table X. are given the total extent under each of the principal crops, the *estimated average* yield per statute acre, and the total produce, for each year from 1853 to 1893, inclusive.

Produce of the Crops, 1892–93.

TABLE VIII.—The *total produce* of the principal Crops in 1892 and 1893, and the increase or decrease in the latter year:—

Crops.	Produce. 1892.	Produce. 1893.	Increase in 1893. Quantity.	Increase in 1893. Percentage.	Decrease in 1893. Quantity.	Decrease in 1893. Percentage.
Wheat, Cwts. of 112 lbs.,	1,186,230	892,270	—	—	293,960	24·8
Oats, " "	18,657,519	20,495,794	1,838,275	7·4	—	—
Barley, " "	2,876,537	2,769,977	—	—	105,560	8·7
Bere, " "	6,853	3,019	—	—	3,834	56·0
Rye, " "	164,439	178,100	13,661	8·3	—	—
Beans, " "	79,846	63,055	—	—	16,791	21·0
Pease, " "	6,153	3,396	—	—	2,757	44·8
Potatoes, in Tons,	2,584,271	3,056,315	472,044	18·5	—	—
Turnips, "	4,070,527	4,848,912	777,385	19·1	—	—
Mangel Wurzel and Beet Root, "	747,041	768,694	21,653	2·9	—	—
Cabbage, "	393,207	461,563	68,356	17·3	—	—
Flax, in Stones of 14 lbs.,	1,550,597	2,461,119	910,522	58·7	—	—
Hay, in Tons. Clover, Sainfoin, and Grasses under Rotation,	1,290,060	1,248,907	—	—	41,153	3·2
Hay, in Tons. Permanent Pasture or Grass not broken up in Rotation,	3,211,168	3,234,380	23,212	0·7	—	—

TABLE IX.—The *estimated average produce* per statute acre of the principal crops in 1892 and 1893, and the *increase* or *decrease* in 1893 compared with 1892:— Average produce of Crops in 1892 and 1893.

Crops.	Produce per Statute Acre. 1892.	1893.	Increase in 1893.	Decrease in 1893.
Wheat, in Cwts. of 112 lbs.,	15·7	16·2	0·5	—
Oats, " "	14·7	15·5	0·8	—
Barley, " "	16·4	16·4	—	—
Bere, " "	16·6	15·4	—	1·2
Rye, " "	13·5	14·2	0·7	—
Beans, " "	20·1	19·2	—	0·9
Peas, " "	13·4	10·5	—	2·9
Potatoes, in Tons,	3·5	4·2	0·7	—
Turnips, "	13·5	16·0	2·5	—
Mangel Wurzel and Beet Root, "	14·5	16·1	1·6	—
Cabbage, "	9·3	10·9	1·6	—
Flax, in Stones of 14 lbs.,	21·9	36·5	14·6	—
Hay, in Tons. Clover, Sainfoin, and Grasses under Rotation,	2·1	1·9	—	0·2
Hay, in Tons. Permanent Pasture or Grass not broken up in Rotation,	2·1	2·1	—	—

The further statement contained in Table X. gives a general view of the state of agriculture during the year 1893 as compared with the preceding ten years. Extent under Crops, produce, &c., 1883–93.

Tables showing the total produce of the Crops in 1893, by counties and provinces, will be found at page 44, and by poor law unions at page 50. The average rates by counties and provinces for each year from 1884 to 1893, are given at pages 59 to 63.

TABLE X.—The extent under each of the principal Crops—the average Yield per Statute Acre, and the total Produce for all Ireland, in each year from 1883 to 1893, inclusive, with the average for the ten years, 1883 to 1892.

Years.	Wheat.	Oats.	Barley.	Bere.	Rye.	Beans.	Potatoes.	Turnips.	Mangel Wurzel and Beet Root.	Cabbage.	Flax.	Hay.
EXTENT UNDER CROPS IN STATUTE MEASURE.												
[illegible]	[illegible]	[illegible]	[illegible]	[illegible]	[illegible]	[illegible]	[illegible]	[illegible]	[illegible]	[illegible]	[illegible]	[illegible]
Average, 1883–92.	[illegible]	[illegible]	[illegible]	[illegible]	[illegible]	[illegible]	[illegible]	[illegible]	[illegible]	[illegible]	[illegible]	[illegible]
1893.	[illegible]	[illegible]	[illegible]	[illegible]	[illegible]	[illegible]	[illegible]	[illegible]	[illegible]	[illegible]	[illegible]	[illegible]
ESTIMATED AVERAGE PRODUCE PER STATUTE ACRE.												
[illegible]	[illegible]	[illegible]	[illegible]	[illegible]	[illegible]	[illegible]	[illegible]	[illegible]	[illegible]	[illegible]	[illegible]	[illegible]
Average, 1883–92.	[illegible]	[illegible]	[illegible]	[illegible]	[illegible]	[illegible]	[illegible]	[illegible]	[illegible]	[illegible]	[illegible]	[illegible]
1893.	[illegible]	[illegible]	[illegible]	[illegible]	[illegible]	[illegible]	[illegible]	[illegible]	[illegible]	[illegible]	[illegible]	[illegible]
TOTAL PRODUCE.												
[illegible]	[illegible]	[illegible]	[illegible]	[illegible]	[illegible]	[illegible]	[illegible]	[illegible]	[illegible]	[illegible]	[illegible]	[illegible]
Average, 1883–92.	[illegible]	[illegible]	[illegible]	[illegible]	[illegible]	[illegible]	[illegible]	[illegible]	[illegible]	[illegible]	[illegible]	[illegible]
1893.	[illegible]	[illegible]	[illegible]	[illegible]	[illegible]	[illegible]	[illegible]	[illegible]	[illegible]	[illegible]	[illegible]	[illegible]

LIVE STOCK.

Number and Ages of Live Stock, 1892 and 1893.

TABLE XI.—The Number and Ages of the Live Stock in Ireland, in 1892 and 1893, and the Increase or Decrease in each description:—

Description of Stock.		Number in 1892.	Number in 1893.	Increase in 1893. In Number.	Increase in 1893. Per Centage.	Decrease in 1893. In Number.	Decrease in 1893. Per Centage.
Horses,	Two years old and upwards,	480,451	486,896	6,445	1·3	—	—
	One year old and under two,	83,521	87,548	4,027	4·8	—	—
	Under one year,	41,938	39,483	—	—	2,455	5·9
Total No. of Horses,		605,910	613,927	8,017	1·3	—	—
Mules,		29,303	29,202	—	—	101	0·3
Asses,		217,600	218,720	1,120	0·5	—	—
Cattle,	Two years old and upwards,	2,498,182	2,538,717	40,535	1·6	—	—
	One year old and under two,	1,016,109	970,502	—	—	45,607	4·5
	Under one year,	1,017,804	956,008	—	—	61,796	6·1
Total No. of Cattle,		4,531,125	4,464,057	—	—	67,068	1·5
Sheep,	One year old and upwards,	2,631,763	2,431,185	—	—	200,578	7·6
	Under one year,	1,966,014	1,710,275	—	—	249,7[illegible]	12·[illegible]
Total No. of Sheep,		4,597,777	4,141,460	—	—	456,3[illegible]	9·1
Pigs,	One year old and upwards,	183,923	189,056	6,133	3·3	—	—
	Under one year,	979,548	1,013,361	33,813	3·5	—	—
Total No. of Pigs,		1,113,471	1,168,417	53,946	5·0	—	—
Goats,		322,786	323,174	—	—	9,563	2·9
Poultry,		15,335,719	16,097,461	761,742	5·0	—	—

Number of Live Stock.

At the period of the enumeration in 1893, the total number of horses in Ireland was 613,927 being an increase of 8,017 compared with 1892. There was an increase of 6,445 in the number "two years old and upwards," and of 4,027 in the "one year old, and under two," but a decrease of 2,455 in those "under one year."

The number of Mules was 29,202, being 101 less than in 1892, and asses numbered 218,720, being an increase of 1,120.

Horses, Mules, and Asses taken together numbered 852,813 in 1892, and 861,849 in 1893, being an increase of 9,036 or 1·1 per cent.; compared with the average number for the ten years 1883–92, they show an increase of 65,129, or 8·2 per cent.

The number of Cattle in 1893 was 4,464,057, showing a decrease of 67,068, or 1·5 per cent. as compared with the number enumerated in 1892, which was the highest number for any of the ten years 1883–92; there was an increase of 40,535 in the "two years old and upwards"; a decrease of 45,607 in the "one year old and under two," and a decrease of 61,796 in the number "under one year." Compared with the average number for the ten years 1883–92, Cattle show an increase of 244,788, or 5·8 per cent.

Sheep numbered 4,491,435 in 1893, being 406,329, or 8·4 per cent. less than the number for the previous year, but 623,646 or 16·4 per cent. over the average for the ten years 1883-92; the "one year old and upwards" decreased by 200,573, or 7·0 per cent. as compared with the number in 1892, and those "under one year" by 205,750, or 10·6 per cent. Number of Live Stock.

Pigs were returned as 1,152,417 in 1893, showing an increase of 38,945, or 3·5 per cent., as compared with the previous year, the number for which was 18·6 per cent. less than that for the year 1891. The "one year old and upwards" increased by 5,162, and those "under one year" by 83,812.

Comparing the number of pigs returned in 1893 with the average for the ten years 1883-92, we find a decrease of 190,148 or 14·2 per cent.

Goats numbered 323,173 in 1893, being 9,553 *less* than in 1892, but 31,601 or 10·8 per cent. over the average for the ten years 1883-92.

The number of poultry in 1893 was 16,097,461, being 761,718 more than in 1892, and 1,726,030 or 12·0 per cent. over the average for the ten years 1883-92. Of the 16,097,461 poultry in 1893, 1,081,954 were turkeys; 2,177,437 geese; 2,909,353 ducks; and 9,978,717 ordinary fowl. Poultry.

Compared with 1892, turkeys increased by 61,238, geese by 61,523, ducks by 43,218, and ordinary fowl by 555,689.

TABLE XII.—The Number of Live Stock in Ireland, in each year from 1883 to 1893 inclusive, with the average numbers for the ten years 1883-92:— Number of Live Stock, 1883 to 1893.

Years.	Horses and Mules.	Asses.	Cattle.	Sheep.	Pigs.	Goats.	Poultry.
1883,	561,497	189,760	4,098,953	3,916,311	1,348,354	263,148	13,258,430
1884,	537,139	191,839	4,112,783	3,843,719	1,306,560	254,411	13,767,440
1885,	576,130	197,170	4,228,531	3,178,058	1,269,093	264,637	13,650,632
1886,	573,899	196,848	4,183,724	3,368,043	1,263,112	266,176	13,909,823
1887,	567,231	198,617	4,167,104	3,377,834	1,408,485	271,780	14,462,643
1888,	596,252	203,153	4,089,185	3,826,640	1,387,935	266,678	14,185,409
1889,	604,109	206,226	4,094,174	3,759,167	1,380,670	263,853	14,644,617
1890,	614,894	213,016	4,140,211	4,323,183	1,570,388	287,144	15,106,438
1891,	621,470	216,348	4,449,311	4,722,613	1,367,712	330,337	15,776,128
1892,	633,813	217,680	4,631,120	4,897,777	1,113,472	332,726	15,335,743
Average 1883-92,	593,697	203,030	4,219,324	3,767,809	1,343,565	291,572	14,371,431
1893,	643,179	218,730	4,464,087	4,491,435	1,152,417	323,173	16,097,461

TABLE XIII.—The proportion per cent. of Horses, Cattle, Sheep, and Pigs in Ireland according to Age, for the years 1883 to 1893, inclusive, and averages for the ten years 1883-92. Number of Live Stock, 1883 to 1893.

Years.	Horses.			Cattle.			Sheep.		Pigs.	
	Percentage at each age.			Percentage at each age.			Percentage at each age.		Percentage at each age.	
	Two Years old and upwards.	One Year old and under Two.	Under One Year.	Two Years old and upwards.	One Year old and under Two.	Under One Year.	One Year old and upwards.	Under One Year.	One Year old and upwards.	Under One Year.
1883,	77·1	10·3	10·5	53·3	20·8	25·9	61·7	38·3	15·4	84·6
1884,	75·9	11·1	12·9	55·3	21·3	23·7	62·5	37·5	12·8	87·2
1885,	75·5	11·9	12·6	54·0	22·6	23·4	61·6	38·4	12·7	87·3
1886,	76·2	12·8	11·5	54·7	21·0	23·3	61·7	38·3	12·7	87·3
1887,	75·8	12·5	11·7	54·7	20·8	23·5	60·2	39·8	12·7	87·3
1888,	74·4	12·1	13·5	54·2	21·3	23·5	59·6	40·4	12·2	87·8
1889,	74·5	13·4	12·2	55·6	21·2	23·2	59·5	40·5	12·2	87·8
1890,	73·3	13·7	13·0	54·7	21·2	24·1	58·7	41·3	12·1	87·9
1891,	72·2	14·3	13·5	54·1	22·0	23·9	59·0	41·0	11·9	88·1
1892,	71·1	14·6	14·4	55·1	22·4	22·5	59·7	40·3	12·0	88·0
Average 1883-92,	75·1	11·9	13·0	55·5	21·3	23·1	60·4	39·6	12·5	87·5
1893,	71·3	15·9	12·8	55·0	21·7	23·3	60·6	39·4	12·1	87·9

MILCH COWS.

The following statement (Table XIV.) shows the number of Milch Cows in Ireland in each year from 1854—the first year in which Milch Cows were separately enumerated—to 1893. The average number for the first five years of the period was 1,579,851, and for the last five years 1,419,793, being a decline of 160,058 or 10·1 per cent. The highest number in any one year was 1,690,289 in 1859, and the lowest 1,348,886 in 1864.

Years.	No. of Milch Cows.	Years.	No. of Milch Cows.	Years.	No. of Milch Cows.	Years.	No. of Milch Cows.
1854, .	1,517,673	1864, .	1,348,886	1874, .	1,491,575	1884, .	1,356,[illegible]
1855, .	1,561,598	1865, .	1,387,446	1875, .	1,630,366	1885, .	1,417,433
1856, .	1,579,879	1866, .	1,463,618	1876, .	1,538,974	1886, .	1,418,644
1857, .	1,628,350	1867, .	1,511,032	1877, .	1,522,511	1887, .	1,394,135
1858, .	1,626,109	1868, .	1,476,333	1878, .	1,484,815	1888, .	1,394,771
1859, .	1,690,289	1869, .	1,506,038	1879, .	1,464,818	1889, .	1,363,760
1860, .	1,624,443	1870, .	1,549,094	1880, .	1,398,017	1890, .	1,400,857
1861, .	1,545,129	1871, .	1,545,969	1881, .	1,392,018	1891, .	1,443,308
1862, .	1,426,833	1872, .	1,481,784	1882, .	1,398,005	1892,	1,451,089
1863, .	1,394,834	1873, .	1,478,116	1883, .	1,402,394	1893, .	1,441,329

Tables showing the number of Live Stock in 1893, by counties and provinces, will be found at page 64; by Poor Law Unions at pages 65–8; and by counties and provinces, for each year from 1884 to 1893 at pages 69–73.

DISEASES OF CATTLE.

The following information has been derived from returns compiled in pursuance of the provisions of the 59th section of the Contagious Diseases (Animals) Act, 1878, for the year ended the 31st December, 1893.

No case of Pleuro-Pneumonia occurred during the year 1893. The numbers for four previous years were 86 for 1892, 133 for 1891, 95 for 1890, and 108 for 1889.

Ireland continues to be free from Foot-and-Mouth Disease. No case has occurred since the year 1884.

As regards the working of the Act relating to Swine Fever it may be observed that, while only 196 outbreaks of the disease were reported during the ten months from 1st January to 1st November, 1893, 488 suspected outbreaks were reported during the remaining months, November and December. The existence of disease was confirmed in 310 of these cases by the Veterinary Officers of the Department who examined the internal organs of the dead or slaughtered swine. The number of outbreaks in the year 1892 was 237, and 278 in 1891.

Six outbreaks of Glanders were reported during the year.

There were 22 outbreaks of Anthrax during the year, as compared with 6 in the previous year, 29 in 1891, 17 in 1890, and 21 in 1889.

The returns show that 424 cases of Rabies were reported in 1893, as compared with 446 in 1892, 470 in 1891, and 353 in 1890.

PRICES OF AGRICULTURAL PRODUCE.

Prices of Agricultural Produce.

TABLE XV.—The information in the following Table is derived from Returns of the Average Prices of Agricultural Produce collected by the Irish Land Commission for the seven years, 1887–93.

Produce.	Average Price for the year 1887.	Average Price for the year 1888.	Average Price for the year 1889.	Average Price for the year 1890.	Average Price for the year 1891.	Average Price for the year 1892.	Average Price for the Year 1893. Quarter ended 31st March.	Quarter ended 30th June.	Quarter ended 30th Sept.	Quarter ended 31st Dec.	Whole Year 1893.
GRAIN:—	s. d.	s. d.	s. d.	s. d.	s. d.	s. d.	s. d.	s. d.	s. d.	s. d.	s. d.
Wheat, per cwt.,	[illegible]	[illegible]	[illegible]	[illegible]	[illegible]	[illegible]	[illegible]	[illegible]	[illegible]	[illegible]	[illegible]
Oats, "	[illegible]	[illegible]	[illegible]	[illegible]	[illegible]	[illegible]	[illegible]	[illegible]	[illegible]	[illegible]	[illegible]
Barley, "	[illegible]	[illegible]	[illegible]	[illegible]	[illegible]	[illegible]	[illegible]	[illegible]	[illegible]	[illegible]	[illegible]
Flax, per stone,	[illegible]	[illegible]	[illegible]	[illegible]	[illegible]	[illegible]	[illegible]	—	[illegible]	[illegible]	[illegible]
Potatoes, per cwt.,	[illegible]	[illegible]	[illegible]	[illegible]	[illegible]	[illegible]	[illegible]	[illegible]	[illegible]	[illegible]	[illegible]
Hay, "	[illegible]	[illegible]	[illegible]	[illegible]	[illegible]	[illegible]	[illegible]	[illegible]	[illegible]	[illegible]	[illegible]
BUTTER, "	[illegible]	[illegible]	[illegible]	[illegible]	[illegible]	[illegible]	[illegible]	[illegible]	[illegible]	[illegible]	[illegible]
BEEF, "	[illegible]	[illegible]	[illegible]	[illegible]	[illegible]	[illegible]	[illegible]	[illegible]	[illegible]	[illegible]	[illegible]
MUTTON, "	[illegible]	[illegible]	[illegible]	[illegible]	[illegible]	[illegible]	[illegible]	[illegible]	[illegible]	[illegible]	[illegible]
PORK (Fresh ...),	[illegible]	[illegible]	[illegible]	[illegible]	[illegible]	[illegible]	[illegible]	[illegible]	[illegible]	[illegible]	[illegible]
WOOL, per lb.,	[illegible]	[illegible]	[illegible]	[illegible]	[illegible]	[illegible]	[illegible]	[illegible]	[illegible]	[illegible]	[illegible]
EGGS, per 120 [illegible]	—	—	—	—	—	—	[illegible]	[illegible]	[illegible]	[illegible]	[illegible]

NOTE.—The prices of beef and mutton in the above [illegible]

(a) Prior to [illegible] August, [illegible]

(b) After [illegible] August, [illegible]

[illegible]

DAIRY INDUSTRIES.

Dairy Industries.

As the increase during recent years in the number of Dairy Factories appeared to render it desirable that some particulars should be obtained regarding what is now an important Agricultural industry, information on several points connected with the subject was collected through the medium of the Enumerators in 1891, 1892, and 1893. Statistics were also had respecting the number of Milk Separators used in private establishments. Except in two or three cases, where the proprietors declined to give any particulars, the details sought for were willingly supplied where available; but in some establishments the accounts kept did not contain information on all the branches inquired into.

The following Table shows, *inter alia*, that the number of Factories from which statistics were obtained in 1893 was 190, being an increase of 15 as compared with the number returned in 1892, and that the number of hands permanently employed amounted to 1,418, or 199 more than the (revised) number for 1892. Of the 190 factories, 95 were owned by individual proprietors, 49 were the property of Joint Stock Companies, and 46 belonged to Co-operative Farmers. In the 190 Factories there were 419 milk separators, of which 357, or 85 per cent., were worked by steam-power. Almost four-fifths of the total number of Factories were in Munster, the number for that province being 151; in Leinster there were 33, in Ulster 4, and in Connaught 2. The quantity of Butter produced during the year ended 30th September, 1893, was 167,185 cwts. (against 141,678 cwts. in the preceding year), and of Cheese 183 cwts., and the number of lbs. of Condensed Milk amounted to 15,154,700.

TABLE XVI.—Showing the number of DAIRY FACTORIES and of CONDENSED MILK FACTORIES, with [illegible] of Butter, Cream, &c., produced;

Provinces and Counties.	Number of Factories.	Number of Factories which secure			Description of Ownership			PUBLIC FACTORIES					
								Total quantity of Milk [illegible] by Factories during the year ended 30th Sept., 189[illegible].	Total quantity of Cream [illegible] by Factories during the year ended 30th Sept., 189[illegible].	Power employed, with number of [illegible]			
		Milk and Cream.	Milk only.	Cream only.	Proprietary.	Joint Stock.	Co-operative [illegible] Farmers.			Hand.	Horse.	Steam.	Water.
LEINSTER:								Gallons.	Gallons.				
Carlow,	[illegible]	.	1	.	.	.	1	[illegible]	.	.	.	[illegible]	.
Dublin,	[illegible]	.	1	.	1	1	.	[illegible]	.	.	.	[illegible]	.
Kildare,	.	.	.	.	.	.	.	.	.	.	.	.	.
Kilkenny,	[illegible]	[illegible]	[illegible]	.	[illegible]	[illegible]	[illegible]	[illegible]	[illegible]*	.	.	[illegible]	[illegible]
King's,	.	.	.	.	.	.	.	.	.	.	.	.	.
Longford,	1	.	1	.	.	1	.	[illegible]	.	.	.	[illegible]	.
Louth and Drogheda, (County of Town),	.	.	.	.	.	.	.	.	.	.	.	.	.
Meath,	.	.	.	.	.	.	.	.	.	.	.	.	.
Queen's,	1	.	1	.	1	.	.	[illegible]	.	.	.	1	.
Westmeath,	.	.	.	.	.	.	.	.	.	.	.	.	.
Wexford,	[illegible]	.	[illegible]	.	[illegible]	.	.	[illegible]	.	.	.	[illegible]	.
Wicklow,	.	.	.	.	.	.	.	.	.	.	.	.	.
Total,	[illegible]	[illegible]	[illegible]	.	[illegible]	[illegible]	1	[illegible]	[illegible]	.	.	[illegible]	[illegible]
MUNSTER:													
Clare,	[illegible]	.	[illegible]	.	[illegible]	.	1	[illegible]	.	.	.	[illegible]	.
Cork,	[illegible]	1	[illegible]	1	[illegible]	[illegible]	[illegible]	[illegible]	[illegible]	.	.	(a) [illegible]	[illegible]
Kerry,	[illegible]	.	[illegible]	.	[illegible]	.	.	[illegible]	.	.	.	[illegible]	.
Limerick,	[illegible]	[illegible]	[illegible]	1	[illegible]	[illegible]	[illegible]	[illegible]	[illegible]	.	.	(a) [illegible]	[illegible]
Tipperary,	[illegible]	[illegible]	[illegible]	.	[illegible]	[illegible]	[illegible]	[illegible]	[illegible]	.	.	(a) [illegible]	[illegible]
Waterford,	[illegible]	.	[illegible]	.	[illegible]	[illegible]	.	[illegible]	.	.	.	[illegible]	[illegible]
Total,	[illegible]	[illegible]	[illegible]	[illegible]	[illegible]	[illegible]	[illegible]	[illegible]	[illegible]	.	.	[illegible]	[illegible]
ULSTER:													
Antrim,	.	.	.	.	.	.	.	.	.	.	.	.	.
Armagh,	.	.	.	.	.	.	.	.	.	.	.	.	.
Cavan,	[illegible]	1	1	.	[illegible]	.	.	[illegible]	.	[illegible]	.	[illegible]	.
Donegal,	.	.	.	.	.	.	.	.	.	.	.	.	.
Down,	[illegible]	.	1	.	1	.	.	[illegible]	.	.	.	1	.
Fermanagh,	.	.	.	.	.	.	.	.	.	.	.	.	.
Londonderry,	.	.	.	.	.	.	.	.	.	.	.	.	.
Monaghan,	1	.	1	.	1	.	.	[illegible]	.	.	.	1	.
Tyrone,	.	.	.	.	.	.	.	.	.	.	.	.	.
Total,	[illegible]	1	[illegible]	.	[illegible]	.	.	[illegible]	.	[illegible]	.	[illegible]	.
CONNAUGHT:													
Galway,	.	.	.	.	.	.	.	.	.	.	.	.	.
Leitrim,	[illegible]	.	.	[illegible]	1	1	.	.	[illegible]	1	.	1	.
Mayo,	.	.	.	.	.	.	.	.	.	.	.	.	.
Roscommon,	.	.	.	.	.	.	.	.	.	.	.	.	.
Sligo,	.	.	.	.	.	.	.	.	.	.	.	.	.
Total,	[illegible]	.	.	[illegible]	1	1	.	.	[illegible]	1	.	1	.
TOTAL OF IRELAND,	[illegible]	[illegible]	[illegible]	[illegible]	[illegible]	[illegible]	[illegible]	[illegible]	[illegible]	[illegible]	.	[illegible]	[illegible]

(a) Exclusive of the quantity used in a [illegible] Factory.
* See note (?), page [illegible].

(a) Including one Factory employing Steam and Water Power.

the number of Milk-Separators in use; the number of hands permanently employed; the quantity and other details.

[illegible]		Total Annual Production. (Year ended 30th September, [illegible].)					Disposal of Skim Milk. Number of Factories in which it is			Number of Milk Suppliers [illegible]	Provinces and Counties.
Total Number of Milk Separators in use.	Number of Hands permanently employed.	Butter in cwts.	Cheese in cwts.: Cream.	Cheese in cwts.: Whole Milk.	Cream and Condensed Milk sold as such: Cream in Gallons.	Cream and Condensed Milk sold as such: Condensed Milk in lb.	Returned to Farmers.	Utilised in Factory in Cheese making.	Otherwise disposed of.		
											Leinster.
[illegible]	7	[illegible]	.	.	.	.	[illegible]	.	.	1	Carlow.
[illegible]	[illegible]	[illegible]	.	.	[illegible]	.	.	.	[illegible]	4	Dublin.
	.	.	.	.	-	.	.	.	.	[illegible]	Kildare.
[illegible]	[illegible]	[illegible]	.	-	[illegible]	.	[illegible]	-	[illegible]	[illegible]	Kilkenny.
.	.	.	.	.	.	-	.	-	.	1	King's.
[illegible]	[illegible]	[illegible]	.	.	.	-	[illegible]	-	.	1	Longford.
-	.	.	.	.	.	.	.	-	.	[illegible]	Louth and Drogheda, County of Town.
-	.	.	.	.	.	.	.	.	.	[illegible]	Meath.
[illegible]	[illegible]	[illegible]	.	.	.	.	[illegible]	.	.	[illegible]	Queen's.
-	.	.	.	.	.	.	.	.	.	.	Westmeath.
[illegible]	[illegible]	[illegible]	.	.	[illegible]	.	[illegible]	.	[illegible]	[illegible]	Wexford.
.	.	-	.	.	.	.	.	-	.	[illegible]	Wicklow.
[illegible]	[illegible]	[illegible]	-	.	[illegible]	.	[illegible]	.	[illegible]	[illegible]	Total.
											Munster.
[illegible]	[illegible]	[illegible]	.	.	.	.	[illegible]	.	[illegible]	[illegible]	Clare.
[illegible]	[illegible]	[illegible]	[illegible]		[illegible]	[illegible]	[illegible]	.	[illegible]	[illegible]	Cork.
7	[illegible]	[illegible]	.	.	.	.	[illegible]	.	.	[illegible]	Kerry.
[illegible]	[illegible]	[illegible]	.	.	[illegible]	[illegible]	[illegible]	.	[illegible]	[illegible]	Limerick.
[illegible]	[illegible]	[illegible]	.	.	[illegible]	[illegible]	[illegible]	.	[illegible]	[illegible]	Tipperary.
[illegible]	[illegible]	[illegible]	.	.	.	[illegible]	[illegible]	.	[illegible]	[illegible]	Waterford.
[illegible]	[illegible]	[illegible]	[illegible]	.	[illegible]	[illegible]	[illegible]	.	[illegible]	[illegible]	Total.
											Ulster.
-	-	.	.	.	-	-		.	.	[illegible]	Antrim.
.	.	.	.	.	-	.	.	.	.	-	Armagh.
[illegible]	[illegible]	[illegible]	.	.	[illegible]	.	[illegible]	.	.	[illegible]	Cavan.
.	.	.	.	.	.	-	.	.	.	.	Donegal.
[illegible]	[illegible]	[illegible]	.	.	[illegible]	.	-	.	[illegible]	.	Down.
.	.	-	.	.	-	.	.	.	.	.	Fermanagh.
.	.	.	.	.	-	.	.	.	.	.	Londonderry.
[illegible]	[illegible]	[illegible]	.	.	.	-	[illegible]	.	.	.	Monaghan.
.	.	.	.	.	-	.	.	.	.	.	Tyrone.
[illegible]	[illegible]	[illegible]	.	.	[illegible]	.	[illegible]	.	[illegible]	[illegible]	Total.
											Connaught.
.	-	.	.	.	.	.	.	.	.	[illegible]	Galway.
[illegible]	[illegible]	[illegible]	.	.	.	.	.	-	.	[illegible]	Leitrim.
.	.	.	.	.	.	.	.	.	.	-	Mayo.
-	.	.	.	.	-	-	.	.	.	-	Roscommon.
-	.	.	.	-	.	-	.	.	.	.	Sligo.
[illegible]	[illegible]	[illegible]	.	.	.	.	.	.	.	[illegible]	Total.
[illegible]	[illegible]	[illegible]	[illegible]	.	[illegible]	[illegible]	[illegible]	.	[illegible]	[illegible]	Total of Ireland.

[illegible] A large portion of this quantity, [illegible] in [illegible], was [illegible] Factory in [illegible] owned by the same proprietor.

EXPORTS AND IMPORTS OF LIVE STOCK.

Exports of Live Stock.

With the view of giving a more accurate idea of the number of live stock produced in Ireland the following statement has been extracted from the Statistical Returns published in the Report for 1893 under the "Contagious Diseases (Animals) Act, 1878."

TABLE XVII.—Number of Cattle, Sheep, and Swine, exported from Ireland to Great Britain during each of the nineteen years, 1875–93:—

Years.	Cattle.						Sheep.			Swine.			Total
	Oxen, Bulls and Cows.				Calves.	Total.	Sheep.	Lambs.	Total.	Fat Animals.	Store Swine.	Total.	
	Fat Cattle.	Store Cattle for Grazing or Breeding Purposes.	Other Cattle.	Total.									
[illegible]	[illegible]	[illegible]	[illegible]	[illegible]	[illegible]	[illegible]	[illegible]	[illegible]	[illegible]	[illegible]	[illegible]	[illegible]	[illegible]
[illegible]	[illegible]	[illegible]	[illegible]	[illegible]	[illegible]	[illegible]	[illegible]	[illegible]	[illegible]	[illegible]	[illegible]	[illegible]	[illegible]
[illegible]	[illegible]	[illegible]	[illegible]	[illegible]	[illegible]	[illegible]	[illegible]	[illegible]	[illegible]	[illegible]	[illegible]	[illegible]	[illegible]
[illegible]	[illegible]	[illegible]	[illegible]	[illegible]	[illegible]	[illegible]	[illegible]	[illegible]	[illegible]	[illegible]	[illegible]	[illegible]	[illegible]
[illegible]	[illegible]	[illegible]	[illegible]	[illegible]	[illegible]	[illegible]	[illegible]	[illegible]	[illegible]	[illegible]	[illegible]	[illegible]	[illegible]
[illegible]	[illegible]	[illegible]	[illegible]	[illegible]	[illegible]	[illegible]	[illegible]	[illegible]	[illegible]	[illegible]	[illegible]	[illegible]	[illegible]
[illegible]	[illegible]	[illegible]	[illegible]	[illegible]	[illegible]	[illegible]	[illegible]	[illegible]	[illegible]	[illegible]	[illegible]	[illegible]	[illegible]
[illegible]	[illegible]	[illegible]	[illegible]	[illegible]	[illegible]	[illegible]	[illegible]	[illegible]	[illegible]	[illegible]	[illegible]	[illegible]	[illegible]
[illegible]	[illegible]	[illegible]	[illegible]	[illegible]	[illegible]	[illegible]	[illegible]	[illegible]	[illegible]	[illegible]	[illegible]	[illegible]	[illegible]
[illegible]	[illegible]	[illegible]	[illegible]	[illegible]	[illegible]	[illegible]	[illegible]	[illegible]	[illegible]	[illegible]	[illegible]	[illegible]	[illegible]
[illegible]	[illegible]	[illegible]	[illegible]	[illegible]	[illegible]	[illegible]	[illegible]	[illegible]	[illegible]	[illegible]	[illegible]	[illegible]	[illegible]
[illegible]	[illegible]	[illegible]	[illegible]	[illegible]	[illegible]	[illegible]	[illegible]	[illegible]	[illegible]	[illegible]	[illegible]	[illegible]	[illegible]
[illegible]	[illegible]	[illegible]	[illegible]	[illegible]	[illegible]	[illegible]	[illegible]	[illegible]	[illegible]	[illegible]	[illegible]	[illegible]	[illegible]
[illegible]	[illegible]	[illegible]	[illegible]	[illegible]	[illegible]	[illegible]	[illegible]	[illegible]	[illegible]	[illegible]	[illegible]	[illegible]	[illegible]
[illegible]	[illegible]	[illegible]	[illegible]	[illegible]	[illegible]	[illegible]	[illegible]	[illegible]	[illegible]	[illegible]	[illegible]	[illegible]	[illegible]
[illegible]	[illegible]	[illegible]	[illegible]	[illegible]	[illegible]	[illegible]	[illegible]	[illegible]	[illegible]	[illegible]	[illegible]	[illegible]	[illegible]
[illegible]	[illegible]	[illegible]	[illegible]	[illegible]	[illegible]	[illegible]	[illegible]	[illegible]	[illegible]	[illegible]	[illegible]	[illegible]	[illegible]
[illegible]	[illegible]	[illegible]	[illegible]	[illegible]	[illegible]	[illegible]	[illegible]	[illegible]	[illegible]	[illegible]	[illegible]	[illegible]	[illegible]
[illegible]	[illegible]	[illegible]	[illegible]	[illegible]	[illegible]	[illegible]	[illegible]	[illegible]	[illegible]	[illegible]	[illegible]	[illegible]	[illegible]

From the foregoing it is evident that some of the younger animals included in the Statistics of Exports must of necessity escape enumeration in June of each year when the returns of live stock are collected for this Department. Viewing the number of animals exported to Great Britain in relation to those enumerated, it is found that in cattle the number exported bears a relation of 15·4 per cent. to those enumerated in 1893, as compared with 13·8 per cent. in 1892; in sheep 25·1 per cent. as compared with 22·4 per cent. in 1892; and in pigs 49·6 per cent. as compared with 45·0 per cent. in 1892.

From the same Report it appears that the number of horses exported to Great Britain in 1893 amounted to 30,390, equal to 5·0 per cent. of those enumerated.

Imports of Live Stock.

It also appears that during the same period there were imported into Ireland, 8,871 horses, 359 cattle (including 31 calves), 10,406 sheep, and 159 pigs.

HONEY PRODUCED IN 1893.

Honey produced in 1893.

The inquiries made in the preceding seven years relative to the extent to which bee-keeping is followed in Ireland, and the degree of success attained in this special branch of rural economy, were repeated last year with reference to the season of 1893.

According to the Returns received there would appear to have been a decrease of 34·1 per cent. in the quantity of honey produced in 1893, as compared with the preceding year.

The quantity of honey produced, according to the Returns, was 192,457 lbs.; of this, 60,129 lbs. were produced in the province of Leinster; 65,369 lbs. in Munster; 49,463 lbs. in Ulster; and 17,496 lbs. in Connaught. Of the 192,457 lbs., 104,336 lbs. were produced "in Hives having Movable Combs," and 88,121 lbs. "in other Hives." It was stated that 101,440 lbs. was "Run Honey," and 91,017 lbs. "Section Honey."

The number of stocks brought through the Winter of 1892–93 amounted to 15,846; of which 7,115 were in hives having movable combs, and 8,731 in other hives.

According to the returns collected there were 4,668 lbs. of wax manufactured in 1892; of which 1,955 lbs. were from hives having movable combs, and 2,713 lbs. from other hives. Honey produced in 1892.

The Returns received in 1892 gave the number of swarms at work during the season of 1891 as 17,578; the quantity of honey as 253,561 lbs.; the number of stocks brought through the winter of 1891–92 as 18,534; and the quantity of wax manufactured in 1891 as 4,586 lbs.

The following Table shows the quantity of Honey returned as produced in Ireland during each of the eight years, 1885–92. It will be observed, that the quantity produced in 1892 was less than that for any of the preceding seven years, and very much below the average.

TABLE XVIII.—Showing for each of the Eight Years 1885–92 the Quantity of HONEY Produced in Ireland, distinguishing the quantity Produced in Hives having Movable Combs from that Produced in other Hives, and RUN HONEY from SECTION HONEY:—

YEARS.	HONEY PRODUCED, IN LBS.						
	In Hives having Movable Combs.			In other Hives.			GENERAL TOTAL.
	Run.	Section.	Total.	Run.	Section.	Total.	
1885	46,196	59,918	106,114	141,[illegible]	54,[illegible]	196,[illegible]	[illegible],297
1886	52,603	76,338	128,941	145,180	59,094	204,274	331,167
1887	77,897	134,357	212,254	168,951	68,161	237,112	449,366
1888	55,783	92,658	148,441	137,801	42,260	179,661	328,012
1889	74,942	143,866	218,808	152,101	53,978	206,080	424,888
1890	47,958	86,138	134,082	118,596	42,489	161,085	295,116
1891	43,087	91,561	134,648	85,[illegible]	30,104	118,913	253,561
1892	34,707	69,629	104,336	66,153	21,848	88,191	192,477

SCUTCHING MILLS.

The number of Mills for scutching Flax in Ireland in 1893 was 970, being a decrease of 23 compared with 1892, and a decrease of 145 since the year 1884. 954 of these Mills in 1893 were in Ulster, 6 in Connaught, 6 in Leinster, and 4 in Munster. There were 396 Mills with from 1 to 4 stocks; 325 having 5 or 6; 222 with from 7 to 12; 25 having from 13 to 18, and 2 having above 18 stocks; 800 were worked by water power; 116 by steam; and 54 by water and steam. The total number of Stocks in Ireland in 1893 amounted to 6,837, and of this number 5,785 were in Mills situated in Ulster. Scutching Mills, 1893.

The following is the number of Scutching Mills, in each year, from 1884 to 1893 inclusive, by Provinces:— Scutching Mills, 1884 to 1893.

Provinces.	1884.	1885.	1886.	1887.	1888.	1889.	1890.	1891.	1892.	1893.
Leinster, . .	9	7	7	7	8	7	7	7	4	6
Munster, . .	13	9	8	6	1	4	5	5	6	4
Ulster, . .	1,086	1,097	1,033	1,063	1,056	1,048	1,048	993	979	954
Connaught, . .	8	9	5	3	8	3	9	9	4	6
IRELAND, .	1,115	1,099	1,053	1,078	1,070	1,062	1,039	1,003	993	970

Scutching Mills, 1893.

TABLE XII.—Number of SCUTCHING MILLS in 1893, by COUNTIES and PROVINCES, classified according to the number of Stocks in each Mill, and the Power used in working them; with the Total Number of Stocks in each County:—

Provinces and Counties in which there were Scutching Mills.	Power Employed.					Total No. of Mills.	Classification of Mills.					Total No. of Stocks.
	Water.	Steam.	Water and Steam.	Horse.	Wind.		Having 1, 2, 3 or 4 Stocks.	Having 5 to 8 Stocks.	Having above 8 and not exceeding 12 Stocks.	Having above 12 and not exceeding 18 Stocks.	Having above 18 Stocks.	
LEINSTER:												
Dublin,	1	.	.	.	.	1	.	1	.	.	.	6
Kildare,	1	.	.	.	.	1	.	.	.	1	.	18
Louth & Drogheda, Co. of Town.	1	.	.	.	.	1	.	1	.	.	.	5
Meath,	3	.	.	.	.	3	.	2	1	.	.	20
Total,	6	.	.	.	.	6	.	4	1	1	.	49
MUNSTER:												
Cork,	3	1	.	.	.	4	3	1	.	.	.	18
Total,	3	1	.	.	.	4	3	1	.	.	.	18
ULSTER:												
Antrim,	117	10	4	.	.	131	57	49	24	1	.	781
Armagh,	64	12	6	.	.	82	10	52	18	2	.	388
Cavan,	34	4	1	.	.	39	10	14	14	1	.	276
Donegal,	125	8	3	.	.	136	103	19	11	.	.	675
Down,	94	33	14	.	.	169	17	68	67	11	1	1,134
Fermanagh,	31	3	.	.	.	34	4	11	8	2	.	167
Londonderry,	139	7	12	.	.	158	63	67	18	1	.	789
Monaghan,	56	13	3	.	.	71	27	28	17	4	.	338
Tyrone,	182	34	31	.	.	247	63	81	90	8	1	1,227
Total,	787	118	64	.	.	964	395	320	316	24	2	4,785
CONNAUGHT:												
Leitrim,	2	.	.	.	.	1	.	.	1	.	.	13
Mayo,	3	.	.	.	.	3	.	.	3	.	.	25
Roscommon,	1	2	.	.	.	3	1	.	3	.	.	20
Total,	6	2	.	.	.	6	1	.	6	.	.	64
TOTAL OF IRELAND,	800	116	64	.	.	970	394	331	322	25	2	5,837

CORN MILLS.

Corn Mills.

As in 1891 and 1892, returns were obtained showing the number of Corn Mills in Ireland, with details as to the power used, the kind of corn chiefly ground, and the average quantity ground per week when the mills are at work. The results are given, by provinces and counties, in the following table, from which it appears that the total number of mills returned is 1,588 (an increase of 36 as compared with the number for 1892) of which

1,342 were worked by water, 93 by steam, 23 by wind, and 77 by water and steam; and that wheat was the chief kind of corn ground in 292 mills, oats in 999, and Indian corn in 236. In 820 of the 1,533 mills the average quantity ground per week, when the mills are at work, exceeds 500 cwts.

TABLE XX.—Number of CORN MILLS in 18[illegible], by COUNTIES and PROVINCES, classified according to the Power used, the kind of Corn chiefly ground, and the average Quantity (in cwts.) ground per week when the Mills are at work.

Counties and Provinces.	Total No. of Mills.	Description of Power used: Water	Steam	Wind	Water and Steam	Kind of Corn chiefly ground: Wheat	Oats	Indian Corn	All others	Average Quantity ground per week when at work: Under 50 cwts.	[illegible]	[illegible]	[illegible]	[illegible]	[illegible]
		Number of Mills.				Number of Mills.				Number of Mills.					
LEINSTER:															
Carlow,	[illegible]	[illegible]	[illegible]	[illegible]	[illegible]	[illegible]	[illegible]	[illegible]	[illegible]	[illegible]	[illegible]	[illegible]	[illegible]	[illegible]	[illegible]
Dublin,	[illegible]	[illegible]	[illegible]	[illegible]	[illegible]	[illegible]	[illegible]	[illegible]	[illegible]	[illegible]	[illegible]	[illegible]	[illegible]	[illegible]	[illegible]
Kildare,	[illegible]	[illegible]	[illegible]	[illegible]	[illegible]	[illegible]	[illegible]	[illegible]	[illegible]	[illegible]	[illegible]	[illegible]	[illegible]	[illegible]	[illegible]
Kilkenny,	[illegible]	[illegible]	[illegible]	[illegible]	[illegible]	[illegible]	[illegible]	[illegible]	[illegible]	[illegible]	[illegible]	[illegible]	[illegible]	[illegible]	[illegible]
King's,	[illegible]	[illegible]	[illegible]	[illegible]	[illegible]	[illegible]	[illegible]	[illegible]	[illegible]	[illegible]	[illegible]	[illegible]	[illegible]	[illegible]	[illegible]
Longford,	[illegible]	[illegible]	[illegible]	[illegible]	[illegible]	[illegible]	[illegible]	[illegible]	[illegible]	[illegible]	[illegible]	[illegible]	[illegible]	[illegible]	[illegible]
Louth and Drogheda, County of Town,	[illegible]	[illegible]	[illegible]	[illegible]	[illegible]	[illegible]	[illegible]	[illegible]	[illegible]	[illegible]	[illegible]	[illegible]	[illegible]	[illegible]	[illegible]
Meath,	[illegible]	[illegible]	[illegible]	[illegible]	[illegible]	[illegible]	[illegible]	[illegible]	[illegible]	[illegible]	[illegible]	[illegible]	[illegible]	[illegible]	[illegible]
Queen's,	[illegible]	[illegible]	[illegible]	[illegible]	[illegible]	[illegible]	[illegible]	[illegible]	[illegible]	[illegible]	[illegible]	[illegible]	[illegible]	[illegible]	[illegible]
Westmeath,	[illegible]	[illegible]	[illegible]	[illegible]	[illegible]	[illegible]	[illegible]	[illegible]	[illegible]	[illegible]	[illegible]	[illegible]	[illegible]	[illegible]	[illegible]
Wexford,	[illegible]	[illegible]	[illegible]	[illegible]	[illegible]	[illegible]	[illegible]	[illegible]	[illegible]	[illegible]	[illegible]	[illegible]	[illegible]	[illegible]	[illegible]
Wicklow,	[illegible]	[illegible]	[illegible]	[illegible]	[illegible]	[illegible]	[illegible]	[illegible]	[illegible]	[illegible]	[illegible]	[illegible]	[illegible]	[illegible]	[illegible]
Total,	[illegible]	[illegible]	[illegible]	[illegible]	[illegible]	[illegible]	[illegible]	[illegible]	[illegible]	[illegible]	[illegible]	[illegible]	[illegible]	[illegible]	[illegible]
MUNSTER:															
Clare,	[illegible]	[illegible]	[illegible]	[illegible]	[illegible]	[illegible]	[illegible]	[illegible]	[illegible]	[illegible]	[illegible]	[illegible]	[illegible]	[illegible]	[illegible]
Cork,	[illegible]	[illegible]	[illegible]	[illegible]	[illegible]	[illegible]	[illegible]	[illegible]	[illegible]	[illegible]	[illegible]	[illegible]	[illegible]	[illegible]	[illegible]
Kerry,	[illegible]	[illegible]	[illegible]	[illegible]	[illegible]	[illegible]	[illegible]	[illegible]	[illegible]	[illegible]	[illegible]	[illegible]	[illegible]	[illegible]	[illegible]
Limerick,	[illegible]	[illegible]	[illegible]	[illegible]	[illegible]	[illegible]	[illegible]	[illegible]	[illegible]	[illegible]	[illegible]	[illegible]	[illegible]	[illegible]	[illegible]
Tipperary,	[illegible]	[illegible]	[illegible]	[illegible]	[illegible]	[illegible]	[illegible]	[illegible]	[illegible]	[illegible]	[illegible]	[illegible]	[illegible]	[illegible]	[illegible]
Waterford,	[illegible]	[illegible]	[illegible]	[illegible]	[illegible]	[illegible]	[illegible]	[illegible]	[illegible]	[illegible]	[illegible]	[illegible]	[illegible]	[illegible]	[illegible]
Total,	[illegible]	[illegible]	[illegible]	[illegible]	[illegible]	[illegible]	[illegible]	[illegible]	[illegible]	[illegible]	[illegible]	[illegible]	[illegible]	[illegible]	[illegible]
ULSTER:															
Antrim,	[illegible]	[illegible]	[illegible]	[illegible]	[illegible]	[illegible]	[illegible]	[illegible]	[illegible]	[illegible]	[illegible]	[illegible]	[illegible]	[illegible]	[illegible]
Armagh,	[illegible]	[illegible]	[illegible]	[illegible]	[illegible]	[illegible]	[illegible]	[illegible]	[illegible]	[illegible]	[illegible]	[illegible]	[illegible]	[illegible]	[illegible]
Cavan,	[illegible]	[illegible]	[illegible]	[illegible]	[illegible]	[illegible]	[illegible]	[illegible]	[illegible]	[illegible]	[illegible]	[illegible]	[illegible]	[illegible]	[illegible]
Donegal,	[illegible]	[illegible]	[illegible]	[illegible]	[illegible]	[illegible]	[illegible]	[illegible]	[illegible]	[illegible]	[illegible]	[illegible]	[illegible]	[illegible]	[illegible]
Down,	[illegible]	[illegible]	[illegible]	[illegible]	[illegible]	[illegible]	[illegible]	[illegible]	[illegible]	[illegible]	[illegible]	[illegible]	[illegible]	[illegible]	[illegible]
Fermanagh,	[illegible]	[illegible]	[illegible]	[illegible]	[illegible]	[illegible]	[illegible]	[illegible]	[illegible]	[illegible]	[illegible]	[illegible]	[illegible]	[illegible]	[illegible]
Londonderry,	[illegible]	[illegible]	[illegible]	[illegible]	[illegible]	[illegible]	[illegible]	[illegible]	[illegible]	[illegible]	[illegible]	[illegible]	[illegible]	[illegible]	[illegible]
Monaghan,	[illegible]	[illegible]	[illegible]	[illegible]	[illegible]	[illegible]	[illegible]	[illegible]	[illegible]	[illegible]	[illegible]	[illegible]	[illegible]	[illegible]	[illegible]
Tyrone,	[illegible]	[illegible]	[illegible]	[illegible]	[illegible]	[illegible]	[illegible]	[illegible]	[illegible]	[illegible]	[illegible]	[illegible]	[illegible]	[illegible]	[illegible]
Total,	[illegible]	[illegible]	[illegible]	[illegible]	[illegible]	[illegible]	[illegible]	[illegible]	[illegible]	[illegible]	[illegible]	[illegible]	[illegible]	[illegible]	[illegible]
CONNAUGHT:															
Galway,	[illegible]	[illegible]	[illegible]	[illegible]	[illegible]	[illegible]	[illegible]	[illegible]	[illegible]	[illegible]	[illegible]	[illegible]	[illegible]	[illegible]	[illegible]
Leitrim,	[illegible]	[illegible]	[illegible]	[illegible]	[illegible]	[illegible]	[illegible]	[illegible]	[illegible]	[illegible]	[illegible]	[illegible]	[illegible]	[illegible]	[illegible]
Mayo,	[illegible]	[illegible]	[illegible]	[illegible]	[illegible]	[illegible]	[illegible]	[illegible]	[illegible]	[illegible]	[illegible]	[illegible]	[illegible]	[illegible]	[illegible]
Roscommon,	[illegible]	[illegible]	[illegible]	[illegible]	[illegible]	[illegible]	[illegible]	[illegible]	[illegible]	[illegible]	[illegible]	[illegible]	[illegible]	[illegible]	[illegible]
Sligo,	[illegible]	[illegible]	[illegible]	[illegible]	[illegible]	[illegible]	[illegible]	[illegible]	[illegible]	[illegible]	[illegible]	[illegible]	[illegible]	[illegible]	[illegible]
Total,	[illegible]	[illegible]	[illegible]	[illegible]	[illegible]	[illegible]	[illegible]	[illegible]	[illegible]	[illegible]	[illegible]	[illegible]	[illegible]	[illegible]	[illegible]
TOTAL OF IRELAND,	[illegible]	[illegible]	[illegible]	[illegible]	[illegible]	[illegible]	[illegible]	[illegible]	[illegible]	[illegible]	[illegible]	[illegible]	[illegible]	[illegible]	[illegible]

SILOS AND ENSILAGE

Following the course adopted in the six previous years relative to Ensilage, I communicated with those Landed Proprietors and Landholders, throughout the country, reported to me as having Silos or otherwise making Ensilage, requesting them to favour me with certain details regarding the methods followed and the results obtained in the year 1893. I received replies to 217 out of 536 circulars issued by me, and I beg to express my obligations to my correspondents for the valuable and interesting information afforded. It will be found set forth in the Appendix, pp. 90 to 119. Many of the replies stated that no ensilage was made during the season of 1893, owing to the weather being so favourable for the saving of hay.

The following Table (XXI.) shows, by Counties and Provinces, for the years 1892 and 1893, the number of Silos or Stacks mentioned in the communications received from the persons who forwarded replies to the circular above referred to:—

Counties.	Number in 1892.	Number in 1893.	Counties.	Number in 1892.	Number in 1893.
Antrim,	11	10	Mayo,	18	11
Armagh,	–	–	Meath,	26	33
Carlow,	8	8	Monaghan,	1	–
Cavan,	3	3	Queen's,	12	7
Clare,	6	5	Roscommon,	10	13
Cork,	19	6	Sligo,	3	9
Donegal,	5	6	Tipperary,	20	11
Down,	4	5	Tyrone,	8	8
Dublin,	8	5	Waterford,	3	8
Fermanagh,	5	4	Westmeath,	10	18
Galway,	14	10	Wexford,	5	1
Kerry,	3	8	Wicklow,	4	4
Kildare,	17	7			
Kilkenny,	11	9	PROVINCES.		
King's,	28	11	Leinster,	184	94
Leitrim,	10	4	Munster,	56	34
Limerick,	6	7	Ulster,	53	46
Londonderry,	9	14	Connaught,	64	39
Longford,	4	3			
Louth,	6	1	TOTAL OF IRELAND,	296	313

FORESTRY OPERATIONS.

The inquiries into Forestry Operations instituted in 1890, and continued in 1891, and 1892, were repeated in 1893. The details are set forth in the GENERAL ABSTRACT of FORESTRY OPERATIONS in IRELAND during the year ended 30th June, 1893. The subjects dealt with in the Abstract are—I. Planting—The area planted during the year ended 30th June, 1893, the total number of trees planted in that period, and the number of each description; II. Felling—The area cleared and the number of trees of each description felled; III. Ages of trees felled; IV. Disposal of timber. The inquiry did not extend to the planting or felling of isolated trees.

It appears that during the period 1851–93 there were some slight fluctuations in the acreage, and that comparing 1893 with 1851 there has been an increase of about 0·8 per cent., the extent under woods and plantations in 1851 being 304,906 statute acres, and in last year 307,336 acres.

During the year ended 30th June, 1893, 1,111 acres were planted with trees, against 1,193 acres in the preceding year. Larch trees constituted 47·3 per cent., fir trees 18·6 per cent., and spruce trees 5·7 per cent., of the total number planted.

In connection with this subject it may be here mentioned that from the passing of the Act 29 and 30 Vic., cap. 40, to the 31st March, 1893, 120 loans for £27,055 have been sanctioned for planting for shelter, and of this number five, amounting to £1,125, were sanctioned in the last year of the period.

The number of trees felled both for clearance and for thinning plantations amounted to 1,190,820. The area returned as cleared is 1,552 acres.

Of the 1,190,820 trees felled, 651,698 were used for "propping," which appears to have been the chief purpose to which the timber of almost all descriptions was applied. The numbers applied to the principal specified uses comprise also:—23,566 trees for sleepers, 158,191 for paling, 3,760 for spools, &c., 9,998 for fuel, 22,625 for furniture and building purposes, 6,816 for carts, wagons, &c., 4,708 for clog soles, and 3,030 for ship-building.

WAGES OF AGRICULTURAL LABOURERS IN 1893.

Enquiries were made as to the Wages paid to Agricultural Labourers in 1893, and the information received from the District Inspectors of the Royal Irish Constabulary with reference to their respective districts is shown in the following Table (XXII.) and notes appended thereto.

I.—PROVINCE OF LEINSTER.

Counties and Constabulary Districts.	Summer.								Winter.							
	Men.		Boys.		Women.		Girls.		Men.		Boys.		Women.		Girls.	
	From	To	From	To	From	To	From	To	From	To	From	To	From	To	From	To
	s. d.	s. d.	s. d.	s. d.	s. d.	s. d.	s. d.	s. d.	s. d.	s. d.	s. d.	s. d.	s. d.	s. d.	s. d.	s. d.
CARLOW COUNTY.																
[illegible] (a).	[illegible]	[illegible]	[illegible]	[illegible]	[illegible]	[illegible]	[illegible]	[illegible]	[illegible]	[illegible]	[illegible]	[illegible]	[illegible]	[illegible]	[illegible]	[illegible]
Carlow,	[illegible]	[illegible]	[illegible]	[illegible]	[illegible]	[illegible]	[illegible]	[illegible]	[illegible]	[illegible]	[illegible]	[illegible]	[illegible]	[illegible]	[illegible]	[illegible]
DUBLIN COUNTY.																
Balbriggan (b).	[illegible]	[illegible]	[illegible]	[illegible]	[illegible]	[illegible]	[illegible]	[illegible]	[illegible]	[illegible]	[illegible]	[illegible]	[illegible]	[illegible]	[illegible]	[illegible]
Clontarf.	[illegible]	[illegible]	[illegible]	[illegible]	[illegible]	[illegible]	[illegible]	[illegible]	[illegible]	[illegible]	[illegible]	[illegible]	[illegible]	[illegible]	[illegible]	[illegible]
Dundrum.	[illegible]	[illegible]	[illegible]	[illegible]	[illegible]	[illegible]	[illegible]	[illegible]	[illegible]	[illegible]	[illegible]	[illegible]	[illegible]	[illegible]	[illegible]	–
Lucan (c).	[illegible]	[illegible]	[illegible]	[illegible]	[illegible]	[illegible]	[illegible]	[illegible]	[illegible]	[illegible]	[illegible]	[illegible]	[illegible]	[illegible]	[illegible]	[illegible]
KILDARE COUNTY.																
Athy.	[illegible]	[illegible]	[illegible]	[illegible]	[illegible]	[illegible]	[illegible]	[illegible]	[illegible]	[illegible]	[illegible]	[illegible]	[illegible]	[illegible]	[illegible]	[illegible]
Kildare.	[illegible]	[illegible]	[illegible]	[illegible]	[illegible]	[illegible]	[illegible]	[illegible]	[illegible]	[illegible]	[illegible]	[illegible]	[illegible]	[illegible]	[illegible]	[illegible]
Naas (d).	[illegible]	[illegible]	[illegible]	[illegible]	[illegible]	[illegible]	[illegible]	[illegible]	[illegible]	[illegible]	[illegible]	[illegible]	[illegible]	[illegible]	[illegible]	[illegible]
Robertstown (d).	[illegible]	[illegible]	[illegible]	[illegible]	[illegible]	[illegible]	[illegible]	[illegible]	[illegible]	[illegible]	[illegible]	[illegible]	–	–	–	–
KILKENNY COUNTY.																
Callan (d).	[illegible]	[illegible]	[illegible]	[illegible]	[illegible]	[illegible]	[illegible]	[illegible]	[illegible]	[illegible]	[illegible]	[illegible]	[illegible]	[illegible]	[illegible]	[illegible]
Castlecomer (e).	[illegible]	[illegible]	[illegible]	[illegible]	[illegible]	[illegible]	[illegible]	[illegible]	[illegible]	[illegible]	[illegible]	[illegible]	[illegible]	[illegible]	[illegible]	[illegible]
Johnstown (b).	[illegible]	[illegible]	[illegible]	[illegible]	[illegible]	[illegible]	[illegible]	[illegible]	[illegible]	[illegible]	[illegible]	[illegible]	[illegible]	[illegible]	[illegible]	[illegible]
Kilkenny.	[illegible]	[illegible]	[illegible]	[illegible]	[illegible]	[illegible]	[illegible]	[illegible]	[illegible]	[illegible]	[illegible]	[illegible]	[illegible]	[illegible]	[illegible]	[illegible]
Piltown.	[illegible]	[illegible]	[illegible]	[illegible]	[illegible]	[illegible]	[illegible]	[illegible]	[illegible]	[illegible]	[illegible]	[illegible]	[illegible]	[illegible]	[illegible]	[illegible]
Thomastown (f).	[illegible]	[illegible]	[illegible]	[illegible]	[illegible]	[illegible]	[illegible]	[illegible]	[illegible]	[illegible]	[illegible]	[illegible]	[illegible]	[illegible]	[illegible]	[illegible]
KING'S COUNTY.																
[illegible].	[illegible]	[illegible]	[illegible]	[illegible]	[illegible]	[illegible]	[illegible]	[illegible]	[illegible]	[illegible]	[illegible]	[illegible]	[illegible]	[illegible]	[illegible]	[illegible]
Edenderry.	[illegible]	[illegible]	[illegible]	[illegible]	[illegible]	[illegible]	[illegible]	[illegible]	[illegible]	[illegible]	[illegible]	[illegible]	[illegible]	[illegible]	[illegible]	[illegible]
Parsonstown.	[illegible]	[illegible]	[illegible]	[illegible]	[illegible]	[illegible]	[illegible]	[illegible]	[illegible]	[illegible]	[illegible]	[illegible]	[illegible]	[illegible]	[illegible]	[illegible]
[illegible] (f).	[illegible]	[illegible]	[illegible]	[illegible]	[illegible]	[illegible]	[illegible]	[illegible]	[illegible]	[illegible]	[illegible]	[illegible]	[illegible]	[illegible]	[illegible]	[illegible]
Tullamore (g).	[illegible]	[illegible]	[illegible]	[illegible]	[illegible]	[illegible]	[illegible]	[illegible]	[illegible]	[illegible]	[illegible]	[illegible]	[illegible]	[illegible]	[illegible]	[illegible]
LONGFORD COUNTY.																
Ballymahon (h).	[illegible]	[illegible]	[illegible]	[illegible]	[illegible]	[illegible]	[illegible]	[illegible]	[illegible]	[illegible]	[illegible]	[illegible]	[illegible]	[illegible]	[illegible]	[illegible]
Granard.	[illegible]	[illegible]	[illegible]	[illegible]	[illegible]	[illegible]	[illegible]	[illegible]	[illegible]	[illegible]	[illegible]	[illegible]	[illegible]	[illegible]	[illegible]	[illegible]
Longford (m).	[illegible]	[illegible]	[illegible]	[illegible]	[illegible]	[illegible]	[illegible]	[illegible]	[illegible]	[illegible]	[illegible]	[illegible]	[illegible]	[illegible]	–	–
LOUTH COUNTY.																
Ardee (n).	[illegible]	[illegible]	[illegible]	[illegible]	[illegible]	[illegible]	[illegible]	[illegible]	[illegible]	[illegible]	[illegible]	[illegible]	[illegible]	[illegible]	[illegible]	[illegible]
Collon (i).	[illegible]	[illegible]	[illegible]	[illegible]	–	–	–	–	[illegible]	[illegible]	[illegible]	[illegible]	–	–	–	–
Dundalk (p).	[illegible]	[illegible]	[illegible]	[illegible]	[illegible]	[illegible]	[illegible]	[illegible]	[illegible]	[illegible]	[illegible]	[illegible]	[illegible]	[illegible]	[illegible]	[illegible]
Drogheda.	[illegible]	[illegible]	[illegible]	[illegible]	[illegible]	[illegible]	[illegible]	[illegible]	[illegible]	[illegible]	[illegible]	[illegible]	[illegible]	[illegible]	[illegible]	[illegible]

(a) The average wages without diet, [illegible]

[illegible]

I.—PROVINCE OF LEINSTER—*continued.*

Counties and Constabulary Districts.	Summer.								Winter.							
	Men.		Boys.		Women.		Girls.		Men.		Boys.		Women.		Girls.	
	From	To	From	To	From	To	From	To	From	To	From	To	From	To	From	To
Meath County.	s. d.	s. d.	s. d.	s. d.	s. d.	s. d.	s. d.	s. d.	s. d.	s. d.	s. d.	s. d.	s. d.	s. d.	s. d.	s. d.
Athboy,	[illegible]	[illegible]	[illegible]	[illegible]	[illegible]	[illegible]	[illegible]	[illegible]	[illegible]	[illegible]	[illegible]	[illegible]	[illegible]	[illegible]	[illegible]	[illegible]
Dunshaughlin (a),	[illegible]	–	[illegible]	–	[illegible]	–	–	–	[illegible]	–	[illegible]	–	–	–	–	–
Kells,	[illegible]	[illegible]	[illegible]	[illegible]	[illegible]	[illegible]	[illegible]	[illegible]	[illegible]	[illegible]	[illegible]	[illegible]	[illegible]	[illegible]	[illegible]	[illegible]
Navan,	[illegible]	[illegible]	[illegible]	[illegible]	[illegible]	[illegible]	[illegible]	[illegible]	[illegible]	[illegible]	[illegible]	[illegible]	[illegible]	[illegible]	[illegible]	[illegible]
Slane (f),	[illegible]	[illegible]	[illegible]	[illegible]	[illegible]	[illegible]	[illegible]	[illegible]	[illegible]	[illegible]	[illegible]	[illegible]	[illegible]	[illegible]	[illegible]	[illegible]
Trim (e),	[illegible]	[illegible]	[illegible]	[illegible]	[illegible]	[illegible]	[illegible]	[illegible]	[illegible]	[illegible]	[illegible]	[illegible]	[illegible]	[illegible]	[illegible]	[illegible]
Queen's County.																
Abbeyleix,	[illegible]	[illegible]	[illegible]	[illegible]	[illegible]	[illegible]	[illegible]	[illegible]	[illegible]	[illegible]	[illegible]	[illegible]	[illegible]	[illegible]	[illegible]	[illegible]
Ballybrittas (h),	[illegible]	[illegible]	[illegible]	[illegible]	[illegible]	[illegible]	[illegible]	[illegible]	[illegible]	[illegible]	[illegible]	[illegible]	[illegible]	[illegible]	[illegible]	[illegible]
Maryborough (k),	[illegible]	[illegible]	[illegible]	[illegible]	[illegible]	[illegible]	[illegible]	[illegible]	[illegible]	[illegible]	[illegible]	[illegible]	[illegible]	[illegible]	[illegible]	[illegible]
Mountrath,	[illegible]	[illegible]	[illegible]	[illegible]	[illegible]	[illegible]	[illegible]	[illegible]	[illegible]	[illegible]	[illegible]	[illegible]	[illegible]	[illegible]	[illegible]	[illegible]
Westmeath County.																
Ballymore,	[illegible]	[illegible]	[illegible]	[illegible]	[illegible]	[illegible]	–	–	[illegible]	[illegible]	[illegible]	[illegible]	–	–	–	–
Castlepollard (l),	[illegible]	[illegible]	[illegible]	[illegible]	[illegible]	[illegible]	[illegible]	[illegible]	[illegible]	[illegible]	[illegible]	[illegible]	[illegible]	[illegible]	[illegible]	[illegible]
Delvin (m),	[illegible]	[illegible]	[illegible]	[illegible]	[illegible]	[illegible]	[illegible]	[illegible]	[illegible]	[illegible]	[illegible]	[illegible]	–	–	–	–
Kilbeggan,	[illegible]	[illegible]	[illegible]	[illegible]	[illegible]	[illegible]	[illegible]	[illegible]	[illegible]	[illegible]	[illegible]	[illegible]	[illegible]	[illegible]	[illegible]	[illegible]
Moate,	[illegible]	[illegible]	[illegible]	[illegible]	[illegible]	[illegible]	[illegible]	[illegible]	[illegible]	[illegible]	[illegible]	[illegible]	[illegible]	[illegible]	[illegible]	[illegible]
Mullingar,	[illegible]	[illegible]	[illegible]	[illegible]	[illegible]	[illegible]	[illegible]	[illegible]	[illegible]	[illegible]	[illegible]	[illegible]	[illegible]	[illegible]	[illegible]	[illegible]
Wexford County.																
Enniscorthy,	[illegible]	[illegible]	[illegible]	[illegible]	[illegible]	[illegible]	[illegible]	[illegible]	[illegible]	[illegible]	[illegible]	[illegible]	[illegible]	[illegible]	[illegible]	[illegible]
Gorey (o),	[illegible]	[illegible]	[illegible]	[illegible]	[illegible]	[illegible]	[illegible]	[illegible]	[illegible]	[illegible]	–	–	–	–	–	–
New Ross (p),	[illegible]	–	[illegible]	–	[illegible]	–	[illegible]	–	[illegible]	–	[illegible]	–	[illegible]	–	[illegible]	–
Taghmon,	[illegible]	[illegible]	[illegible]	[illegible]	[illegible]	[illegible]	[illegible]	[illegible]	[illegible]	[illegible]	[illegible]	[illegible]	[illegible]	[illegible]	[illegible]	[illegible]
Wexford,	[illegible]	[illegible]	[illegible]	[illegible]	[illegible]	[illegible]	[illegible]	[illegible]	[illegible]	[illegible]	[illegible]	[illegible]	[illegible]	[illegible]	[illegible]	[illegible]
Wicklow County.																
Arklow (q),	[illegible]	[illegible]	[illegible]	[illegible]	[illegible]	[illegible]	[illegible]	[illegible]	[illegible]	[illegible]	[illegible]	[illegible]	[illegible]	[illegible]	[illegible]	[illegible]
Bray (r),	[illegible]	[illegible]	[illegible]	[illegible]	[illegible]	[illegible]	[illegible]	[illegible]	[illegible]	[illegible]	[illegible]	[illegible]	[illegible]	[illegible]	[illegible]	[illegible]
Dunlavin,	[illegible]	[illegible]	[illegible]	[illegible]	[illegible]	[illegible]	[illegible]	[illegible]	[illegible]	[illegible]	[illegible]	[illegible]	[illegible]	[illegible]	[illegible]	[illegible]
Wicklow,	[illegible]	[illegible]	[illegible]	[illegible]	[illegible]	[illegible]	[illegible]	[illegible]	[illegible]	[illegible]	[illegible]	[illegible]	[illegible]	[illegible]	[illegible]	[illegible]

II.—PROVINCE OF MUNSTER.

Counties and Constabulary Districts.	Men From	Men To	Boys From	Boys To	Women From	Women To	Girls From	Girls To	Men From	Men To	Boys From	Boys To	Women From	Women To	Girls From	Girls To
Clare County.																
Ballyvaughan (s),	[illegible]	[illegible]	[illegible]	[illegible]	[illegible]	[illegible]	[illegible]	[illegible]	[illegible]	[illegible]	[illegible]	[illegible]	–	–	–	–
Corofin (sa),	[illegible]	[illegible]	[illegible]	[illegible]	–	–	–	–	[illegible]	[illegible]	[illegible]	[illegible]	–	–	–	–
Ennis,	[illegible]	[illegible]	[illegible]	[illegible]	[illegible]	[illegible]	[illegible]	[illegible]	[illegible]	[illegible]	[illegible]	[illegible]	[illegible]	[illegible]	[illegible]	[illegible]
Ennistymon,	[illegible]	–	[illegible]	–	[illegible]	–	[illegible]	–	[illegible]	–	[illegible]	–	[illegible]	–	[illegible]	–
Killadysert,	[illegible]	[illegible]	[illegible]	[illegible]	[illegible]	[illegible]	[illegible]	[illegible]	[illegible]	[illegible]	[illegible]	[illegible]	[illegible]	[illegible]	[illegible]	[illegible]
Kilkee,	[illegible]	[illegible]	[illegible]	[illegible]	[illegible]	[illegible]	[illegible]	[illegible]	[illegible]	[illegible]	[illegible]	[illegible]	[illegible]	[illegible]	[illegible]	[illegible]
Kilrush,	[illegible]	[illegible]	[illegible]	[illegible]	[illegible]	[illegible]	[illegible]	[illegible]	[illegible]	[illegible]	[illegible]	[illegible]	[illegible]	[illegible]	[illegible]	[illegible]
Sixmilebridge,	[illegible]	[illegible]	[illegible]	[illegible]	[illegible]	[illegible]	[illegible]	[illegible]	[illegible]	[illegible]	[illegible]	[illegible]	[illegible]	[illegible]	[illegible]	[illegible]
Tulla,	[illegible]	[illegible]	[illegible]	[illegible]	[illegible]	[illegible]	[illegible]	[illegible]	[illegible]	[illegible]	[illegible]	[illegible]	[illegible]	[illegible]	[illegible]	[illegible]

(a) [illegible]

[illegible]

II.—PROVINCE OF MUNSTER—continued.

Counties and Constabulary Districts.	Summer.								Winter.							
	Men.		Boys.		Women.		Girls.		Men.		Boys.		Women.		Girls.	
	From	To	From	To	From	To	From	To	From	To	From	To	From	To	From	To
	s. d.	s. d.	s. d.	s. d.	s. d.	s. d.	s. d.	s. d.	s. d.	s. d.	s. d.	s. d.	s. d.	s. d.	s. d.	s. d.
CORK COUNTY (E.R.)																
Ballincollig (a),	[illegible]	-	[illegible]	-	[illegible]	-	[illegible]	-	[illegible]	-	[illegible]	-	[illegible]	-	[illegible]	-
Charleville,	[illegible]	[illegible]	[illegible]	[illegible]	[illegible]	[illegible]	[illegible]	[illegible]	[illegible]	[illegible]	[illegible]	[illegible]	[illegible]	[illegible]	[illegible]	[illegible]
Cork, North,	[illegible]	[illegible]	[illegible]	[illegible]	[illegible]	[illegible]	[illegible]	[illegible]	[illegible]	[illegible]	[illegible]	[illegible]	[illegible]	[illegible]	[illegible]	[illegible]
Cork, South,	[illegible]	[illegible]	[illegible]	[illegible]	[illegible]	[illegible]	[illegible]	[illegible]	[illegible]	[illegible]	[illegible]	[illegible]	[illegible]	[illegible]	[illegible]	[illegible]
Fermoy	[illegible]	[illegible]	[illegible]	[illegible]	[illegible]	[illegible]	[illegible]	[illegible]	[illegible]	[illegible]	[illegible]	[illegible]	[illegible]	[illegible]	[illegible]	[illegible]
Kanturk,	[illegible]	[illegible]	[illegible]	[illegible]	[illegible]	[illegible]	[illegible]	[illegible]	[illegible]	[illegible]	[illegible]	[illegible]	[illegible]	[illegible]	[illegible]	[illegible]
Kinsale (b),	[illegible]	[illegible]	[illegible]	[illegible]	[illegible]	[illegible]	[illegible]	[illegible]	[illegible]	[illegible]	[illegible]	[illegible]	[illegible]	[illegible]	[illegible]	[illegible]
Mallow (c),	[illegible]	[illegible]	[illegible]	[illegible]	[illegible]	[illegible]	[illegible]	[illegible]	[illegible]	[illegible]	[illegible]	[illegible]	[illegible]	[illegible]	[illegible]	[illegible]
Middleton,	[illegible]	[illegible]	[illegible]	[illegible]	[illegible]	[illegible]	[illegible]	[illegible]	[illegible]	[illegible]	[illegible]	[illegible]	[illegible]	[illegible]	[illegible]	[illegible]
Mitchelstown (d),	[illegible]	[illegible]	[illegible]	[illegible]	[illegible]	[illegible]	[illegible]	[illegible]	[illegible]	[illegible]	[illegible]	[illegible]	[illegible]	[illegible]	[illegible]	[illegible]
Newmarket (e),	[illegible]	[illegible]	[illegible]	[illegible]	[illegible]	[illegible]	[illegible]	[illegible]	[illegible]	[illegible]	[illegible]	[illegible]	[illegible]	[illegible]	[illegible]	[illegible]
Queenstown (f),	[illegible]	[illegible]	[illegible]	[illegible]	[illegible]	[illegible]	[illegible]	[illegible]	[illegible]	[illegible]	[illegible]	[illegible]	[illegible]	[illegible]	[illegible]	[illegible]
Youghal (g),	[illegible]	[illegible]	[illegible]	[illegible]	[illegible]	[illegible]	[illegible]	[illegible]	[illegible]	[illegible]	[illegible]	[illegible]	[illegible]	[illegible]	[illegible]	[illegible]
CORK COUNTY (W.R.)																
Bandon,	[illegible]	[illegible]	[illegible]	[illegible]	[illegible]	[illegible]	[illegible]	[illegible]	[illegible]	[illegible]	[illegible]	[illegible]	[illegible]	[illegible]	[illegible]	[illegible]
Bantry (h),	[illegible]	[illegible]	[illegible]	[illegible]	[illegible]	[illegible]	-	-	[illegible]	[illegible]	[illegible]	[illegible]	-	-	-	-
Castletown Bere,	[illegible]	[illegible]	[illegible]	[illegible]	[illegible]	[illegible]	[illegible]	[illegible]	[illegible]	[illegible]	[illegible]	[illegible]	[illegible]	[illegible]	[illegible]	[illegible]
Clonakilty (i),	[illegible]	[illegible]	[illegible]	[illegible]	[illegible]	[illegible]	[illegible]	[illegible]	[illegible]	[illegible]	[illegible]	[illegible]	[illegible]	[illegible]	[illegible]	[illegible]
Dunmanway,	[illegible]	[illegible]	[illegible]	[illegible]	[illegible]	[illegible]	[illegible]	[illegible]	[illegible]	[illegible]	[illegible]	[illegible]	[illegible]	[illegible]	[illegible]	[illegible]
Macroom,	[illegible]	[illegible]	[illegible]	[illegible]	[illegible]	[illegible]	[illegible]	[illegible]	[illegible]	[illegible]	[illegible]	[illegible]	-	-	-	-
Millstreet,	[illegible]	[illegible]	[illegible]	[illegible]	[illegible]	[illegible]	[illegible]	[illegible]	[illegible]	[illegible]	[illegible]	[illegible]	[illegible]	[illegible]	[illegible]	[illegible]
Skibbereen (k),	[illegible]	[illegible]	[illegible]	-	[illegible]	-	[illegible]	-	[illegible]	[illegible]	[illegible]	-	[illegible]	-	[illegible]	-
Skull (l),	[illegible]	[illegible]	[illegible]	[illegible]	[illegible]	[illegible]	[illegible]	[illegible]	[illegible]	[illegible]	[illegible]	[illegible]	[illegible]	[illegible]	[illegible]	[illegible]
KERRY COUNTY.																
Cahersiveen (m),	[illegible]	[illegible]	[illegible]	[illegible]	[illegible]	[illegible]	[illegible]	[illegible]	[illegible]	[illegible]	[illegible]	[illegible]	[illegible]	[illegible]	[illegible]	[illegible]
Castleisland,	[illegible]	[illegible]	[illegible]	[illegible]	[illegible]	[illegible]	[illegible]	[illegible]	[illegible]	[illegible]	[illegible]	[illegible]	[illegible]	[illegible]	[illegible]	[illegible]
Dingle,	[illegible]	[illegible]	[illegible]	[illegible]	[illegible]	[illegible]	[illegible]	[illegible]	[illegible]	[illegible]	[illegible]	[illegible]	[illegible]	[illegible]	[illegible]	[illegible]
Kenmare,	[illegible]	[illegible]	[illegible]	[illegible]	[illegible]	[illegible]	[illegible]	[illegible]	[illegible]	[illegible]	[illegible]	[illegible]	[illegible]	[illegible]	-	-
Killarney (n),	[illegible]	[illegible]	[illegible]	[illegible]	[illegible]	[illegible]	[illegible]	[illegible]	[illegible]	[illegible]	[illegible]	[illegible]	[illegible]	[illegible]	[illegible]	[illegible]
Killorglin,	[illegible]	[illegible]	[illegible]	[illegible]	[illegible]	[illegible]	[illegible]	[illegible]	[illegible]	[illegible]	[illegible]	[illegible]	[illegible]	[illegible]	[illegible]	[illegible]
Listowel,	[illegible]	[illegible]	[illegible]	[illegible]	[illegible]	[illegible]	[illegible]	[illegible]	[illegible]	[illegible]	[illegible]	[illegible]	[illegible]	[illegible]	[illegible]	[illegible]
Tralee (o),	[illegible]	[illegible]	[illegible]	[illegible]	[illegible]	[illegible]	[illegible]	[illegible]	[illegible]	[illegible]	[illegible]	[illegible]	[illegible]	[illegible]	[illegible]	[illegible]
LIMERICK COUNTY.																
Abbeyfeale (r),	[illegible]	[illegible]	[illegible]	[illegible]	[illegible]	[illegible]	[illegible]	[illegible]	[illegible]	[illegible]	[illegible]	[illegible]	[illegible]	[illegible]	[illegible]	[illegible]
Adare (p),	[illegible]	[illegible]	[illegible]	[illegible]	[illegible]	[illegible]	[illegible]	[illegible]	[illegible]	[illegible]	[illegible]	[illegible]	[illegible]	[illegible]	[illegible]	[illegible]
Bruff (q),	[illegible]	[illegible]	[illegible]	[illegible]	[illegible]	[illegible]	[illegible]	[illegible]	[illegible]	[illegible]	[illegible]	[illegible]	[illegible]	[illegible]	[illegible]	[illegible]
Kilmallock,	[illegible]	[illegible]	[illegible]	[illegible]	[illegible]	[illegible]	[illegible]	[illegible]	[illegible]	[illegible]	[illegible]	[illegible]	[illegible]	[illegible]	[illegible]	[illegible]
Limerick,	[illegible]	[illegible]	[illegible]	[illegible]	[illegible]	[illegible]	[illegible]	[illegible]	[illegible]	[illegible]	[illegible]	[illegible]	[illegible]	[illegible]	[illegible]	[illegible]
Newcastle (t),	[illegible]	[illegible]	[illegible]	[illegible]	[illegible]	[illegible]	[illegible]	[illegible]	[illegible]	[illegible]	[illegible]	[illegible]	[illegible]	[illegible]	[illegible]	[illegible]
New Pallas (u),	[illegible]	[illegible]	[illegible]	[illegible]	[illegible]	[illegible]	[illegible]	[illegible]	[illegible]	[illegible]	[illegible]	[illegible]	[illegible]	[illegible]	[illegible]	[illegible]
Rathkeale (v),	[illegible]	[illegible]	[illegible]	[illegible]	[illegible]	[illegible]	[illegible]	[illegible]	[illegible]	[illegible]	[illegible]	[illegible]	[illegible]	[illegible]	[illegible]	[illegible]

II.—PROVINCE OF MUNSTER—continued.

Counties and Chief Market Districts.	Summer. Men. From	To	Boys. From	To	Women. From	To	Girls. From	To	Winter. Men. From	To	Boys. From	To	Women. From	To	Girls. From	To
	s. d.	s. d.	s. d.	s. d.	s. d.	s. d.	s. d.	s. d.	s. d.	s. d.	s. d.	s. d.	s. d.	s. d.	s. d.	s. d.
TIPPERARY Co., N.R.																
Borrisokane,	[illegible]	[illegible]	[illegible]	[illegible]	[illegible]	[illegible]	[illegible]	[illegible]	[illegible]	[illegible]	[illegible]	[illegible]	[illegible]	[illegible]	[illegible]	[illegible]
Nenagh,	[illegible]	[illegible]	[illegible]	[illegible]	[illegible]	[illegible]	[illegible]	[illegible]	[illegible]	[illegible]	[illegible]	[illegible]	[illegible]	[illegible]	[illegible]	[illegible]
Newport (e),	[illegible]	[illegible]	[illegible]	[illegible]	[illegible]	[illegible]	[illegible]	[illegible]	[illegible]	[illegible]	[illegible]	[illegible]	[illegible]	[illegible]	[illegible]	[illegible]
Roscrea (f),	[illegible]	[illegible]	[illegible]	[illegible]	[illegible]	[illegible]	[illegible]	[illegible]	[illegible]	[illegible]	[illegible]	[illegible]	[illegible]	[illegible]	[illegible]	[illegible]
[illegible]	[illegible]	[illegible]	[illegible]	[illegible]	[illegible]	[illegible]	[illegible]	[illegible]	[illegible]	[illegible]	[illegible]	[illegible]	[illegible]	[illegible]	[illegible]	[illegible]
Thurles (h),	[illegible]	[illegible]	[illegible]	[illegible]	[illegible]	[illegible]	[illegible]	[illegible]	[illegible]	[illegible]	[illegible]	[illegible]	[illegible]	[illegible]	–	–
TIPPERARY Co., S.R.																
[illegible]	[illegible]	[illegible]	[illegible]	[illegible]	[illegible]	[illegible]	[illegible]	[illegible]	[illegible]	[illegible]	[illegible]	[illegible]	[illegible]	[illegible]	[illegible]	[illegible]
[illegible]	[illegible]	[illegible]	[illegible]	[illegible]	[illegible]	[illegible]	[illegible]	[illegible]	[illegible]	[illegible]	[illegible]	[illegible]	[illegible]	[illegible]	[illegible]	[illegible]
Carrick-on-Suir (f),	[illegible]	[illegible]	[illegible]	[illegible]	[illegible]	[illegible]	[illegible]	[illegible]	[illegible]	[illegible]	[illegible]	[illegible]	[illegible]	[illegible]	[illegible]	[illegible]
Cashel,	[illegible]	[illegible]	[illegible]	[illegible]	[illegible]	[illegible]	[illegible]	[illegible]	[illegible]	[illegible]	[illegible]	[illegible]	[illegible]	[illegible]	[illegible]	[illegible]
Clonmel,	[illegible]	[illegible]	[illegible]	[illegible]	[illegible]	[illegible]	[illegible]	[illegible]	[illegible]	[illegible]	[illegible]	[illegible]	[illegible]	[illegible]	[illegible]	[illegible]
[illegible]	[illegible]	[illegible]	[illegible]	[illegible]	[illegible]	[illegible]	[illegible]	[illegible]	[illegible]	[illegible]	[illegible]	[illegible]	[illegible]	[illegible]	[illegible]	[illegible]
Tipperary,	[illegible]	[illegible]	[illegible]	[illegible]	[illegible]	[illegible]	[illegible]	[illegible]	[illegible]	[illegible]	[illegible]	[illegible]	[illegible]	[illegible]	[illegible]	[illegible]
WATERFORD Co.																
[illegible]	[illegible]	[illegible]	[illegible]	[illegible]	[illegible]	[illegible]	[illegible]	[illegible]	[illegible]	[illegible]	[illegible]	[illegible]	[illegible]	[illegible]	[illegible]	[illegible]
Dungarvan (h),	[illegible]	[illegible]	[illegible]	[illegible]	[illegible]	[illegible]	[illegible]	[illegible]	[illegible]	[illegible]	[illegible]	[illegible]	[illegible]	[illegible]	[illegible]	[illegible]
[illegible]	[illegible]	[illegible]	[illegible]	[illegible]	[illegible]	[illegible]	[illegible]	[illegible]	[illegible]	[illegible]	[illegible]	[illegible]	[illegible]	[illegible]	[illegible]	[illegible]
Waterford (i),	[illegible]	[illegible]	[illegible]	[illegible]	[illegible]	[illegible]	[illegible]	[illegible]	[illegible]	[illegible]	[illegible]	[illegible]	[illegible]	[illegible]	[illegible]	[illegible]

III.—PROVINCE OF ULSTER.

Counties and Chief Market Districts.	Summer. Men. From	To	Boys. From	To	Women. From	To	Girls. From	To	Winter. Men. From	To	Boys. From	To	Women. From	To	Girls. From	To
ANTRIM COUNTY.																
Antrim,	[illegible]	[illegible]	[illegible]	[illegible]	[illegible]	[illegible]	[illegible]	[illegible]	[illegible]	[illegible]	[illegible]	[illegible]	[illegible]	[illegible]	[illegible]	[illegible]
Ballycastle,	[illegible]	[illegible]	[illegible]	[illegible]	[illegible]	[illegible]	[illegible]	[illegible]	[illegible]	[illegible]	[illegible]	[illegible]	[illegible]	[illegible]	[illegible]	[illegible]
Ballymena (j),	[illegible]	[illegible]	[illegible]	[illegible]	[illegible]	[illegible]	[illegible]	[illegible]	[illegible]	[illegible]	[illegible]	[illegible]	[illegible]	[illegible]	[illegible]	–
Belfast East,	[illegible]	[illegible]	[illegible]	[illegible]	[illegible]	[illegible]	[illegible]	[illegible]	[illegible]	[illegible]	[illegible]	[illegible]	[illegible]	[illegible]	[illegible]	[illegible]
Belfast North,	[illegible]	[illegible]	[illegible]	[illegible]	–	–	–	–	[illegible]	[illegible]	[illegible]	[illegible]	–	–	–	–
Belfast South (k),	[illegible]	[illegible]	–	–	[illegible]	[illegible]	–	–	[illegible]	[illegible]	–	–	[illegible]	[illegible]	–	–
Belfast West (l),	[illegible]	[illegible]	[illegible]	[illegible]	[illegible]	[illegible]	[illegible]	[illegible]	[illegible]	[illegible]	[illegible]	[illegible]	–	–	–	–
Larne (m),	[illegible]	[illegible]	[illegible]	[illegible]	[illegible]	[illegible]	[illegible]	[illegible]	[illegible]	[illegible]	[illegible]	[illegible]	[illegible]	[illegible]	[illegible]	[illegible]
Lisburn,	[illegible]	[illegible]	[illegible]	[illegible]	[illegible]	[illegible]	[illegible]	[illegible]	[illegible]	[illegible]	[illegible]	[illegible]	[illegible]	[illegible]	[illegible]	[illegible]
ARMAGH COUNTY.																
Armagh (n),	[illegible]	[illegible]	[illegible]	[illegible]	[illegible]	[illegible]	[illegible]	[illegible]	[illegible]	[illegible]	[illegible]	[illegible]	[illegible]	[illegible]	[illegible]	[illegible]
Lurgan (o),	[illegible]	[illegible]	[illegible]	[illegible]	[illegible]	[illegible]	[illegible]	[illegible]	[illegible]	[illegible]	[illegible]	[illegible]	–	–	–	–
Newry,	[illegible]	[illegible]	[illegible]	[illegible]	[illegible]	[illegible]	[illegible]	[illegible]	[illegible]	[illegible]	[illegible]	[illegible]	[illegible]	[illegible]	[illegible]	[illegible]
Portadown,	[illegible]	[illegible]	[illegible]	[illegible]	[illegible]	[illegible]	[illegible]	[illegible]	[illegible]	[illegible]	[illegible]	[illegible]	[illegible]	[illegible]	[illegible]	[illegible]
CAVAN COUNTY.																
Bailieborough (p),	[illegible]	[illegible]	[illegible]	[illegible]	[illegible]	[illegible]	[illegible]	[illegible]	[illegible]	[illegible]	[illegible]	[illegible]	[illegible]	[illegible]	[illegible]	[illegible]
Cavan (q),	[illegible]	[illegible]	[illegible]	[illegible]	–	–	–	–	[illegible]	[illegible]	[illegible]	[illegible]	–	–	–	–
[illegible]	[illegible]	[illegible]	[illegible]	[illegible]	[illegible]	[illegible]	[illegible]	[illegible]	[illegible]	[illegible]	[illegible]	[illegible]	[illegible]	[illegible]	[illegible]	[illegible]
[illegible]	[illegible]	[illegible]	[illegible]	[illegible]	[illegible]	[illegible]	[illegible]	[illegible]	[illegible]	[illegible]	[illegible]	[illegible]	[illegible]	[illegible]	[illegible]	[illegible]
Virginia,	[illegible]	[illegible]	[illegible]	[illegible]	[illegible]	[illegible]	[illegible]	[illegible]	[illegible]	[illegible]	[illegible]	[illegible]	[illegible]	[illegible]	[illegible]	[illegible]

[illegible]

III.—PROVINCE OF ULSTER—*continued.*

Counties and Poor-Law Unions	Summer								Winter							
	Men		Boys		Women		Girls		Men		Boys		Women		Girls	
	From	To	From	To	From	To	From	To	From	To	From	To	From	To	From	To
	s. d.	s. d.	s. d.	s. d.	s. d.	s. d.	s. d.	s. d.	s. d.	s. d.	s. d.	s. d.	s. d.	s. d.	s. d.	s. d.
DONEGAL COUNTY.																
[illegible]	[illegible]	[illegible]	[illegible]	[illegible]	[illegible]	[illegible]	[illegible]	[illegible]	[illegible]	[illegible]	[illegible]	[illegible]	[illegible]	[illegible]	[illegible]	[illegible]
[illegible]	[illegible]	[illegible]	[illegible]	[illegible]	[illegible]	[illegible]	[illegible]	[illegible]	[illegible]	[illegible]	[illegible]	[illegible]	[illegible]	[illegible]	[illegible]	[illegible]
[illegible]	[illegible]	[illegible]	[illegible]	[illegible]	[illegible]	[illegible]	[illegible]	[illegible]	[illegible]	[illegible]	[illegible]	[illegible]	-	-	-	-
[illegible]	[illegible]	[illegible]	[illegible]	[illegible]	[illegible]	[illegible]	[illegible]	[illegible]	[illegible]	[illegible]	[illegible]	[illegible]	[illegible]	[illegible]	[illegible]	[illegible]
[illegible]	[illegible]	[illegible]	[illegible]	[illegible]	[illegible]	[illegible]	[illegible]	[illegible]	[illegible]	[illegible]	[illegible]	[illegible]	[illegible]	[illegible]	[illegible]	[illegible]
[illegible]	[illegible]	[illegible]	[illegible]	[illegible]	[illegible]	[illegible]	[illegible]	[illegible]	[illegible]	[illegible]	[illegible]	[illegible]	[illegible]	[illegible]	[illegible]	[illegible]
[illegible]	[illegible]	[illegible]	[illegible]	[illegible]	[illegible]	[illegible]	[illegible]	[illegible]	[illegible]	[illegible]	[illegible]	[illegible]	[illegible]	[illegible]	[illegible]	[illegible]
[illegible]	[illegible]	[illegible]	[illegible]	[illegible]	[illegible]	[illegible]	[illegible]	[illegible]	[illegible]	[illegible]	[illegible]	[illegible]	[illegible]	[illegible]	[illegible]	[illegible]
[illegible]	[illegible]	[illegible]	[illegible]	[illegible]	[illegible]	[illegible]	[illegible]	[illegible]	[illegible]	[illegible]	[illegible]	[illegible]	[illegible]	[illegible]	[illegible]	[illegible]
DOWN COUNTY.																
[illegible]	[illegible]	[illegible]	[illegible]	[illegible]	[illegible]	[illegible]	[illegible]	[illegible]	[illegible]	[illegible]	[illegible]	[illegible]	[illegible]	[illegible]	[illegible]	[illegible]
[illegible]	[illegible]	[illegible]	[illegible]	[illegible]	[illegible]	[illegible]	[illegible]	[illegible]	[illegible]	[illegible]	[illegible]	[illegible]	[illegible]	[illegible]	[illegible]	[illegible]
[illegible]	[illegible]	[illegible]	[illegible]	[illegible]	[illegible]	[illegible]	[illegible]	[illegible]	[illegible]	[illegible]	[illegible]	[illegible]	[illegible]	[illegible]	[illegible]	[illegible]
[illegible]	[illegible]	[illegible]	[illegible]	[illegible]	[illegible]	[illegible]	[illegible]	[illegible]	[illegible]	[illegible]	[illegible]	[illegible]	[illegible]	[illegible]	[illegible]	[illegible]
FERMANAGH COUNTY.																
[illegible]	[illegible]	[illegible]	[illegible]	[illegible]	[illegible]	[illegible]	[illegible]	[illegible]	[illegible]	[illegible]	[illegible]	[illegible]	[illegible]	[illegible]	[illegible]	[illegible]
[illegible]	[illegible]	[illegible]	[illegible]	[illegible]	[illegible]	[illegible]	[illegible]	[illegible]	[illegible]	[illegible]	[illegible]	[illegible]	[illegible]	[illegible]	[illegible]	[illegible]
[illegible]	[illegible]	[illegible]	[illegible]	[illegible]	[illegible]	[illegible]	[illegible]	[illegible]	[illegible]	[illegible]	[illegible]	[illegible]	[illegible]	[illegible]	[illegible]	[illegible]
[illegible]	[illegible]	[illegible]	[illegible]	[illegible]	[illegible]	[illegible]	[illegible]	[illegible]	[illegible]	[illegible]	[illegible]	[illegible]	[illegible]	[illegible]	[illegible]	[illegible]
LONDONDERRY CO.																
[illegible]	[illegible]	[illegible]	[illegible]	[illegible]	[illegible]	[illegible]	[illegible]	[illegible]	[illegible]	[illegible]	[illegible]	[illegible]	[illegible]	[illegible]	[illegible]	[illegible]
[illegible]	[illegible]	[illegible]	[illegible]	[illegible]	[illegible]	[illegible]	[illegible]	[illegible]	[illegible]	[illegible]	[illegible]	[illegible]	[illegible]	[illegible]	[illegible]	[illegible]
[illegible]	[illegible]	[illegible]	[illegible]	[illegible]	[illegible]	[illegible]	[illegible]	[illegible]	[illegible]	[illegible]	[illegible]	[illegible]	[illegible]	[illegible]	[illegible]	[illegible]
[illegible]	[illegible]	[illegible]	[illegible]	[illegible]	[illegible]	[illegible]	[illegible]	[illegible]	[illegible]	[illegible]	[illegible]	[illegible]	[illegible]	[illegible]	[illegible]	[illegible]
MONAGHAN COUNTY.																
[illegible]	[illegible]	[illegible]	[illegible]	[illegible]	[illegible]	[illegible]	[illegible]	[illegible]	[illegible]	[illegible]	[illegible]	[illegible]	[illegible]	[illegible]	[illegible]	[illegible]
[illegible]	[illegible]	[illegible]	[illegible]	[illegible]	[illegible]	[illegible]	[illegible]	[illegible]	[illegible]	[illegible]	[illegible]	[illegible]	[illegible]	[illegible]	[illegible]	[illegible]
[illegible]	[illegible]	[illegible]	[illegible]	[illegible]	[illegible]	[illegible]	[illegible]	[illegible]	[illegible]	[illegible]	[illegible]	[illegible]	[illegible]	[illegible]	[illegible]	[illegible]
TYRONE COUNTY.																
[illegible]	[illegible]	[illegible]	[illegible]	[illegible]	[illegible]	[illegible]	[illegible]	[illegible]	[illegible]	[illegible]	[illegible]	[illegible]	[illegible]	[illegible]	[illegible]	[illegible]
[illegible]	[illegible]	[illegible]	[illegible]	[illegible]	[illegible]	[illegible]	[illegible]	[illegible]	[illegible]	[illegible]	[illegible]	[illegible]	[illegible]	[illegible]	[illegible]	[illegible]
[illegible]	[illegible]	[illegible]	[illegible]	[illegible]	[illegible]	[illegible]	[illegible]	[illegible]	[illegible]	[illegible]	[illegible]	[illegible]	[illegible]	[illegible]	[illegible]	[illegible]
[illegible]	[illegible]	[illegible]	[illegible]	[illegible]	[illegible]	[illegible]	[illegible]	[illegible]	[illegible]	[illegible]	[illegible]	[illegible]	[illegible]	[illegible]	[illegible]	[illegible]
[illegible]	[illegible]	[illegible]	[illegible]	[illegible]	[illegible]	[illegible]	[illegible]	[illegible]	[illegible]	[illegible]	[illegible]	[illegible]	[illegible]	[illegible]	[illegible]	[illegible]
[illegible]	[illegible]	[illegible]	[illegible]	[illegible]	[illegible]	[illegible]	[illegible]	[illegible]	[illegible]	[illegible]	[illegible]	[illegible]	[illegible]	[illegible]	[illegible]	[illegible]

[illegible]

IV.—PROVINCE OF CONNAUGHT.

Counties and Poor Law Unions	Summer.								Winter.							
	Men.		Boys.		Women.		Girls.		Men.		Boys.		Women.		Girls.	
	From	To	From	To	From	To	From	To	From	To	From	To	From	To	From	To
	s. d.	s. d.	s. d.	s. d.	s. d.	s. d.	s. d.	s. d.	s. d.	s. d.	s. d.	s. d.	s. d.	s. d.	s. d.	s. d.
GALWAY COUNTY.																
Athenry,	[illegible]	[illegible]	[illegible]	[illegible]	[illegible]	[illegible]	[illegible]	[illegible]	[illegible]	[illegible]	–	–	–	–	–	–
Ballinasloe (a),	[illegible]	[illegible]	[illegible]	[illegible]	[illegible]	[illegible]	[illegible]	[illegible]	[illegible]	[illegible]	[illegible]	[illegible]	[illegible]	[illegible]	[illegible]	[illegible]
Clifden,	[illegible]	[illegible]	[illegible]	[illegible]	[illegible]	[illegible]	[illegible]	[illegible]	[illegible]	[illegible]	[illegible]	[illegible]	[illegible]	[illegible]	[illegible]	[illegible]
Glenamaddy (b),	[illegible]	[illegible]	[illegible]	[illegible]	[illegible]	[illegible]	[illegible]	[illegible]	[illegible]	[illegible]	[illegible]	[illegible]	[illegible]	[illegible]	[illegible]	[illegible]
Dunmore,	[illegible]	[illegible]	[illegible]	[illegible]	[illegible]	[illegible]	[illegible]	[illegible]	[illegible]	[illegible]	[illegible]	[illegible]	[illegible]	[illegible]	[illegible]	[illegible]
Galway,	[illegible]	[illegible]	[illegible]	[illegible]	[illegible]	[illegible]	[illegible]	[illegible]	[illegible]	[illegible]	[illegible]	[illegible]	[illegible]	[illegible]	[illegible]	[illegible]
Gort,	[illegible]	[illegible]	[illegible]	[illegible]	[illegible]	[illegible]	[illegible]	[illegible]	[illegible]	[illegible]	[illegible]	[illegible]	[illegible]	[illegible]	[illegible]	[illegible]
Loughrea (c),	[illegible]	[illegible]	[illegible]	[illegible]	[illegible]	–	[illegible]	–	[illegible]	[illegible]	[illegible]	[illegible]	[illegible]	–	[illegible]	[illegible]
Mountbellew,	[illegible]	[illegible]	[illegible]	[illegible]	[illegible]	[illegible]	[illegible]	[illegible]	[illegible]	[illegible]	[illegible]	[illegible]	[illegible]	[illegible]	[illegible]	[illegible]
Oughterard,	[illegible]	[illegible]	[illegible]	[illegible]	[illegible]	[illegible]	[illegible]	[illegible]	[illegible]	[illegible]	[illegible]	[illegible]	[illegible]	[illegible]	[illegible]	[illegible]
Portumna (d),	[illegible]	[illegible]	[illegible]	[illegible]	[illegible]	[illegible]	–	–	[illegible]	[illegible]	[illegible]	[illegible]	[illegible]	[illegible]	–	–
[illegible]	[illegible]	[illegible]	[illegible]	[illegible]	[illegible]	[illegible]	[illegible]	[illegible]	[illegible]	[illegible]	[illegible]	[illegible]	[illegible]	[illegible]	[illegible]	[illegible]
[illegible] (e),	[illegible]	[illegible]	[illegible]	[illegible]	[illegible]	[illegible]	[illegible]	[illegible]	[illegible]	[illegible]	[illegible]	[illegible]	[illegible]	[illegible]	[illegible]	[illegible]
Tuam,	[illegible]	[illegible]	[illegible]	[illegible]	[illegible]	[illegible]	[illegible]	[illegible]	[illegible]	[illegible]	[illegible]	[illegible]	[illegible]	[illegible]	[illegible]	[illegible]
Woodford (f),	[illegible]	[illegible]	[illegible]	[illegible]	[illegible]	[illegible]	[illegible]	[illegible]	[illegible]	[illegible]	–	–	[illegible]	[illegible]	[illegible]	[illegible]
LEITRIM COUNTY.																
Ballinamore (g),	[illegible]	[illegible]	[illegible]	[illegible]	[illegible]	[illegible]	[illegible]	[illegible]	[illegible]	[illegible]	[illegible]	[illegible]	[illegible]	[illegible]	[illegible]	[illegible]
Carrick-on-Shannon,	[illegible]	[illegible]	[illegible]	[illegible]	[illegible]	[illegible]	[illegible]	[illegible]	[illegible]	[illegible]	[illegible]	[illegible]	[illegible]	[illegible]	[illegible]	[illegible]
Drumshanbo (h),	[illegible]	[illegible]	[illegible]	[illegible]	[illegible]	[illegible]	[illegible]	[illegible]	[illegible]	[illegible]	[illegible]	[illegible]	[illegible]	[illegible]	[illegible]	[illegible]
Manorhamilton (i),	[illegible]	[illegible]	[illegible]	[illegible]	–	–	–	–	[illegible]	[illegible]	[illegible]	[illegible]	–	–	–	–
Mohill (j),	[illegible]	[illegible]	[illegible]	[illegible]	[illegible]	[illegible]	[illegible]	[illegible]	[illegible]	[illegible]	[illegible]	[illegible]	[illegible]	[illegible]	[illegible]	[illegible]
MAYO COUNTY.																
Ballaghaderreen (k),	[illegible]	[illegible]	[illegible]	[illegible]	[illegible]	[illegible]	[illegible]	[illegible]	[illegible]	[illegible]	[illegible]	[illegible]	[illegible]	[illegible]	[illegible]	[illegible]
Ballina (l),	[illegible]	[illegible]	[illegible]	[illegible]	[illegible]	[illegible]	[illegible]	[illegible]	[illegible]	[illegible]	[illegible]	[illegible]	[illegible]	[illegible]	[illegible]	[illegible]
Ballinrobe,	[illegible]	[illegible]	[illegible]	[illegible]	[illegible]	[illegible]	[illegible]	[illegible]	[illegible]	[illegible]	[illegible]	[illegible]	[illegible]	[illegible]	[illegible]	[illegible]
Belmullet,	[illegible]	[illegible]	[illegible]	[illegible]	[illegible]	[illegible]	[illegible]	[illegible]	[illegible]	[illegible]	[illegible]	[illegible]	[illegible]	[illegible]	[illegible]	[illegible]
Castlebar (m),	[illegible]	[illegible]	[illegible]	[illegible]	[illegible]	[illegible]	–	–	[illegible]	[illegible]	[illegible]	[illegible]	–	–	–	–
Claremorris (n),	[illegible]	[illegible]	[illegible]	[illegible]	[illegible]	[illegible]	[illegible]	[illegible]	[illegible]	[illegible]	[illegible]	[illegible]	[illegible]	[illegible]	[illegible]	[illegible]
Newport,	[illegible]	[illegible]	[illegible]	[illegible]	[illegible]	[illegible]	[illegible]	[illegible]	[illegible]	[illegible]	[illegible]	[illegible]	[illegible]	[illegible]	[illegible]	[illegible]
Swinford (o),	[illegible]	[illegible]	[illegible]	[illegible]	[illegible]	[illegible]	[illegible]	[illegible]	[illegible]	[illegible]	[illegible]	[illegible]	[illegible]	[illegible]	[illegible]	[illegible]
Westport (p),	[illegible]	[illegible]	[illegible]	[illegible]	[illegible]	[illegible]	[illegible]	[illegible]	[illegible]	[illegible]	[illegible]	[illegible]	–	–	–	–
ROSCOMMON COUNTY.																
Athlone,	[illegible]	[illegible]	[illegible]	[illegible]	[illegible]	[illegible]	[illegible]	[illegible]	[illegible]	[illegible]	[illegible]	[illegible]	[illegible]	[illegible]	[illegible]	[illegible]
Boyle (q),	[illegible]	[illegible]	[illegible]	[illegible]	[illegible]	[illegible]	[illegible]	[illegible]	[illegible]	[illegible]	[illegible]	[illegible]	–	–	–	–
Castlereagh (r),	[illegible]	[illegible]	[illegible]	[illegible]	–	–	–	–	[illegible]	[illegible]	[illegible]	[illegible]	–	–	–	–
Roscommon (s),	[illegible]	–	[illegible]	[illegible]	–	–	–	–	[illegible]	[illegible]	[illegible]	[illegible]	–	–	–	–
Strokestown (t),	[illegible]	[illegible]	[illegible]	[illegible]	[illegible]	[illegible]	[illegible]	[illegible]	[illegible]	[illegible]	[illegible]	[illegible]	[illegible]	[illegible]	[illegible]	[illegible]
SLIGO COUNTY.																
Ballymote (u),	[illegible]	[illegible]	[illegible]	[illegible]	[illegible]	–	[illegible]	–	[illegible]	[illegible]	[illegible]	–	–	–	–	–
[illegible] (v),	[illegible]	[illegible]	[illegible]	[illegible]	[illegible]	[illegible]	[illegible]	[illegible]	[illegible]	[illegible]	[illegible]	[illegible]	[illegible]	[illegible]	[illegible]	[illegible]
Sligo,	[illegible]	[illegible]	[illegible]	[illegible]	[illegible]	[illegible]	[illegible]	[illegible]	[illegible]	[illegible]	[illegible]	[illegible]	[illegible]	[illegible]	[illegible]	[illegible]
[illegible] (w),	[illegible]	[illegible]	[illegible]	[illegible]	[illegible]	[illegible]	–	–	[illegible]	[illegible]	[illegible]	[illegible]	[illegible]	[illegible]	–	–
Tobercurry,	[illegible]	[illegible]	[illegible]	[illegible]	[illegible]	[illegible]	[illegible]	[illegible]	[illegible]	[illegible]	[illegible]	[illegible]	[illegible]	[illegible]	[illegible]	[illegible]

(a) [illegible]

(b) [illegible]

[illegible]

Loans for Labourers' Dwellings under Labourers Acts.

Loans for Labourers' Dwellings.

It would appear from the report of the Local Government Board for Ireland for the year ended 31st March, 1894, that from the inception of these Acts up to that date, 23,304 cottages were applied for by various Boards of Guardians; that of this number 12,987 have been finally authorized and 563 others provisionally; and that the total amount of loans sanctioned for the purpose of the Acts was £1,121,961 2s. 5d.

Out of the 12,987 houses authorized, 10,352 have been provided, and 10,279 of these actually let (at weekly rents varying from 8d. to 2s.), and 640 others were in process of erection at the date of the Report.

It is also stated in the same report that further improvement schemes under consideration are about to be submitted, embracing 7,788 cottages at an estimated cost of about £362,966.

From the report of the Commissioners of Public Works for the year ended 31st March, 1894, it appears that 738 loans to private persons, for this class of work, were sanctioned since the passing of the Act 23 Vic., c. 19, the total amount of the loans being £345,860.

Agricultural Schools.

School Farms, &c.

The following information has been obtained from the Commissioners of National Education in Ireland for the year 1893:—

The total number of School Farms in connection with Ordinary National Schools on the 31st December, 1893, was 45. The total number of pupils examined in Practical Agriculture in this class of Schools was 667, of whom 551 passed in the Agricultural Programme.

There were also 30 Schools having School Gardens attached; the number of pupils examined in these School Gardens was 495, of whom 419 passed.

Dairy Management.

The number of pupils who attended at the Glasnevin Dairy School during the two Sessions of 1893, was 60. The Royal Dublin Society has continued its aid by offering money prizes for competition amongst the pupils.

The attendances at the Munster Dairy School at Cork have been 65 at the 1st Session, 66 at the 2nd, and 67 at the 3rd, respectively.

The Dairy School at the Marlborough-street Training College continues to be largely attended and to be efficiently conducted.

In view of the important development of the Creamery System of Dairying in Ireland, the Government sanctioned the appointment, from the 1st of April, 1893, by the Commissioners of National Education, of an experienced Dairy Instructor to visit and organize the Creameries throughout Ireland and to give instruction in the best methods of Creamery management. This Officer's duties include general instruction in butter-making and cheese-making to the Students of the Model Farms under the control of the Commissioners.

Female Instructors in Dairying have also been appointed to visit districts where their services may be desired by Local Committees, and where they may be usefully employed, at suitable centres, in giving practical instruction in Dairying.

Arrangements have also been made at the Commissioners' Model Farms for the practical instruction of Managers of Creameries, and others in the management of Creameries, Butter Factories, &c.

Experiments in reference to Potato Disease, Cattle-feeding, Manuring, &c., are carried on at the Board's Farms, and also at some of the ordinary National Schools with recognised School Farms attached.

In conclusion I have to thank the occupiers and owners of land in general, and also the proprietors and managers of Scutching Mills, Corn Mills, and Dairy Factories, for their courtesy in supplying the information required for the various Returns to the Enumerators. I have also to express my thanks to the District Inspectors of the Royal Irish Constabulary and the Sergeants of the Metropolitan Police, who have furnished the valuable notes on the local circumstances affecting agriculture in the various parts of the country, which will be found at pages 76 to 89; and to add, as I do with much pleasure, that the Enumerators discharged their duty with their usual efficiency.

I have the honour to remain

Your Excellency's faithful servant,

T. W. GRIMSHAW,

Registrar-General.

TILLAGE; MEADOW AND CLOVER; &c.

TABLE 1.—Showing, by Counties and Provinces, the Number of Holdings, their Size in Statute Acres, and the Division of Land in the Year 1873.

[illegible]

TABLE [illegible].—SHOWING, BY COUNTIES AND PROVINCES, THE EXTENT OF LAND

[illegible]	[illegible]	[illegible]	[illegible]	[illegible]	[illegible]	[illegible]	[illegible]	[illegible]	[illegible]	[illegible]
Acres.	Acres.	Acres.	Acres.	Acres.	Acres.	Acres.	Acres.	Acres.	Acres.	Acres.
[illegible]	[illegible]	[illegible]	.	[illegible]	[illegible]	[illegible]	[illegible]	[illegible]	[illegible]	[illegible]
[illegible]	[illegible]	[illegible]	[illegible]	[illegible]	[illegible]	[illegible]	[illegible]	[illegible]	[illegible]	[illegible]
[illegible]	[illegible]	[illegible]	-	[illegible]	.	.	[illegible]	[illegible]	[illegible]	[illegible]
[illegible]	[illegible]	[illegible]	.	[illegible]	[illegible]	[illegible]	[illegible]	[illegible]	[illegible]	[illegible]
[illegible]	[illegible]	[illegible]	[illegible]	[illegible]	[illegible]	[illegible]	[illegible]	[illegible]	[illegible]	[illegible]
[illegible]	[illegible]	[illegible]	[illegible]	[illegible]	[illegible]	[illegible]	[illegible]	[illegible]	[illegible]	[illegible]
[illegible]	[illegible]	[illegible]	[illegible]	[illegible]	[illegible]	[illegible]	[illegible]	[illegible]	[illegible]	[illegible]
[illegible]	[illegible]	[illegible]	[illegible]	[illegible]	[illegible]	[illegible]	[illegible]	[illegible]	[illegible]	[illegible]
[illegible]	[illegible]	[illegible]	[illegible]	[illegible]	[illegible]	[illegible]	[illegible]	[illegible]	[illegible]	[illegible]
[illegible]	[illegible]	[illegible]	[illegible]	[illegible]	[illegible]	[illegible]	[illegible]	[illegible]	[illegible]	[illegible]
[illegible]	[illegible]	[illegible]	[illegible]	[illegible]	[illegible]	[illegible]	[illegible]	[illegible]	[illegible]	[illegible]
[illegible]	[illegible]	[illegible]	[illegible]	[illegible]	[illegible]	-	[illegible]	[illegible]	[illegible]	[illegible]
[illegible]	[illegible]	[illegible]	[illegible]	[illegible]	[illegible]	[illegible]	[illegible]	[illegible]	[illegible]	[illegible]
[illegible]	[illegible]	[illegible]	.	.	.	.	[illegible]	[illegible]	[illegible]	[illegible]
[illegible]	[illegible]	[illegible]	[illegible]	[illegible]	-	.	[illegible]	[illegible]	[illegible]	[illegible]
[illegible]	[illegible]	[illegible]	[illegible]	[illegible]	.	.	[illegible]	[illegible]	[illegible]	[illegible]
[illegible]	[illegible]	[illegible]	[illegible]	[illegible]	-	-	[illegible]	[illegible]	[illegible]	[illegible]
[illegible]	[illegible]	[illegible]	[illegible]	[illegible]	[illegible]	[illegible]	[illegible]	[illegible]	[illegible]	[illegible]
[illegible]	[illegible]	[illegible]	[illegible]	[illegible]	-	.	[illegible]	[illegible]	[illegible]	[illegible]
[illegible]	[illegible]	[illegible]	.	[illegible]	[illegible]	[illegible]	[illegible]	[illegible]	[illegible]	[illegible]
[illegible]	[illegible]	[illegible]	[illegible]	[illegible]	.	[illegible]	[illegible]	[illegible]	[illegible]	[illegible]
[illegible]	[illegible]	[illegible]	[illegible]	[illegible]	[illegible]	[illegible]	[illegible]	[illegible]	[illegible]	[illegible]
[illegible]	[illegible]	[illegible]	[illegible]	[illegible]	.	-	[illegible]	[illegible]	[illegible]	[illegible]
[illegible]	[illegible]	[illegible]	[illegible]	[illegible]	[illegible]	[illegible]	[illegible]	[illegible]	[illegible]	[illegible]
[illegible]	[illegible]	[illegible]	[illegible]	[illegible]	[illegible]	-	[illegible]	[illegible]	[illegible]	[illegible]
[illegible]	[illegible]	[illegible]	[illegible]	[illegible]	.	.	[illegible]	[illegible]	[illegible]	[illegible]
[illegible]	[illegible]	[illegible]	[illegible]	[illegible]	[illegible]	[illegible]	[illegible]	[illegible]	[illegible]	[illegible]
[illegible]	[illegible]	[illegible]	[illegible]	[illegible]	[illegible]	[illegible]	[illegible]	[illegible]	[illegible]	[illegible]
[illegible]	[illegible]	[illegible]	[illegible]	[illegible]	[illegible]	.	[illegible]	[illegible]	[illegible]	[illegible]
[illegible]	[illegible]	[illegible]	[illegible]	[illegible]	[illegible]	[illegible]	[illegible]	[illegible]	[illegible]	[illegible]
[illegible]	[illegible]	[illegible]	[illegible]	[illegible]	[illegible]	[illegible]	[illegible]	[illegible]	[illegible]	[illegible]
[illegible]	[illegible]	[illegible]	-	[illegible]	-	.	[illegible]	[illegible]	[illegible]	[illegible]

[illegible] Crops in the Year 18[illegible]; the Valuation in 18[illegible]; and the Population in 18[illegible].

[illegible] Statute Acres.

[illegible]	[illegible]	[illegible]	[illegible]	[illegible]	[illegible]	[illegible]	[illegible]	[illegible]	[illegible]	Valuation in 18[illegible].	Population in 18[illegible].	COUNTIES.
[illegible]	[illegible]	[illegible]	[illegible]	[illegible]	[illegible]	[illegible]	[illegible]	[illegible]	[illegible]	[illegible]	[illegible]	Antrim.
[illegible]	[illegible]	[illegible]	[illegible]	[illegible]	[illegible]	[illegible]	[illegible]	[illegible]	[illegible]	[illegible]	[illegible]	Armagh.
[illegible]	[illegible]	[illegible]	[illegible]	[illegible]	[illegible]	[illegible]	[illegible]	[illegible]	[illegible]	[illegible]	[illegible]	Carlow.
[illegible]	[illegible]	[illegible]	[illegible]	[illegible]	[illegible]	[illegible]	[illegible]	[illegible]	[illegible]	[illegible]	[illegible]	Cavan.
[illegible]	[illegible]	[illegible]	[illegible]	[illegible]	[illegible]	[illegible]	[illegible]	[illegible]	[illegible]	[illegible]	[illegible]	Clare.
[illegible]	[illegible]	[illegible]	[illegible]	[illegible]	[illegible]	[illegible]	[illegible]	[illegible]	[illegible]	[illegible]	[illegible]	Cork.
[illegible]	[illegible]	[illegible]	[illegible]	[illegible]	[illegible]	[illegible]	[illegible]	[illegible]	[illegible]	[illegible]	[illegible]	Donegal.
[illegible]	[illegible]	[illegible]	[illegible]	[illegible]	[illegible]	[illegible]	[illegible]	[illegible]	[illegible]	[illegible]	[illegible]	Down.
[illegible]	[illegible]	[illegible]	[illegible]	[illegible]	[illegible]	[illegible]	[illegible]	[illegible]	[illegible]	[illegible]	[illegible]	Dublin.
[illegible]	[illegible]	[illegible]	[illegible]	[illegible]	[illegible]	[illegible]	[illegible]	[illegible]	[illegible]	[illegible]	[illegible]	Fermanagh.
[illegible]	[illegible]	[illegible]	[illegible]	[illegible]	[illegible]	[illegible]	[illegible]	[illegible]	[illegible]	[illegible]	[illegible]	Galway.
[illegible]	[illegible]	[illegible]	[illegible]	[illegible]	[illegible]	[illegible]	[illegible]	[illegible]	[illegible]	[illegible]	[illegible]	Kerry.
[illegible]	[illegible]	[illegible]	[illegible]	[illegible]	[illegible]	[illegible]	[illegible]	[illegible]	[illegible]	[illegible]	[illegible]	Kildare.
[illegible]	[illegible]	[illegible]	[illegible]	[illegible]	[illegible]	[illegible]	[illegible]	[illegible]	[illegible]	[illegible]	[illegible]	Kilkenny.
[illegible]	[illegible]	[illegible]	[illegible]	[illegible]	[illegible]	[illegible]	[illegible]	[illegible]	[illegible]	[illegible]	[illegible]	King's.
[illegible]	[illegible]	[illegible]	[illegible]	[illegible]	[illegible]	[illegible]	[illegible]	[illegible]	[illegible]	[illegible]	[illegible]	Leitrim.
[illegible]	[illegible]	[illegible]	[illegible]	[illegible]	[illegible]	[illegible]	[illegible]	[illegible]	[illegible]	[illegible]	[illegible]	Limerick.
[illegible]	[illegible]	[illegible]	[illegible]	[illegible]	[illegible]	[illegible]	[illegible]	[illegible]	[illegible]	[illegible]	[illegible]	Londonderry.
[illegible]	[illegible]	[illegible]	[illegible]	[illegible]	[illegible]	[illegible]	[illegible]	[illegible]	[illegible]	[illegible]	[illegible]	Longford.
[illegible]	[illegible]	[illegible]	[illegible]	[illegible]	[illegible]	[illegible]	[illegible]	[illegible]	[illegible]	[illegible]	[illegible]	Louth & Drogheda, County of Town.
[illegible]	[illegible]	[illegible]	[illegible]	[illegible]	[illegible]	[illegible]	[illegible]	[illegible]	[illegible]	[illegible]	[illegible]	Mayo.
[illegible]	[illegible]	[illegible]	[illegible]	[illegible]	[illegible]	[illegible]	[illegible]	[illegible]	[illegible]	[illegible]	[illegible]	Meath.
[illegible]	[illegible]	[illegible]	[illegible]	[illegible]	[illegible]	[illegible]	[illegible]	[illegible]	[illegible]	[illegible]	[illegible]	Monaghan.
[illegible]	[illegible]	[illegible]	[illegible]	[illegible]	[illegible]	[illegible]	[illegible]	[illegible]	[illegible]	[illegible]	[illegible]	Queen's.
[illegible]	[illegible]	[illegible]	[illegible]	[illegible]	[illegible]	[illegible]	[illegible]	[illegible]	[illegible]	[illegible]	[illegible]	Roscommon.
[illegible]	[illegible]	[illegible]	[illegible]	[illegible]	[illegible]	[illegible]	[illegible]	[illegible]	[illegible]	[illegible]	[illegible]	Sligo.
[illegible]	[illegible]	[illegible]	[illegible]	[illegible]	[illegible]	[illegible]	[illegible]	[illegible]	[illegible]	[illegible]	[illegible]	Tipperary.
[illegible]	[illegible]	[illegible]	[illegible]	[illegible]	[illegible]	[illegible]	[illegible]	[illegible]	[illegible]	[illegible]	[illegible]	Tyrone.
[illegible]	[illegible]	[illegible]	[illegible]	[illegible]	[illegible]	[illegible]	[illegible]	[illegible]	[illegible]	[illegible]	[illegible]	Waterford.
[illegible]	[illegible]	[illegible]	[illegible]	[illegible]	[illegible]	[illegible]	[illegible]	[illegible]	[illegible]	[illegible]	[illegible]	Westmeath.
[illegible]	[illegible]	[illegible]	[illegible]	[illegible]	[illegible]	[illegible]	[illegible]	[illegible]	[illegible]	[illegible]	[illegible]	Wexford.
[illegible]	[illegible]	[illegible]	[illegible]	[illegible]	[illegible]	[illegible]	[illegible]	[illegible]	[illegible]	[illegible]	[illegible]	Wicklow.
												PROVINCES.
[illegible]	[illegible]	[illegible]	[illegible]	[illegible]	[illegible]	[illegible]	[illegible]	[illegible]	[illegible]	[illegible]	[illegible]	Leinster.
[illegible]	[illegible]	[illegible]	[illegible]	[illegible]	[illegible]	[illegible]	[illegible]	[illegible]	[illegible]	[illegible]	[illegible]	Munster.
[illegible]	[illegible]	[illegible]	[illegible]	[illegible]	[illegible]	[illegible]	[illegible]	[illegible]	[illegible]	[illegible]	[illegible]	Ulster.
[illegible]	[illegible]	[illegible]	[illegible]	[illegible]	[illegible]	[illegible]	[illegible]	[illegible]	[illegible]	[illegible]	[illegible]	Connaught.
[illegible]	[illegible]	[illegible]	[illegible]	[illegible]	[illegible]	[illegible]	[illegible]	[illegible]	[illegible]	[illegible]	[illegible]	Total.

TABLE 6.—SHOWING, BY COUNTIES AND PROVINCES, THE PRODUCE OF

COUNTIES.	Corn, Grain, and Pulse.						
	Wheat.	Oats.	Barley.	Bere.	Rye.	Beans.	Peas.
Antrim,	[illegible]	[illegible]	[illegible]	.	[illegible]	[illegible]	[illegible]
Armagh,	[illegible]	[illegible]	[illegible]	[illegible]	[illegible]	[illegible]	[illegible]
Carlow,	[illegible]	[illegible]	[illegible]	.	[illegible]	.	.
Cavan,	[illegible]	[illegible]	[illegible]	.	[illegible]	[illegible]	[illegible]
Clare,	[illegible]	[illegible]	[illegible]	[illegible]	[illegible]	[illegible]	[illegible]
Cork,	[illegible]	[illegible]	[illegible]	[illegible]	[illegible]	[illegible]	[illegible]
Donegal,	[illegible]	[illegible]	[illegible]	[illegible]	[illegible]	[illegible]	[illegible]
Down,	[illegible]	[illegible]	[illegible]	[illegible]	[illegible]	[illegible]	[illegible]
Dublin,	[illegible]	[illegible]	[illegible]	[illegible]	[illegible]	[illegible]	[illegible]
Fermanagh,	[illegible]	[illegible]	[illegible]	[illegible]	[illegible]	[illegible]	[illegible]
Galway,	[illegible]	[illegible]	[illegible]	[illegible]	[illegible]	[illegible]	[illegible]
Kerry,	[illegible]	[illegible]	[illegible]	[illegible]	[illegible]	[illegible]	.
Kildare,	[illegible]	[illegible]	[illegible]	[illegible]	[illegible]	[illegible]	[illegible]
Kilkenny,	[illegible]	[illegible]	[illegible]	.	.	.	.
King's,	[illegible]	[illegible]	[illegible]	[illegible]	[illegible]	.	.
Leitrim,	[illegible]	[illegible]	[illegible]	[illegible]	[illegible]	.	.
Limerick,	[illegible]	[illegible]	[illegible]	[illegible]	[illegible]	.	.
Londonderry,	[illegible]	[illegible]	[illegible]	[illegible]	[illegible]	[illegible]	[illegible]
Longford,	[illegible]	[illegible]	[illegible]	[illegible]	[illegible]	.	.
Louth and Drogheda, County of Town,	[illegible]	[illegible]	[illegible]	.	[illegible]	[illegible]	[illegible]
Mayo,	[illegible]	[illegible]	[illegible]	[illegible]	[illegible]	.	[illegible]
Meath,	[illegible]	[illegible]	[illegible]	[illegible]	[illegible]	[illegible]	[illegible]
Monaghan,	[illegible]	[illegible]	[illegible]	[illegible]	[illegible]	[illegible]	.
Queen's,	[illegible]	[illegible]	[illegible]	[illegible]	[illegible]	[illegible]	[illegible]
Roscommon,	[illegible]	[illegible]	[illegible]	[illegible]	[illegible]	[illegible]	.
Sligo,	[illegible]	[illegible]	[illegible]	[illegible]	[illegible]	-	.
Tipperary,	[illegible]	[illegible]	[illegible]	[illegible]	[illegible]	[illegible]	[illegible]
Tyrone,	[illegible]	[illegible]	[illegible]	[illegible]	[illegible]	[illegible]	[illegible]
Waterford,	[illegible]	[illegible]	[illegible]	[illegible]	[illegible]	[illegible]	-
Westmeath,	[illegible]	[illegible]	[illegible]	[illegible]	[illegible]	[illegible]	[illegible]
Wexford,	[illegible]	[illegible]	[illegible]	[illegible]	[illegible]	[illegible]	[illegible]
Wicklow,	[illegible]	[illegible]	[illegible]	.	[illegible]	.	.
PROVINCES.							
Leinster,	[illegible]	[illegible]	[illegible]	[illegible]	[illegible]	[illegible]	[illegible]
Munster,	[illegible]	[illegible]	[illegible]	[illegible]	[illegible]	[illegible]	[illegible]
Ulster,	[illegible]	[illegible]	[illegible]	[illegible]	[illegible]	[illegible]	[illegible]
Connaught,	[illegible]	[illegible]	[illegible]	[illegible]	[illegible]	[illegible]	[illegible]
Total,	[illegible]	[illegible]	[illegible]	[illegible]	[illegible]	[illegible]	[illegible]

Produce of the Crops in the Year 1858.

[illegible]

Green Crops.							Flax.	Hay.		Counties.
[illegible]	[illegible]	[illegible]	[illegible]	[illegible]	[illegible]	[illegible]		[illegible]	[illegible]	
[illegible]	[illegible]	[illegible]	[illegible]	[illegible]	[illegible]	[illegible]	[illegible]	[illegible]	[illegible]	
[illegible]	[illegible]	[illegible]	[illegible]	[illegible]	[illegible]	[illegible]	[illegible]	[illegible]	[illegible]	Antrim.
[illegible]	[illegible]	[illegible]	[illegible]	[illegible]	[illegible]	[illegible]	[illegible]	[illegible]	[illegible]	Armagh.
[illegible]	[illegible]	[illegible]	[illegible]	[illegible]	[illegible]	[illegible]	.	[illegible]	[illegible]	Carlow.
[illegible]	[illegible]	[illegible]	[illegible]	[illegible]	[illegible]	[illegible]	[illegible]	[illegible]	[illegible]	Cavan.
[illegible]	[illegible]	[illegible]	[illegible]	[illegible]	[illegible]	[illegible]	[illegible]	[illegible]	[illegible]	Clare.
[illegible]	[illegible]	[illegible]	[illegible]	[illegible]	[illegible]	[illegible]	[illegible]	[illegible]	[illegible]	Cork.
[illegible]	[illegible]	[illegible]	[illegible]	[illegible]	[illegible]	[illegible]	[illegible]	[illegible]	[illegible]	Donegal.
[illegible]	[illegible]	[illegible]	[illegible]	[illegible]	[illegible]	[illegible]	[illegible]	[illegible]	[illegible]	Down.
[illegible]	[illegible]	[illegible]	[illegible]	[illegible]	[illegible]	[illegible]	.	[illegible]	[illegible]	Dublin.
[illegible]	[illegible]	[illegible]	[illegible]	[illegible]	[illegible]	[illegible]	[illegible]	[illegible]	[illegible]	Fermanagh.
[illegible]	[illegible]	[illegible]	[illegible]	[illegible]	[illegible]	[illegible]	[illegible]	[illegible]	[illegible]	Galway.
[illegible]	[illegible]	[illegible]	[illegible]	[illegible]	[illegible]	[illegible]	[illegible]	[illegible]	[illegible]	Kerry.
[illegible]	[illegible]	[illegible]	[illegible]	[illegible]	[illegible]	[illegible]	.	[illegible]	[illegible]	Kildare.
[illegible]	[illegible]	[illegible]	[illegible]	[illegible]	[illegible]	[illegible]	.	[illegible]	[illegible]	Kilkenny.
[illegible]	[illegible]	[illegible]	[illegible]	[illegible]	[illegible]	[illegible]	[illegible]	[illegible]	[illegible]	King's.
[illegible]	[illegible]	[illegible]	[illegible]	[illegible]	[illegible]	[illegible]	[illegible]	[illegible]	[illegible]	Leitrim.
[illegible]	[illegible]	[illegible]	[illegible]	[illegible]	[illegible]	[illegible]	[illegible]	[illegible]	[illegible]	Limerick.
[illegible]	[illegible]	[illegible]	[illegible]	[illegible]	[illegible]	[illegible]	[illegible]	[illegible]	[illegible]	Londonderry.
[illegible]	[illegible]	[illegible]	[illegible]	[illegible]	[illegible]	[illegible]	[illegible]	[illegible]	[illegible]	Longford.
[illegible]	[illegible]	[illegible]	[illegible]	[illegible]	[illegible]	[illegible]	[illegible]	[illegible]	[illegible]	Louth and Drogheda, County of Town.
[illegible]	[illegible]	[illegible]	[illegible]	[illegible]	[illegible]	[illegible]	[illegible]	[illegible]	[illegible]	Mayo.
[illegible]	[illegible]	[illegible]	[illegible]	[illegible]	[illegible]	[illegible]	[illegible]	[illegible]	[illegible]	Meath.
[illegible]	[illegible]	[illegible]	[illegible]	[illegible]	[illegible]	[illegible]	[illegible]	[illegible]	[illegible]	Monaghan.
[illegible]	[illegible]	[illegible]	[illegible]	[illegible]	[illegible]	[illegible]	.	[illegible]	[illegible]	Queen's.
[illegible]	[illegible]	[illegible]	[illegible]	[illegible]	[illegible]	[illegible]	[illegible]	[illegible]	[illegible]	Roscommon.
[illegible]	[illegible]	[illegible]	[illegible]	[illegible]	[illegible]	[illegible]	[illegible]	[illegible]	[illegible]	Sligo.
[illegible]	[illegible]	[illegible]	[illegible]	[illegible]	[illegible]	[illegible]	.	[illegible]	[illegible]	Tipperary.
[illegible]	[illegible]	[illegible]	[illegible]	[illegible]	[illegible]	[illegible]	[illegible]	[illegible]	[illegible]	Tyrone.
[illegible]	[illegible]	[illegible]	[illegible]	[illegible]	[illegible]	[illegible]	.	[illegible]	[illegible]	Waterford.
[illegible]	[illegible]	[illegible]	[illegible]	[illegible]	[illegible]	[illegible]	.	[illegible]	[illegible]	Westmeath.
[illegible]	[illegible]	[illegible]	[illegible]	[illegible]	[illegible]	[illegible]	[illegible]	[illegible]	[illegible]	Wexford.
[illegible]	[illegible]	[illegible]	[illegible]	[illegible]	[illegible]	[illegible]	.	[illegible]	[illegible]	Wicklow.
										PROVINCES.
[illegible]	[illegible]	[illegible]	[illegible]	[illegible]	[illegible]	[illegible]	[illegible]	[illegible]	[illegible]	Leinster.
[illegible]	[illegible]	[illegible]	[illegible]	[illegible]	[illegible]	[illegible]	[illegible]	[illegible]	[illegible]	Munster.
[illegible]	[illegible]	[illegible]	[illegible]	[illegible]	[illegible]	[illegible]	[illegible]	[illegible]	[illegible]	Ulster.
[illegible]	[illegible]	[illegible]	[illegible]	[illegible]	[illegible]	[illegible]	[illegible]	[illegible]	[illegible]	Connaught.
[illegible]	[illegible]	[illegible]	[illegible]	[illegible]	[illegible]	[illegible]	[illegible]	[illegible]	[illegible]	Total.

TABLE 7.—Showing, by Poor Law Unions, the Extent of Land under

Table 7.—Showing, by Poor Law Unions, the Extent of Land under Crops

Extent under Crops										
Corn, Beans, and Peas.										
Wheat.	Oats.	Barley.	Bere.	Rye.	Beans.	Peas.	Total.	Potatoes.	Turnips.	Mangel Wurzel and Beet-root.
Acres.	Acres.	Acres.	Acres.	Acres.	Acres.	Acres.	Acres.	Acres.	Acres.	Acres.
[illegible]	[illegible]	[illegible]	[illegible]	[illegible]	[illegible]	[illegible]	[illegible]	[illegible]	[illegible]	[illegible]

PRODUCE OF THE CROPS IN THE YEAR 1893.

[illegible] OF THE CROPS.

Green Crops.								Hay.		POOR LAW UNIONS.
[illegible]	[illegible]	[illegible]	[illegible]	[illegible]	[illegible]	[illegible]	[illegible]	[illegible]	[illegible]	
[illegible]	[illegible]	[illegible]	[illegible]	[illegible]	[illegible]	[illegible]	[illegible]	[illegible]	[illegible]	
[illegible]	[illegible]	[illegible]	[illegible]	[illegible]	[illegible]	[illegible]	[illegible]	[illegible]	[illegible]	Abbeyleix.
[illegible]	[illegible]	[illegible]	[illegible]	[illegible]	[illegible]	[illegible]	[illegible]	[illegible]	[illegible]	Antrim.
[illegible]	[illegible]	[illegible]	[illegible]	[illegible]	[illegible]	[illegible]	[illegible]	[illegible]	[illegible]	Ardee.
[illegible]	[illegible]	[illegible]	[illegible]	[illegible]	[illegible]	[illegible]	[illegible]	[illegible]	[illegible]	Armagh.
[illegible]	[illegible]	[illegible]	[illegible]	[illegible]	[illegible]	[illegible]	[illegible]	[illegible]	[illegible]	Athlone.
[illegible]	[illegible]	[illegible]	[illegible]	[illegible]	[illegible]	[illegible]	[illegible]	[illegible]	[illegible]	Athy.
[illegible]	[illegible]	[illegible]	[illegible]	[illegible]	[illegible]	[illegible]	[illegible]	[illegible]	[illegible]	[illegible]
[illegible]	[illegible]	[illegible]	[illegible]	[illegible]	[illegible]	[illegible]	[illegible]	[illegible]	[illegible]	Ballina.
[illegible]	[illegible]	[illegible]	[illegible]	[illegible]	[illegible]	[illegible]	[illegible]	[illegible]	[illegible]	[illegible]
[illegible]	[illegible]	[illegible]	[illegible]	[illegible]	[illegible]	[illegible]	[illegible]	[illegible]	[illegible]	[illegible]
[illegible]	[illegible]	[illegible]	[illegible]	[illegible]	[illegible]	[illegible]	[illegible]	[illegible]	[illegible]	[illegible]
[illegible]	[illegible]	[illegible]	[illegible]	[illegible]	[illegible]	[illegible]	[illegible]	[illegible]	[illegible]	[illegible]
[illegible]	[illegible]	[illegible]	[illegible]	[illegible]	[illegible]	[illegible]	[illegible]	[illegible]	[illegible]	[illegible]
[illegible]	[illegible]	[illegible]	[illegible]	[illegible]	[illegible]	[illegible]	[illegible]	[illegible]	[illegible]	[illegible]
[illegible]	[illegible]	[illegible]	[illegible]	[illegible]	[illegible]	[illegible]	[illegible]	[illegible]	[illegible]	[illegible]
[illegible]	[illegible]	[illegible]	[illegible]	[illegible]	[illegible]	[illegible]	[illegible]	[illegible]	[illegible]	[illegible]
[illegible]	[illegible]	[illegible]	[illegible]	[illegible]	[illegible]	[illegible]	[illegible]	[illegible]	[illegible]	[illegible]
[illegible]	[illegible]	[illegible]	[illegible]	[illegible]	[illegible]	[illegible]	[illegible]	[illegible]	[illegible]	[illegible]
[illegible]	[illegible]	[illegible]	[illegible]	[illegible]	[illegible]	[illegible]	[illegible]	[illegible]	[illegible]	[illegible]
[illegible]	[illegible]	[illegible]	[illegible]	[illegible]	[illegible]	[illegible]	[illegible]	[illegible]	[illegible]	Bantry.
[illegible]	[illegible]	[illegible]	[illegible]	[illegible]	[illegible]	[illegible]	[illegible]	[illegible]	[illegible]	Bawnboy.
[illegible]	[illegible]	[illegible]	[illegible]	[illegible]	[illegible]	[illegible]	[illegible]	[illegible]	[illegible]	Belfast.
[illegible]	[illegible]	[illegible]	[illegible]	[illegible]	[illegible]	[illegible]	[illegible]	[illegible]	[illegible]	[illegible]
[illegible]	[illegible]	[illegible]	[illegible]	[illegible]	[illegible]	[illegible]	[illegible]	[illegible]	[illegible]	[illegible]
[illegible]	[illegible]	[illegible]	[illegible]	[illegible]	[illegible]	[illegible]	[illegible]	[illegible]	[illegible]	Boyle.
[illegible]	[illegible]	[illegible]	[illegible]	[illegible]	[illegible]	[illegible]	[illegible]	[illegible]	[illegible]	[illegible]
[illegible]	[illegible]	[illegible]	[illegible]	[illegible]	[illegible]	[illegible]	[illegible]	[illegible]	[illegible]	Callan.
[illegible]	[illegible]	[illegible]	[illegible]	[illegible]	[illegible]	[illegible]	[illegible]	[illegible]	[illegible]	Carlow.
[illegible]	[illegible]	[illegible]	[illegible]	[illegible]	[illegible]	[illegible]	[illegible]	[illegible]	[illegible]	[illegible]
[illegible]	[illegible]	[illegible]	[illegible]	[illegible]	[illegible]	[illegible]	[illegible]	[illegible]	[illegible]	[illegible]
[illegible]	[illegible]	[illegible]	[illegible]	[illegible]	[illegible]	[illegible]	[illegible]	[illegible]	[illegible]	[illegible]
[illegible]	[illegible]	[illegible]	[illegible]	[illegible]	[illegible]	[illegible]	[illegible]	[illegible]	[illegible]	[illegible]
[illegible]	[illegible]	[illegible]	[illegible]	[illegible]	[illegible]	[illegible]	[illegible]	[illegible]	[illegible]	[illegible]
[illegible]	[illegible]	[illegible]	[illegible]	[illegible]	[illegible]	[illegible]	[illegible]	[illegible]	[illegible]	[illegible]
[illegible]	[illegible]	[illegible]	[illegible]	[illegible]	[illegible]	[illegible]	[illegible]	[illegible]	[illegible]	[illegible]
[illegible]	[illegible]	[illegible]	[illegible]	[illegible]	[illegible]	[illegible]	[illegible]	[illegible]	[illegible]	[illegible]
[illegible]	[illegible]	[illegible]	[illegible]	[illegible]	[illegible]	[illegible]	[illegible]	[illegible]	[illegible]	[illegible]
[illegible]	[illegible]	[illegible]	[illegible]	[illegible]	[illegible]	[illegible]	[illegible]	[illegible]	[illegible]	[illegible]
[illegible]	[illegible]	[illegible]	[illegible]	[illegible]	[illegible]	[illegible]	[illegible]	[illegible]	[illegible]	Cavan.
[illegible]	[illegible]	[illegible]	[illegible]	[illegible]	[illegible]	[illegible]	[illegible]	[illegible]	[illegible]	[illegible]
[illegible]	[illegible]	[illegible]	[illegible]	[illegible]	[illegible]	[illegible]	[illegible]	[illegible]	[illegible]	[illegible]
[illegible]	[illegible]	[illegible]	[illegible]	[illegible]	[illegible]	[illegible]	[illegible]	[illegible]	[illegible]	[illegible]
[illegible]	[illegible]	[illegible]	[illegible]	[illegible]	[illegible]	[illegible]	[illegible]	[illegible]	[illegible]	[illegible]
[illegible]	[illegible]	[illegible]	[illegible]	[illegible]	[illegible]	[illegible]	[illegible]	[illegible]	[illegible]	[illegible]
[illegible]	[illegible]	[illegible]	[illegible]	[illegible]	[illegible]	[illegible]	[illegible]	[illegible]	[illegible]	[illegible]
[illegible]	[illegible]	[illegible]	[illegible]	[illegible]	[illegible]	[illegible]	[illegible]	[illegible]	[illegible]	[illegible]
[illegible]	[illegible]	[illegible]	[illegible]	[illegible]	[illegible]	[illegible]	[illegible]	[illegible]	[illegible]	[illegible]
[illegible]	[illegible]	[illegible]	[illegible]	[illegible]	[illegible]	[illegible]	[illegible]	[illegible]	[illegible]	[illegible]
[illegible]	[illegible]	[illegible]	[illegible]	[illegible]	[illegible]	[illegible]	[illegible]	[illegible]	[illegible]	[illegible]
[illegible]	[illegible]	[illegible]	[illegible]	[illegible]	[illegible]	[illegible]	[illegible]	[illegible]	[illegible]	[illegible]
[illegible]	[illegible]	[illegible]	[illegible]	[illegible]	[illegible]	[illegible]	[illegible]	[illegible]	[illegible]	Cork.
[illegible]	[illegible]	[illegible]	[illegible]	[illegible]	[illegible]	[illegible]	[illegible]	[illegible]	[illegible]	[illegible]
[illegible]	[illegible]	[illegible]	[illegible]	[illegible]	[illegible]	[illegible]	[illegible]	[illegible]	[illegible]	[illegible]
[illegible]	[illegible]	[illegible]	[illegible]	[illegible]	[illegible]	[illegible]	[illegible]	[illegible]	[illegible]	[illegible]
[illegible]	[illegible]	[illegible]	[illegible]	[illegible]	[illegible]	[illegible]	[illegible]	[illegible]	[illegible]	Dingle.
[illegible]	[illegible]	[illegible]	[illegible]	[illegible]	[illegible]	[illegible]	[illegible]	[illegible]	[illegible]	[illegible]
[illegible]	[illegible]	[illegible]	[illegible]	[illegible]	[illegible]	[illegible]	[illegible]	[illegible]	[illegible]	[illegible]
[illegible]	[illegible]	[illegible]	[illegible]	[illegible]	[illegible]	[illegible]	[illegible]	[illegible]	[illegible]	[illegible]
[illegible]	[illegible]	[illegible]	[illegible]	[illegible]	[illegible]	[illegible]	[illegible]	[illegible]	[illegible]	[illegible]
[illegible]	[illegible]	[illegible]	[illegible]	[illegible]	[illegible]	[illegible]	[illegible]	[illegible]	[illegible]	[illegible]
[illegible]	[illegible]	[illegible]	[illegible]	[illegible]	[illegible]	[illegible]	[illegible]	[illegible]	[illegible]	[illegible]
[illegible]	[illegible]	[illegible]	[illegible]	[illegible]	[illegible]	[illegible]	[illegible]	[illegible]	[illegible]	[illegible]
[illegible]	[illegible]	[illegible]	[illegible]	[illegible]	[illegible]	[illegible]	[illegible]	[illegible]	[illegible]	[illegible]
[illegible]	[illegible]	[illegible]	[illegible]	[illegible]	[illegible]	[illegible]	[illegible]	[illegible]	[illegible]	[illegible]
[illegible]	[illegible]	[illegible]	[illegible]	[illegible]	[illegible]	[illegible]	[illegible]	[illegible]	[illegible]	[illegible]
[illegible]	[illegible]	[illegible]	[illegible]	[illegible]	[illegible]	[illegible]	[illegible]	[illegible]	[illegible]	[illegible]
[illegible]	[illegible]	[illegible]	[illegible]	[illegible]	[illegible]	[illegible]	[illegible]	[illegible]	[illegible]	[illegible]
[illegible]	[illegible]	[illegible]	[illegible]	[illegible]	[illegible]	[illegible]	[illegible]	[illegible]	[illegible]	Ennis.
[illegible]	[illegible]	[illegible]	[illegible]	[illegible]	[illegible]	[illegible]	[illegible]	[illegible]	[illegible]	[illegible]
[illegible]	[illegible]	[illegible]	[illegible]	[illegible]	[illegible]	[illegible]	[illegible]	[illegible]	[illegible]	[illegible]
[illegible]	[illegible]	[illegible]	[illegible]	[illegible]	[illegible]	[illegible]	[illegible]	[illegible]	[illegible]	[illegible]
[illegible]	[illegible]	[illegible]	[illegible]	[illegible]	[illegible]	[illegible]	[illegible]	[illegible]	[illegible]	[illegible]
[illegible]	[illegible]	[illegible]	[illegible]	[illegible]	[illegible]	[illegible]	[illegible]	[illegible]	[illegible]	Galway.
[illegible]	[illegible]	[illegible]	[illegible]	[illegible]	[illegible]	[illegible]	[illegible]	[illegible]	[illegible]	[illegible]
[illegible]	[illegible]	[illegible]	[illegible]	[illegible]	[illegible]	[illegible]	[illegible]	[illegible]	[illegible]	[illegible]
[illegible]	[illegible]	[illegible]	[illegible]	[illegible]	[illegible]	[illegible]	[illegible]	[illegible]	[illegible]	[illegible]
[illegible]	[illegible]	[illegible]	[illegible]	[illegible]	[illegible]	[illegible]	[illegible]	[illegible]	[illegible]	Gort.

TABLE 3.—SHOWING, BY POOR LAW UNIONS, THE

POOR LAW UNIONS.	PRODUCE						
	Corn, Beans, and Pease.						
	Wheat.	Oats.	Barley.	Bere.	Rye.	Beans.	Pease.
[illegible]	[illegible]	[illegible]	[illegible]	[illegible]	[illegible]	[illegible]	[illegible]

PRODUCE OF THE CROPS OF THE YEAR 1893—continued.

Green Crops.								Hay.		Poor Law Unions.
Potatoes.	Turnips.	Mangel Wurzel and Beet Root.	[illegible]	Cabbage.	[illegible]	[illegible]	Flax.	[illegible]	[illegible]	
[illegible]	Tons.	Tons.	Tons.	Tons.	[illegible]	[illegible]	Stones (14 lbs.)	Tons.	Tons.	
[illegible]	[illegible]	[illegible]	[illegible]	[illegible]	[illegible]	[illegible]	[illegible]	[illegible]	[illegible]	[illegible]
[illegible]	[illegible]	[illegible]	[illegible]	[illegible]	[illegible]	[illegible]	[illegible]	[illegible]	[illegible]	[illegible]
[illegible]	[illegible]	[illegible]	[illegible]	[illegible]	[illegible]	[illegible]	[illegible]	[illegible]	[illegible]	[illegible]
[illegible]	[illegible]	[illegible]	[illegible]	[illegible]	[illegible]	[illegible]	[illegible]	[illegible]	[illegible]	[illegible]
[illegible]	[illegible]	[illegible]	[illegible]	[illegible]	[illegible]	[illegible]	[illegible]	[illegible]	[illegible]	[illegible]
[illegible]	[illegible]	[illegible]	[illegible]	[illegible]	[illegible]	[illegible]	[illegible]	[illegible]	[illegible]	[illegible]
[illegible]	[illegible]	[illegible]	[illegible]	[illegible]	[illegible]	[illegible]	[illegible]	[illegible]	[illegible]	[illegible]
[illegible]	[illegible]	[illegible]	[illegible]	[illegible]	[illegible]	[illegible]	[illegible]	[illegible]	[illegible]	[illegible]
[illegible]	[illegible]	[illegible]	[illegible]	[illegible]	[illegible]	[illegible]	[illegible]	[illegible]	[illegible]	[illegible]
[illegible]	[illegible]	[illegible]	[illegible]	[illegible]	[illegible]	[illegible]	[illegible]	[illegible]	[illegible]	[illegible]
[illegible]	[illegible]	[illegible]	[illegible]	[illegible]	[illegible]	[illegible]	[illegible]	[illegible]	[illegible]	[illegible]
[illegible]	[illegible]	[illegible]	[illegible]	[illegible]	[illegible]	[illegible]	[illegible]	[illegible]	[illegible]	[illegible]
[illegible]	[illegible]	[illegible]	[illegible]	[illegible]	[illegible]	[illegible]	[illegible]	[illegible]	[illegible]	[illegible]
[illegible]	[illegible]	[illegible]	[illegible]	[illegible]	[illegible]	[illegible]	[illegible]	[illegible]	[illegible]	[illegible]
[illegible]	[illegible]	[illegible]	[illegible]	[illegible]	[illegible]	[illegible]	[illegible]	[illegible]	[illegible]	[illegible]
Total	[illegible]	[illegible]	[illegible]	[illegible]	[illegible]	[illegible]	[illegible]	[illegible]	[illegible]	Total.

TABLE 2.—SHOWING THE NUMBER OF HOLDINGS EXCEEDING ONE ACRE, AND EXTENT OF LAND UNDER CROPS IN EACH YEAR FROM 1884 TO 1893, BY COUNTIES AND PROVINCES.

COUNTIES.	Years.	No. of Holdings	Corn, Beans, and Peas: [illegible]	[illegible]	[illegible]	[illegible]	[illegible]	[illegible]	[illegible]	Green Crops: [illegible]	[illegible]	[illegible]	[illegible]	[illegible]	[illegible]	[illegible]	[illegible]
ANTRIM: Area, [illegible] Acres.	[illegible]	[illegible]	[illegible]	[illegible]	[illegible]	[illegible]	[illegible]	[illegible]	[illegible]	[illegible]	[illegible]	[illegible]	[illegible]	[illegible]	[illegible]	[illegible]	[illegible]
ARMAGH: Area, [illegible] Acres.	[illegible]	[illegible]	[illegible]	[illegible]	[illegible]	[illegible]	[illegible]	[illegible]	[illegible]	[illegible]	[illegible]	[illegible]	[illegible]	[illegible]	[illegible]	[illegible]	[illegible]
CARLOW: Area, [illegible] Acres.	[illegible]	[illegible]	[illegible]	[illegible]	[illegible]	[illegible]	[illegible]	[illegible]	[illegible]	[illegible]	[illegible]	[illegible]	[illegible]	[illegible]	[illegible]	[illegible]	[illegible]
CAVAN: Area, [illegible] Acres.	[illegible]	[illegible]	[illegible]	[illegible]	[illegible]	[illegible]	[illegible]	[illegible]	[illegible]	[illegible]	[illegible]	[illegible]	[illegible]	[illegible]	[illegible]	[illegible]	[illegible]
CLARE: Area, [illegible] Acres.	[illegible]	[illegible]	[illegible]	[illegible]	[illegible]	[illegible]	[illegible]	[illegible]	[illegible]	[illegible]	[illegible]	[illegible]	[illegible]	[illegible]	[illegible]	[illegible]	[illegible]
CORK: Area, [illegible] Acres.	[illegible]	[illegible]	[illegible]	[illegible]	[illegible]	[illegible]	[illegible]	[illegible]	[illegible]	[illegible]	[illegible]	[illegible]	[illegible]	[illegible]	[illegible]	[illegible]	[illegible]
DONEGAL: Area, [illegible] Acres.	[illegible]	[illegible]	[illegible]	[illegible]	[illegible]	[illegible]	[illegible]	[illegible]	[illegible]	[illegible]	[illegible]	[illegible]	[illegible]	[illegible]	[illegible]	[illegible]	[illegible]
DOWN: Area, [illegible] Acres.	[illegible]	[illegible]	[illegible]	[illegible]	[illegible]	[illegible]	[illegible]	[illegible]	[illegible]	[illegible]	[illegible]	[illegible]	[illegible]	[illegible]	[illegible]	[illegible]	[illegible]

[illegible]	[illegible]	[illegible]	[illegible]	[illegible]
[illegible]	[illegible]	[illegible]	[illegible]	[illegible]
[illegible]	[illegible]	[illegible]	[illegible]	[illegible]
[illegible]	[illegible]	[illegible]	[illegible]	[illegible]

[illegible]	[illegible]	[illegible]	[illegible]
[illegible]	[illegible]	[illegible]	[illegible]
[illegible]	[illegible]	[illegible]	[illegible]
[illegible]	[illegible]	[illegible]	[illegible]
[illegible]	[illegible]	[illegible]	[illegible]

TABLE 10.—SHOWING THE AVERAGE RATES OF PRODUCE TO THE STATUTE ACRE—continued.

Counties.	Years.	Wheat.	Oats.	Barley.	Bere.	Rye.	Beans.	Peas.	Potatoes.	Turnips.	Mangel Wurzel and Beet Root.	Cabbage.	Flax.	Hay.
		Cwt.	Cwt.	Cwt.	Cwt.	Cwt.	Cwt.	Cwt.	Tons.	Tons.	Tons.	Tons.	Stones.	Tons.
Dublin,	[illegible]	[illegible]	[illegible]	[illegible]	[illegible]	[illegible]	[illegible]	[illegible]	[illegible]	[illegible]	[illegible]	[illegible]	[illegible]	[illegible]
Fermanagh,	[illegible]	[illegible]	[illegible]	[illegible]	[illegible]	[illegible]	[illegible]	[illegible]	[illegible]	[illegible]	[illegible]	[illegible]	[illegible]	[illegible]
Galway,	[illegible]	[illegible]	[illegible]	[illegible]	[illegible]	[illegible]	[illegible]	[illegible]	[illegible]	[illegible]	[illegible]	[illegible]	[illegible]	[illegible]
Kerry,	[illegible]	[illegible]	[illegible]	[illegible]	[illegible]	[illegible]	[illegible]	[illegible]	[illegible]	[illegible]	[illegible]	[illegible]	[illegible]	[illegible]
Kildare,	[illegible]	[illegible]	[illegible]	[illegible]	[illegible]	[illegible]	[illegible]	[illegible]	[illegible]	[illegible]	[illegible]	[illegible]	[illegible]	[illegible]
Kilkenny,	[illegible]	[illegible]	[illegible]	[illegible]	[illegible]	[illegible]	[illegible]	[illegible]	[illegible]	[illegible]	[illegible]	[illegible]	[illegible]	[illegible]
King's,	[illegible]	[illegible]	[illegible]	[illegible]	[illegible]	[illegible]	[illegible]	[illegible]	[illegible]	[illegible]	[illegible]	[illegible]	[illegible]	[illegible]
Leitrim,	[illegible]	[illegible]	[illegible]	[illegible]	[illegible]	[illegible]	[illegible]	[illegible]	[illegible]	[illegible]	[illegible]	[illegible]	[illegible]	[illegible]

[illegible]	[illegible]	[illegible]	[illegible]	[illegible]	[illegible]	[illegible]	[illegible]	[illegible]	[illegible]	[illegible]
[illegible]	[illegible]	[illegible]	[illegible]	[illegible]	[illegible]	[illegible]	[illegible]	[illegible]	[illegible]	[illegible]
[illegible]	[illegible]	[illegible]	[illegible]	[illegible]	[illegible]	[illegible]	[illegible]	[illegible]	[illegible]	[illegible]
[illegible]	[illegible]	[illegible]	[illegible]	[illegible]	[illegible]	[illegible]	[illegible]	[illegible]	[illegible]	[illegible]
[illegible]	[illegible]	[illegible]	[illegible]	[illegible]	[illegible]	[illegible]	[illegible]	[illegible]	[illegible]	[illegible]
[illegible]	[illegible]	[illegible]	[illegible]	[illegible]	[illegible]	[illegible]	[illegible]	[illegible]	[illegible]	[illegible]

[illegible]
[illegible]
[illegible]
[illegible]
[illegible]
[illegible]
[illegible]
[illegible]
[illegible]
[illegible]

TABLE 12.—Showing the Number of [illegible] and the Quantity of Live Stock in each Poor Law Union of Ireland, in [illegible]—continued.

TABLE 15.—SHOWING THE QUANTITY OF LIVE STOCK IN EACH YEAR FROM [illegible] TO [illegible], BY COUNTIES AND PROVINCES.

Counties.	Years.	No. of Horses.			Mules and Asses.		No. of Cattle.			No. of Sheep.		No. of Pigs.		No. of Goats.	No. of Poultry.
		[illegible]	[illegible]	[illegible]	No. of Mules.	No. of Asses.	[illegible]	[illegible]	[illegible]	[illegible]	[illegible]	[illegible]	[illegible]		
ANTRIM: Area, [illegible] Acres.	[illegible]	[illegible]	[illegible]	[illegible]	[illegible]	[illegible]	[illegible]	[illegible]	[illegible]	[illegible]	[illegible]	[illegible]	[illegible]	[illegible]	[illegible]
ARMAGH: Area, [illegible] Acres.	[illegible]	[illegible]	[illegible]	[illegible]	[illegible]	[illegible]	[illegible]	[illegible]	[illegible]	[illegible]	[illegible]	[illegible]	[illegible]	[illegible]	[illegible]
CARLOW: Area, [illegible] Acres.	[illegible]	[illegible]	[illegible]	[illegible]	[illegible]	[illegible]	[illegible]	[illegible]	[illegible]	[illegible]	[illegible]	[illegible]	[illegible]	[illegible]	[illegible]
CAVAN: Area, [illegible] Acres.	[illegible]	[illegible]	[illegible]	[illegible]	[illegible]	[illegible]	[illegible]	[illegible]	[illegible]	[illegible]	[illegible]	[illegible]	[illegible]	[illegible]	[illegible]
CLARE: Area, [illegible] Acres.	[illegible]	[illegible]	[illegible]	[illegible]	[illegible]	[illegible]	[illegible]	[illegible]	[illegible]	[illegible]	[illegible]	[illegible]	[illegible]	[illegible]	[illegible]
CORK: Area, [illegible] Acres.	[illegible]	[illegible]	[illegible]	[illegible]	[illegible]	[illegible]	[illegible]	[illegible]	[illegible]	[illegible]	[illegible]	[illegible]	[illegible]	[illegible]	[illegible]
DONEGAL: Area, [illegible] Acres.	[illegible]	[illegible]	[illegible]	[illegible]	[illegible]	[illegible]	[illegible]	[illegible]	[illegible]	[illegible]	[illegible]	[illegible]	[illegible]	[illegible]	[illegible]
DOWN: Area, [illegible] Acres.	[illegible]	[illegible]	[illegible]	[illegible]	[illegible]	[illegible]	[illegible]	[illegible]	[illegible]	[illegible]	[illegible]	[illegible]	[illegible]	[illegible]	[illegible]

TABLE 13.—Showing the Quantity of Live Stock in each Year from 1884 to 1893, by Counties and Provinces—continued.

Counties.	Years.	No. of Horses.			Mules and Asses.		No. of Cattle.			No. of Sheep.		No. of Pigs.		No. of Goats.	No. of Poultry.
		[illegible]	[illegible]	[illegible]	[illegible]	[illegible]	[illegible]	[illegible]	[illegible]	[illegible]	[illegible]	[illegible]	[illegible]		
Dublin: Area, [illegible] Acres.	1884–1893	[illegible]	[illegible]	[illegible]	[illegible]	[illegible]	[illegible]	[illegible]	[illegible]	[illegible]	[illegible]	[illegible]	[illegible]	[illegible]	[illegible]
Fermanagh: Area, [illegible] Acres.	1884–1893	[illegible]	[illegible]	[illegible]	[illegible]	[illegible]	[illegible]	[illegible]	[illegible]	[illegible]	[illegible]	[illegible]	[illegible]	[illegible]	[illegible]
Galway: Area, [illegible] Acres.	1884–1893	[illegible]	[illegible]	[illegible]	[illegible]	[illegible]	[illegible]	[illegible]	[illegible]	[illegible]	[illegible]	[illegible]	[illegible]	[illegible]	[illegible]
Kerry: Area, [illegible] Acres.	1884–1893	[illegible]	[illegible]	[illegible]	[illegible]	[illegible]	[illegible]	[illegible]	[illegible]	[illegible]	[illegible]	[illegible]	[illegible]	[illegible]	[illegible]
Kildare: Area, [illegible] Acres.	1884–1893	[illegible]	[illegible]	[illegible]	[illegible]	[illegible]	[illegible]	[illegible]	[illegible]	[illegible]	[illegible]	[illegible]	[illegible]	[illegible]	[illegible]
Kilkenny: Area, [illegible] Acres.	1884–1893	[illegible]	[illegible]	[illegible]	[illegible]	[illegible]	[illegible]	[illegible]	[illegible]	[illegible]	[illegible]	[illegible]	[illegible]	[illegible]	[illegible]
King's: Area, [illegible] Acres.	1884–1893	[illegible]	[illegible]	[illegible]	[illegible]	[illegible]	[illegible]	[illegible]	[illegible]	[illegible]	[illegible]	[illegible]	[illegible]	[illegible]	[illegible]
Leitrim: Area, [illegible] Acres.	1884–1893	[illegible]	[illegible]	[illegible]	[illegible]	[illegible]	[illegible]	[illegible]	[illegible]	[illegible]	[illegible]	[illegible]	[illegible]	[illegible]	[illegible]

Table 13.—Showing the Quantity of Live Stock in each Year from 1884 to 1893, by Counties and Provinces—continued.

Counties.	[illegible]
Limerick: Area, [illegible] Acres.	[illegible]
Londonderry: Area, [illegible] Acres.	[illegible]
Longford: Area, [illegible] Acres.	[illegible]
Louth & Drogheda Co. of Town: Area, [illegible] Acres.	[illegible]
Mayo: Area, [illegible] Acres.	[illegible]
Meath: Area, [illegible] Acres.	[illegible]
Monaghan: Area, [illegible] Acres.	[illegible]
Queen's: Area, [illegible] Acres.	[illegible]

TABLE 11.—SHOWING THE QUANTITY OF LIVE STOCK IN EACH YEAR FROM 1854 TO 1863, BY COUNTIES AND PROVINCES—continued.

Counties.	Years.	No. of Horses.			Mules and Asses.		No. of Cattle.			No. of Sheep.		No. of Pigs.		No. of Goats.	No. of Poultry.
		[illegible]	[illegible]	[illegible]	No. of Mules.	No. of Asses.	[illegible]	[illegible]	[illegible]	[illegible]	[illegible]	[illegible]	[illegible]		
Roscommon: Area, [illegible] Acres.	[illegible]	[illegible]	[illegible]	[illegible]	[illegible]	[illegible]	[illegible]	[illegible]	[illegible]	[illegible]	[illegible]	[illegible]	[illegible]	[illegible]	[illegible]
Sligo: Area, [illegible] Acres.	[illegible]	[illegible]	[illegible]	[illegible]	[illegible]	[illegible]	[illegible]	[illegible]	[illegible]	[illegible]	[illegible]	[illegible]	[illegible]	[illegible]	[illegible]
Tipperary: Area, [illegible] Acres.	[illegible]	[illegible]	[illegible]	[illegible]	[illegible]	[illegible]	[illegible]	[illegible]	[illegible]	[illegible]	[illegible]	[illegible]	[illegible]	[illegible]	[illegible]
Tyrone: Area, [illegible] Acres.	[illegible]	[illegible]	[illegible]	[illegible]	[illegible]	[illegible]	[illegible]	[illegible]	[illegible]	[illegible]	[illegible]	[illegible]	[illegible]	[illegible]	[illegible]
Waterford: Area, [illegible] Acres.	[illegible]	[illegible]	[illegible]	[illegible]	[illegible]	[illegible]	[illegible]	[illegible]	[illegible]	[illegible]	[illegible]	[illegible]	[illegible]	[illegible]	[illegible]
Westmeath: Area, [illegible] Acres.	[illegible]	[illegible]	[illegible]	[illegible]	[illegible]	[illegible]	[illegible]	[illegible]	[illegible]	[illegible]	[illegible]	[illegible]	[illegible]	[illegible]	[illegible]
Wexford: Area, [illegible] Acres.	[illegible]	[illegible]	[illegible]	[illegible]	[illegible]	[illegible]	[illegible]	[illegible]	[illegible]	[illegible]	[illegible]	[illegible]	[illegible]	[illegible]	[illegible]
Wicklow: Area, [illegible] Acres.	[illegible]	[illegible]	[illegible]	[illegible]	[illegible]	[illegible]	[illegible]	[illegible]	[illegible]	[illegible]	[illegible]	[illegible]	[illegible]	[illegible]	[illegible]

TABLE 15.—Showing the Quantity of Live Stock in each Year from [illegible] to [illegible], in Counties and Provinces—continued.

PROVINCES.

Provinces.	Year.	No. of Horses.			Mules and Asses.		No. of Cattle.			No. of Sheep.		No. of Pigs.		No. of Goats.	No. of Poultry.
		[illegible]	[illegible]	[illegible]	No. of Mules.	No. of Asses.	[illegible]	[illegible]	[illegible]	[illegible]	[illegible]	[illegible]	[illegible]		
Leinster:	[illegible]	[illegible]	[illegible]	[illegible]	[illegible]	[illegible]	[illegible]	[illegible]	[illegible]	[illegible]	[illegible]	[illegible]	[illegible]	[illegible]	[illegible]
	[illegible]	[illegible]	[illegible]	[illegible]	[illegible]	[illegible]	[illegible]	[illegible]	[illegible]	[illegible]	[illegible]	[illegible]	[illegible]	[illegible]	[illegible]
	[illegible]	[illegible]	[illegible]	[illegible]	[illegible]	[illegible]	[illegible]	[illegible]	[illegible]	[illegible]	[illegible]	[illegible]	[illegible]	[illegible]	[illegible]
Area, [illegible] Acres.	[illegible]	[illegible]	[illegible]	[illegible]	[illegible]	[illegible]	[illegible]	[illegible]	[illegible]	[illegible]	[illegible]	[illegible]	[illegible]	[illegible]	[illegible]
	[illegible]	[illegible]	[illegible]	[illegible]	[illegible]	[illegible]	[illegible]	[illegible]	[illegible]	[illegible]	[illegible]	[illegible]	[illegible]	[illegible]	[illegible]
	[illegible]	[illegible]	[illegible]	[illegible]	[illegible]	[illegible]	[illegible]	[illegible]	[illegible]	[illegible]	[illegible]	[illegible]	[illegible]	[illegible]	[illegible]
	[illegible]	[illegible]	[illegible]	[illegible]	[illegible]	[illegible]	[illegible]	[illegible]	[illegible]	[illegible]	[illegible]	[illegible]	[illegible]	[illegible]	[illegible]
	[illegible]	[illegible]	[illegible]	[illegible]	[illegible]	[illegible]	[illegible]	[illegible]	[illegible]	[illegible]	[illegible]	[illegible]	[illegible]	[illegible]	[illegible]
	[illegible]	[illegible]	[illegible]	[illegible]	[illegible]	[illegible]	[illegible]	[illegible]	[illegible]	[illegible]	[illegible]	[illegible]	[illegible]	[illegible]	[illegible]
	[illegible]	[illegible]	[illegible]	[illegible]	[illegible]	[illegible]	[illegible]	[illegible]	[illegible]	[illegible]	[illegible]	[illegible]	[illegible]	[illegible]	[illegible]
Munster:	[illegible]	[illegible]	[illegible]	[illegible]	[illegible]	[illegible]	[illegible]	[illegible]	[illegible]	[illegible]	[illegible]	[illegible]	[illegible]	[illegible]	[illegible]
	[illegible]	[illegible]	[illegible]	[illegible]	[illegible]	[illegible]	[illegible]	[illegible]	[illegible]	[illegible]	[illegible]	[illegible]	[illegible]	[illegible]	[illegible]
	[illegible]	[illegible]	[illegible]	[illegible]	[illegible]	[illegible]	[illegible]	[illegible]	[illegible]	[illegible]	[illegible]	[illegible]	[illegible]	[illegible]	[illegible]
Area, [illegible] Acres.	[illegible]	[illegible]	[illegible]	[illegible]	[illegible]	[illegible]	[illegible]	[illegible]	[illegible]	[illegible]	[illegible]	[illegible]	[illegible]	[illegible]	[illegible]
	[illegible]	[illegible]	[illegible]	[illegible]	[illegible]	[illegible]	[illegible]	[illegible]	[illegible]	[illegible]	[illegible]	[illegible]	[illegible]	[illegible]	[illegible]
	[illegible]	[illegible]	[illegible]	[illegible]	[illegible]	[illegible]	[illegible]	[illegible]	[illegible]	[illegible]	[illegible]	[illegible]	[illegible]	[illegible]	[illegible]
	[illegible]	[illegible]	[illegible]	[illegible]	[illegible]	[illegible]	[illegible]	[illegible]	[illegible]	[illegible]	[illegible]	[illegible]	[illegible]	[illegible]	[illegible]
	[illegible]	[illegible]	[illegible]	[illegible]	[illegible]	[illegible]	[illegible]	[illegible]	[illegible]	[illegible]	[illegible]	[illegible]	[illegible]	[illegible]	[illegible]
	[illegible]	[illegible]	[illegible]	[illegible]	[illegible]	[illegible]	[illegible]	[illegible]	[illegible]	[illegible]	[illegible]	[illegible]	[illegible]	[illegible]	[illegible]
	[illegible]	[illegible]	[illegible]	[illegible]	[illegible]	[illegible]	[illegible]	[illegible]	[illegible]	[illegible]	[illegible]	[illegible]	[illegible]	[illegible]	[illegible]
Ulster:	[illegible]	[illegible]	[illegible]	[illegible]	[illegible]	[illegible]	[illegible]	[illegible]	[illegible]	[illegible]	[illegible]	[illegible]	[illegible]	[illegible]	[illegible]
	[illegible]	[illegible]	[illegible]	[illegible]	[illegible]	[illegible]	[illegible]	[illegible]	[illegible]	[illegible]	[illegible]	[illegible]	[illegible]	[illegible]	[illegible]
	[illegible]	[illegible]	[illegible]	[illegible]	[illegible]	[illegible]	[illegible]	[illegible]	[illegible]	[illegible]	[illegible]	[illegible]	[illegible]	[illegible]	[illegible]
Area, [illegible] Acres.	[illegible]	[illegible]	[illegible]	[illegible]	[illegible]	[illegible]	[illegible]	[illegible]	[illegible]	[illegible]	[illegible]	[illegible]	[illegible]	[illegible]	[illegible]
	[illegible]	[illegible]	[illegible]	[illegible]	[illegible]	[illegible]	[illegible]	[illegible]	[illegible]	[illegible]	[illegible]	[illegible]	[illegible]	[illegible]	[illegible]
	[illegible]	[illegible]	[illegible]	[illegible]	[illegible]	[illegible]	[illegible]	[illegible]	[illegible]	[illegible]	[illegible]	[illegible]	[illegible]	[illegible]	[illegible]
	[illegible]	[illegible]	[illegible]	[illegible]	[illegible]	[illegible]	[illegible]	[illegible]	[illegible]	[illegible]	[illegible]	[illegible]	[illegible]	[illegible]	[illegible]
	[illegible]	[illegible]	[illegible]	[illegible]	[illegible]	[illegible]	[illegible]	[illegible]	[illegible]	[illegible]	[illegible]	[illegible]	[illegible]	[illegible]	[illegible]
	[illegible]	[illegible]	[illegible]	[illegible]	[illegible]	[illegible]	[illegible]	[illegible]	[illegible]	[illegible]	[illegible]	[illegible]	[illegible]	[illegible]	[illegible]
	[illegible]	[illegible]	[illegible]	[illegible]	[illegible]	[illegible]	[illegible]	[illegible]	[illegible]	[illegible]	[illegible]	[illegible]	[illegible]	[illegible]	[illegible]
Connaught:	[illegible]	[illegible]	[illegible]	[illegible]	[illegible]	[illegible]	[illegible]	[illegible]	[illegible]	[illegible]	[illegible]	[illegible]	[illegible]	[illegible]	[illegible]
	[illegible]	[illegible]	[illegible]	[illegible]	[illegible]	[illegible]	[illegible]	[illegible]	[illegible]	[illegible]	[illegible]	[illegible]	[illegible]	[illegible]	[illegible]
	[illegible]	[illegible]	[illegible]	[illegible]	[illegible]	[illegible]	[illegible]	[illegible]	[illegible]	[illegible]	[illegible]	[illegible]	[illegible]	[illegible]	[illegible]
Area, [illegible] Acres.	[illegible]	[illegible]	[illegible]	[illegible]	[illegible]	[illegible]	[illegible]	[illegible]	[illegible]	[illegible]	[illegible]	[illegible]	[illegible]	[illegible]	[illegible]
	[illegible]	[illegible]	[illegible]	[illegible]	[illegible]	[illegible]	[illegible]	[illegible]	[illegible]	[illegible]	[illegible]	[illegible]	[illegible]	[illegible]	[illegible]
	[illegible]	[illegible]	[illegible]	[illegible]	[illegible]	[illegible]	[illegible]	[illegible]	[illegible]	[illegible]	[illegible]	[illegible]	[illegible]	[illegible]	[illegible]
	[illegible]	[illegible]	[illegible]	[illegible]	[illegible]	[illegible]	[illegible]	[illegible]	[illegible]	[illegible]	[illegible]	[illegible]	[illegible]	[illegible]	[illegible]
	[illegible]	[illegible]	[illegible]	[illegible]	[illegible]	[illegible]	[illegible]	[illegible]	[illegible]	[illegible]	[illegible]	[illegible]	[illegible]	[illegible]	[illegible]
	[illegible]	[illegible]	[illegible]	[illegible]	[illegible]	[illegible]	[illegible]	[illegible]	[illegible]	[illegible]	[illegible]	[illegible]	[illegible]	[illegible]	[illegible]
	[illegible]	[illegible]	[illegible]	[illegible]	[illegible]	[illegible]	[illegible]	[illegible]	[illegible]	[illegible]	[illegible]	[illegible]	[illegible]	[illegible]	[illegible]

TOTAL OF IRELAND.

Ireland.	Year.	No. of Horses.			Mules and Asses.		No. of Cattle.			No. of Sheep.		No. of Pigs.		No. of Goats.	No. of Poultry.
		[illegible]	[illegible]	[illegible]	No. of Mules.	No. of Asses.	[illegible]	[illegible]	[illegible]	[illegible]	[illegible]	[illegible]	[illegible]		
Total of Ireland:	[illegible]	[illegible]	[illegible]	[illegible]	[illegible]	[illegible]	[illegible]	[illegible]	[illegible]	[illegible]	[illegible]	[illegible]	[illegible]	[illegible]	[illegible]
	[illegible]	[illegible]	[illegible]	[illegible]	[illegible]	[illegible]	[illegible]	[illegible]	[illegible]	[illegible]	[illegible]	[illegible]	[illegible]	[illegible]	[illegible]
	[illegible]	[illegible]	[illegible]	[illegible]	[illegible]	[illegible]	[illegible]	[illegible]	[illegible]	[illegible]	[illegible]	[illegible]	[illegible]	[illegible]	[illegible]
Area, [illegible] Acres.	[illegible]	[illegible]	[illegible]	[illegible]	[illegible]	[illegible]	[illegible]	[illegible]	[illegible]	[illegible]	[illegible]	[illegible]	[illegible]	[illegible]	[illegible]
	[illegible]	[illegible]	[illegible]	[illegible]	[illegible]	[illegible]	[illegible]	[illegible]	[illegible]	[illegible]	[illegible]	[illegible]	[illegible]	[illegible]	[illegible]
	[illegible]	[illegible]	[illegible]	[illegible]	[illegible]	[illegible]	[illegible]	[illegible]	[illegible]	[illegible]	[illegible]	[illegible]	[illegible]	[illegible]	[illegible]
	[illegible]	[illegible]	[illegible]	[illegible]	[illegible]	[illegible]	[illegible]	[illegible]	[illegible]	[illegible]	[illegible]	[illegible]	[illegible]	[illegible]	[illegible]
	[illegible]	[illegible]	[illegible]	[illegible]	[illegible]	[illegible]	[illegible]	[illegible]	[illegible]	[illegible]	[illegible]	[illegible]	[illegible]	[illegible]	[illegible]
	[illegible]	[illegible]	[illegible]	[illegible]	[illegible]	[illegible]	[illegible]	[illegible]	[illegible]	[illegible]	[illegible]	[illegible]	[illegible]	[illegible]	[illegible]
	[illegible]	[illegible]	[illegible]	[illegible]	[illegible]	[illegible]	[illegible]	[illegible]	[illegible]	[illegible]	[illegible]	[illegible]	[illegible]	[illegible]	[illegible]

TABLE 14.—SHOWING, by COUNTIES and PROVINCES, the Total Area under POTATOES in 1893, and the Extent in Statute Acres under each description of that crop.

COUNTIES.	Total Area under Potatoes in Statute Acres	General Names of the different kinds of Potatoes planted															
	Acres.	Acres.	Acres.	Acres.	Acres.	Acres.	Acres.	Acres.	Acres.	Acres.	Acres.	Acres.	Acres.	Acres.	Acres.	Acres.	Acres.
Antrim	[illegible]	[illegible]	[illegible]	[illegible]	[illegible]	[illegible]	[illegible]	[illegible]	[illegible]	[illegible]	[illegible]	[illegible]	[illegible]	[illegible]	[illegible]	[illegible]	[illegible]
Armagh	[illegible]	[illegible]	[illegible]	[illegible]	[illegible]	[illegible]	[illegible]	[illegible]	[illegible]	[illegible]	[illegible]	[illegible]	[illegible]	[illegible]	[illegible]	[illegible]	[illegible]
Carlow	[illegible]	[illegible]	[illegible]	[illegible]	[illegible]	[illegible]	[illegible]	[illegible]	[illegible]	[illegible]	[illegible]	[illegible]	[illegible]	[illegible]	[illegible]	[illegible]	[illegible]
Cavan	[illegible]	[illegible]	[illegible]	[illegible]	[illegible]	[illegible]	[illegible]	[illegible]	[illegible]	[illegible]	[illegible]	[illegible]	[illegible]	[illegible]	[illegible]	[illegible]	[illegible]
Clare	[illegible]	[illegible]	[illegible]	[illegible]	[illegible]	[illegible]	[illegible]	[illegible]	[illegible]	[illegible]	[illegible]	[illegible]	[illegible]	[illegible]	[illegible]	[illegible]	[illegible]
Cork	[illegible]	[illegible]	[illegible]	[illegible]	[illegible]	[illegible]	[illegible]	[illegible]	[illegible]	[illegible]	[illegible]	[illegible]	[illegible]	[illegible]	[illegible]	[illegible]	[illegible]
Donegal	[illegible]	[illegible]	[illegible]	[illegible]	[illegible]	[illegible]	[illegible]	[illegible]	[illegible]	[illegible]	[illegible]	[illegible]	[illegible]	[illegible]	[illegible]	[illegible]	[illegible]
Down	[illegible]	[illegible]	[illegible]	[illegible]	[illegible]	[illegible]	[illegible]	[illegible]	[illegible]	[illegible]	[illegible]	[illegible]	[illegible]	[illegible]	[illegible]	[illegible]	[illegible]
Dublin	[illegible]	[illegible]	[illegible]	[illegible]	[illegible]	[illegible]	[illegible]	[illegible]	[illegible]	[illegible]	[illegible]	[illegible]	[illegible]	[illegible]	[illegible]	[illegible]	[illegible]
Fermanagh	[illegible]	[illegible]	[illegible]	[illegible]	[illegible]	[illegible]	[illegible]	[illegible]	[illegible]	[illegible]	[illegible]	[illegible]	[illegible]	[illegible]	[illegible]	[illegible]	[illegible]
Galway	[illegible]	[illegible]	[illegible]	[illegible]	[illegible]	[illegible]	[illegible]	[illegible]	[illegible]	[illegible]	[illegible]	[illegible]	[illegible]	[illegible]	[illegible]	[illegible]	[illegible]
Kerry	[illegible]	[illegible]	[illegible]	[illegible]	[illegible]	[illegible]	[illegible]	[illegible]	[illegible]	[illegible]	[illegible]	[illegible]	[illegible]	[illegible]	[illegible]	[illegible]	[illegible]
Kildare	[illegible]	[illegible]	[illegible]	[illegible]	[illegible]	[illegible]	[illegible]	[illegible]	[illegible]	[illegible]	[illegible]	[illegible]	[illegible]	[illegible]	[illegible]	[illegible]	[illegible]
Kilkenny	[illegible]	[illegible]	[illegible]	[illegible]	[illegible]	[illegible]	[illegible]	[illegible]	[illegible]	[illegible]	[illegible]	[illegible]	[illegible]	[illegible]	[illegible]	[illegible]	[illegible]
King's	[illegible]	[illegible]	[illegible]	[illegible]	[illegible]	[illegible]	[illegible]	[illegible]	[illegible]	[illegible]	[illegible]	[illegible]	[illegible]	[illegible]	[illegible]	[illegible]	[illegible]
Leitrim	[illegible]	[illegible]	[illegible]	[illegible]	[illegible]	[illegible]	[illegible]	[illegible]	[illegible]	[illegible]	[illegible]	[illegible]	[illegible]	[illegible]	[illegible]	[illegible]	[illegible]
Limerick	[illegible]	[illegible]	[illegible]	[illegible]	[illegible]	[illegible]	[illegible]	[illegible]	[illegible]	[illegible]	[illegible]	[illegible]	[illegible]	[illegible]	[illegible]	[illegible]	[illegible]
Londonderry	[illegible]	[illegible]	[illegible]	[illegible]	[illegible]	[illegible]	[illegible]	[illegible]	[illegible]	[illegible]	[illegible]	[illegible]	[illegible]	[illegible]	[illegible]	[illegible]	[illegible]
Longford	[illegible]	[illegible]	[illegible]	[illegible]	[illegible]	[illegible]	[illegible]	[illegible]	[illegible]	[illegible]	[illegible]	[illegible]	[illegible]	[illegible]	[illegible]	[illegible]	[illegible]
Louth and Drogheda, County of Town	[illegible]	[illegible]	[illegible]	[illegible]	[illegible]	[illegible]	[illegible]	[illegible]	[illegible]	[illegible]	[illegible]	[illegible]	[illegible]	[illegible]	[illegible]	[illegible]	[illegible]
Mayo	[illegible]	[illegible]	[illegible]	[illegible]	[illegible]	[illegible]	[illegible]	[illegible]	[illegible]	[illegible]	[illegible]	[illegible]	[illegible]	[illegible]	[illegible]	[illegible]	[illegible]
Meath	[illegible]	[illegible]	[illegible]	[illegible]	[illegible]	[illegible]	[illegible]	[illegible]	[illegible]	[illegible]	[illegible]	[illegible]	[illegible]	[illegible]	[illegible]	[illegible]	[illegible]
Monaghan	[illegible]	[illegible]	[illegible]	[illegible]	[illegible]	[illegible]	[illegible]	[illegible]	[illegible]	[illegible]	[illegible]	[illegible]	[illegible]	[illegible]	[illegible]	[illegible]	[illegible]
Queen's	[illegible]	[illegible]	[illegible]	[illegible]	[illegible]	[illegible]	[illegible]	[illegible]	[illegible]	[illegible]	[illegible]	[illegible]	[illegible]	[illegible]	[illegible]	[illegible]	[illegible]
Roscommon	[illegible]	[illegible]	[illegible]	[illegible]	[illegible]	[illegible]	[illegible]	[illegible]	[illegible]	[illegible]	[illegible]	[illegible]	[illegible]	[illegible]	[illegible]	[illegible]	[illegible]
Sligo	[illegible]	[illegible]	[illegible]	[illegible]	[illegible]	[illegible]	[illegible]	[illegible]	[illegible]	[illegible]	[illegible]	[illegible]	[illegible]	[illegible]	[illegible]	[illegible]	[illegible]
Tipperary	[illegible]	[illegible]	[illegible]	[illegible]	[illegible]	[illegible]	[illegible]	[illegible]	[illegible]	[illegible]	[illegible]	[illegible]	[illegible]	[illegible]	[illegible]	[illegible]	[illegible]
Tyrone	[illegible]	[illegible]	[illegible]	[illegible]	[illegible]	[illegible]	[illegible]	[illegible]	[illegible]	[illegible]	[illegible]	[illegible]	[illegible]	[illegible]	[illegible]	[illegible]	[illegible]
Waterford	[illegible]	[illegible]	[illegible]	[illegible]	[illegible]	[illegible]	[illegible]	[illegible]	[illegible]	[illegible]	[illegible]	[illegible]	[illegible]	[illegible]	[illegible]	[illegible]	[illegible]
Westmeath	[illegible]	[illegible]	[illegible]	[illegible]	[illegible]	[illegible]	[illegible]	[illegible]	[illegible]	[illegible]	[illegible]	[illegible]	[illegible]	[illegible]	[illegible]	[illegible]	[illegible]
Wexford	[illegible]	[illegible]	[illegible]	[illegible]	[illegible]	[illegible]	[illegible]	[illegible]	[illegible]	[illegible]	[illegible]	[illegible]	[illegible]	[illegible]	[illegible]	[illegible]	[illegible]
Wicklow	[illegible]	[illegible]	[illegible]	[illegible]	[illegible]	[illegible]	[illegible]	[illegible]	[illegible]	[illegible]	[illegible]	[illegible]	[illegible]	[illegible]	[illegible]	[illegible]	[illegible]
PROVINCES.																	
Leinster	[illegible]	[illegible]	[illegible]	[illegible]	[illegible]	[illegible]	[illegible]	[illegible]	[illegible]	[illegible]	[illegible]	[illegible]	[illegible]	[illegible]	[illegible]	[illegible]	[illegible]
Munster	[illegible]	[illegible]	[illegible]	[illegible]	[illegible]	[illegible]	[illegible]	[illegible]	[illegible]	[illegible]	[illegible]	[illegible]	[illegible]	[illegible]	[illegible]	[illegible]	[illegible]
Ulster	[illegible]	[illegible]	[illegible]	[illegible]	[illegible]	[illegible]	[illegible]	[illegible]	[illegible]	[illegible]	[illegible]	[illegible]	[illegible]	[illegible]	[illegible]	[illegible]	[illegible]
Connaught	[illegible]	[illegible]	[illegible]	[illegible]	[illegible]	[illegible]	[illegible]	[illegible]	[illegible]	[illegible]	[illegible]	[illegible]	[illegible]	[illegible]	[illegible]	[illegible]	[illegible]
Total of Ireland, 1893	[illegible]	[illegible]	[illegible]	[illegible]	[illegible]	[illegible]	[illegible]	[illegible]	[illegible]	[illegible]	[illegible]	[illegible]	[illegible]	[illegible]	[illegible]	[illegible]	[illegible]
Percentage in 1893	[illegible]	[illegible]	[illegible]	[illegible]	[illegible]	[illegible]	[illegible]	[illegible]	[illegible]	[illegible]	3·6						
Total of Ireland, 1892	[illegible]	[illegible]	[illegible]	[illegible]	[illegible]	[illegible]	[illegible]	[illegible]	[illegible]	[illegible]	[illegible]	[illegible]	[illegible]	[illegible]	[illegible]	[illegible]	[illegible]
Percentage in 1892	[illegible]	[illegible]	[illegible]	[illegible]	[illegible]	[illegible]	[illegible]	[illegible]	[illegible]	[illegible]	[illegible]						

TABLE 16.—SHOWING, by COUNTIES, the average rate of Produce per acre of the principal descriptions of POTATOES planted in Ireland in 1893.

COUNTIES.	General Names of the different kinds of Potatoes planted in each County.															
	[illegible]	[illegible]	[illegible]	[illegible]	[illegible]	[illegible]	[illegible]	[illegible]	[illegible]	[illegible]	[illegible]	[illegible]	[illegible]	[illegible]	[illegible]	[illegible]
	Cwts.	Cwts.	Cwts.	Cwts.	Cwts.	Cwts.	Cwts.	Cwts.	Cwts.	Cwts.	Cwts.	Cwts.	Cwts.	Cwts.	Cwts.	Cwts.
Antrim,	[illegible]	[illegible]	[illegible]	[illegible]	[illegible]	[illegible]	[illegible]	[illegible]	[illegible]	[illegible]	.	.	.	.	.	.
Armagh,	[illegible]	[illegible]	[illegible]	[illegible]	79	[illegible]	[illegible]	[illegible]	[illegible]	[illegible]	.	.	.	.	.	.
Carlow,	[illegible]	71	.	.	.	[illegible]	[illegible]	[illegible]	[illegible]	.	.	.	.	.	.	.
Cavan,	[illegible]	[illegible]	[illegible]	.	[illegible]	[illegible]	[illegible]	[illegible]	[illegible]	.	.	.	.	.	.	.
Clare,	[illegible]	[illegible]	.	.	[illegible]	[illegible]	[illegible]	[illegible]	71	.	.	[illegible]	.	.	.	.
Cork,	[illegible]	77	.	.	[illegible]	[illegible]	[illegible]	[illegible]	[illegible]	.	.	.	.	.	.	.
Donegal,	[illegible]	[illegible]	[illegible]	[illegible]	[illegible]	[illegible]	[illegible]	[illegible]	117	[illegible]	[illegible]	.	.	.	[illegible]	[illegible]
Down,	[illegible]	[illegible]	[illegible]	.	[illegible]	[illegible]	71	[illegible]	[illegible]	[illegible]	.	.	.	.	.	.
Dublin,	[illegible]	[illegible]	[illegible]	.	[illegible]	[illegible]	[illegible]	[illegible]	[illegible]	.	.	.	.	.	.	.
Fermanagh,	[illegible]	[illegible]	[illegible]	[illegible]	[illegible]	[illegible]	[illegible]	[illegible]	[illegible]	.	.	.	.	.	.	.
Galway,	[illegible]	[illegible]	.	.	[illegible]	[illegible]	[illegible]	[illegible]	.	.	.	.	[illegible]	.	.	.
Kerry,	[illegible]	[illegible]	.	146	[illegible]	[illegible]	.	[illegible]	.	.	.	.	.	.	.	.
Kildare,	[illegible]	[illegible]	.	.	[illegible]	74	[illegible]	[illegible]	[illegible]	.	.	.	.	.	.	.
Kilkenny,	[illegible]	[illegible]	.	.	[illegible]	[illegible]	[illegible]	[illegible]	[illegible]	.	.	.	.	.	.	.
King's,	[illegible]	[illegible]	.	.	.	71	[illegible]	[illegible]	[illegible]	.	.	.	[illegible]	.	.	.
Leitrim,	[illegible]	[illegible]	[illegible]	.	[illegible]	[illegible]	[illegible]	[illegible]	[illegible]	.	.	.	.	115	.	.
Limerick,	[illegible]	[illegible]	.	.	[illegible]	77	[illegible]	[illegible]	.	.	.	[illegible]	.	.	.	.
Londonderry,	[illegible]	[illegible]	[illegible]	[illegible]	[illegible]	[illegible]	[illegible]	[illegible]	[illegible]	[illegible]	[illegible]	.	.	.	.	.
Longford,	[illegible]	[illegible]	[illegible]	.	[illegible]	[illegible]	[illegible]	[illegible]	[illegible]	.	.	.	.	.	.	.
Louth and Drogheda, County of Town,	[illegible]	[illegible]	77	.	[illegible]	[illegible]	[illegible]	[illegible]	.	.	[illegible]	.	.	.	.	.
Mayo,	[illegible]	[illegible]	[illegible]	.	[illegible]	[illegible]	[illegible]	[illegible]	[illegible]	.	.	.	.	.	.	.
Meath,	[illegible]	[illegible]	[illegible]	.	[illegible]	[illegible]	[illegible]	[illegible]	[illegible]	.	.	.	.	.	.	.
Monaghan,	[illegible]	[illegible]	[illegible]	.	[illegible]	[illegible]	[illegible]	.	[illegible]	.	.	.	.	.	.	.
Queen's,	[illegible]	[illegible]	.	.	111	[illegible]	[illegible]	[illegible]	[illegible]	.	.	.	.	.	.	.
Roscommon,	[illegible]	[illegible]	[illegible]	.	[illegible]	[illegible]	[illegible]	73	[illegible]	.	.	.	[illegible]	.	.	.
Sligo,	[illegible]	[illegible]	[illegible]	.	[illegible]	[illegible]	[illegible]	[illegible]	.	.	.	.	.	.	.	.
Tipperary,	[illegible]	[illegible]	[illegible]	.	[illegible]	[illegible]	[illegible]	[illegible]	[illegible]	.	.	[illegible]	.	[illegible]	.	.
Tyrone,	[illegible]	[illegible]	[illegible]	[illegible]	[illegible]	[illegible]	[illegible]	[illegible]	77	.	[illegible]	.	.	.	.	.
Waterford,	[illegible]	[illegible]	.	.	[illegible]	[illegible]	[illegible]	110	.	.	.	.	.	.	.	.
Westmeath,	[illegible]	77	[illegible]	.	[illegible]	[illegible]	[illegible]	[illegible]	[illegible]	.	.	.	.	.	.	.
Wexford,	[illegible]	[illegible]	[illegible]	.	[illegible]	[illegible]	[illegible]	[illegible]	[illegible]	.	.	.	.	.	.	.
Wicklow,	[illegible]	71	[illegible]	.	.	[illegible]	[illegible]	[illegible]	.	.	.	.	.	.	.	.

OBSERVATIONS

OF THE

DISTRICT INSPECTORS OF THE ROYAL IRISH CONSTABULARY AND OF THE SERGEANTS OF THE METROPOLITAN POLICE,

WHO ACTED AS SUPERINTENDENTS OF THE AGRICULTURAL STATISTICS;

IN REPLY TO A CIRCULAR DATED 9TH OCTOBER, 18[illegible], ON THE PROBABLE CAUSES TO WHICH THE GOOD OR BAD YIELD OF THE VARIOUS CROPS IN EACH OF THEIR DISTRICTS MAY BE ATTRIBUTED.

PROVINCE OF LEINSTER.

Province of Leinster.

CARLOW COUNTY. *Bagenalstown D.*—The crop would rate as follows:—Wheat.—None sown. Oats.—A good crop, though short in straw owing to want of moisture. Barley.—A good sound crop, above the average, straw short. Bere, Rye, Beans, Peas.—None sown. Potatoes.—A good crop, and owing to the absence of blight, the yield has been quite up to the average. Turnips.—This was a variable crop, as in some places the return was bad, while in others there was an excellent crop. Mangel Wurzel.—An average crop all round. Hay.—Generally a light crop, though well saved. The crops have not been injured to any extent by insects or fungi. *Carlow D.*—Potatoes are excellent everywhere. The yield both in quality and quantity is much above the average, and there is no disease. This is due to the unusual dryness of the season. Oats.—A very good heavy crop, well saved. Barley.—A good average crop, very well saved. Wheat.—Very little grown. A good yield up to average. The straw of all the grain crops is light owing to the drought. Turnips and Mangolds.—Fair on the whole. Roots rather small owing to drought. Cabbage.—Good in parts. In some places affected in quantity by drought. Hay.—A very light crop owing to drought, but good in quality, and well and cheaply saved. No special injury has been done by insects or fungi.

DUBLIN COUNTY. *Balbriggan D.*—The crops are [illegible] good and productive; the want of rain during the year caused wheat and the hay crop to be much less than the average, and also affected the grass on grazing lands. Green crops and oats are very good, and altogether the year has been most prosperous for farmers and fruit-growers. The potatoes in the district are a good crop, but have not escaped blight, though the ravages of the disease have not been serious. *Clontarf D.*—With the exception of the hay crop, all the others are this year more than an average. Potato crop is abundant, and of good quality. Grain crops have been placed over an average, although I have heard complaints as to the quality, as the ear had not filled owing to the dry weather. The green crops, except in very light soil, look very flourishing. In the early part of the year these crops promised to be a failure, but they revived when rain fell in August. The hay crop was deficient in quantity owing to the exceptionally dry weather experienced this year, but it was well saved, and the quality is very good. The cabbage crop in this district is very good, and promises a great yield. I have heard some complaints from farmers in the neighbourhood of Rahany, complaining of their potatoes being injured by wireworm. In no other part of the district has there been any complaint of a similar nature, as in general all the farms are very highly cultivated, and kept free from weeds and fungi. *Clonskeagh Lane D.*—The carrot yield was not quite so good as last year owing to the damage done to the young sprouts by the "blue fly" on account of the summer being so warm. The cabbage did not give as good a return owing to same cause. The potatoes were somewhat better crop, and a great deal better as an article of food—the principal cause was warm weather in July. Turnips and Mangel wurzel were not as good as last year owing to very dry weather. *Kingstown D.*—The yield of crops is above the average of previous years; this increase may be attributed to the unusually dry season. There is no special injury to crops from insects or fungi. *Rathdrum D.*—The farmers and others state that their crops are of a fair average character this year. Oats was not so heavy a crop this season owing to the very dry summer; little sown here. Potatoes are about the same as last year. Hay is said to be lighter owing to the long drought, but not much lighter than other seasons. Other crops are about the same average this year as last year. *Dundrum D.*—All crops were up to the average, except turnips and hay. The remarkably dry summer caused the former crop to be stunted in growth, and was also the reason why the hay crop, especially the old meadows, was not heavy. I have noticed also that the leaves of the turnips were affected by insects, which gave them a faded white appearance, but I do not think the roots were affected by them. Of course pasture land suffered also from the continued dry season, but, on the whole, complaints in general are few. *Lucan D.*—With the one exception of hay the yield of crops has been considerably above the average. There has not been such a return of wheat for many years. This is attributed to the fine dry weather during the season. The early hay crop was short owing to want of rain, and the present yield was therefore under the average. There was no injury from insects or fungi.

KILDARE COUNTY. *Athy D.*—The yield of all crops was above the average, with the exception of the hay and grass. The dry spring was very favourable to the various corn and root crops, but very unfavourable to the hay and grass. No crops seem to have suffered from the long continued drought except grass. All cereals were well and quickly harvested owing to the fine weather. There was a good deal of mildew on turnips owing to the drought which prevented growth, but on the whole the crop is good. I have not heard of any special injury to crops from insects or fungi. Hay is scarce and dear, as much as £4 10s. per ton being paid in Athy market, which is considerably above the average. There was a good deal of hay made out of clover seeds and aftergrass, more than I have seen previously. This second crop was very fair, and did a great service to the farmers. *Kildare D.*—The crops have been in general good, owing to fine season. No injury from insects or fungi, except that in a few places turnips were attacked by fly, but not to any extent. *Naas D.*—The good yield of the various crops (hay excepted) is due to the exceptionally favourable season; the weather was in most places too dry for hay, but it was as a rule well saved. The potatoes and other root crops were as a rule exactly suited by the weather. *Robertstown D.*—The good yield of crops may be attributed to the good weather at spring and autumn, and also to the good harvest weather. The want of rain of course made the meadows short. But every other crop is good. The hay crop in the district was very little below the average, it was exceptionally well saved, and is being exported and sent to Dublin, and the Curragh, etc., in large quantities. Turnip crop a very good one.

KILKENNY COUNTY. *Callan D.*—The various crops have yielded about average produce, and thus need no special remarks. There has been no special injury to crops from insects or fungi. *Castlecomer D.*—Wheat is not extensively cultivated here, and farmers say that what was sown was affected less or more with "smut," and from this cause the yield was not so good as it might have been. Oats.—This was a very good crop, owing to the dryness of the season—which dryness continued until the crop was gathered into the haggards. Barley.—This crop is cultivated in a good many electoral divisions, and the yield has been very good, owing to the favourable season. Bere, Rye, Beans, Peas—not cultivated. Potatoes.—The dry season favoured this crop also. The yield has been good, and the farmers of these in this year, number, but farmers complain that after the crop had ripened, a kind of dry rot set in, and a good many of the tubers rotted away. This rot is attributed to the dryness of the autumn. Turnips, mangel-wurzel, and cabbage—these crops are very good owing to the favourable season. Green vetches, rape, and flax—not cultivated. Hay.—New meadows were rather light owing to the dry hot summer, but old meadows were in general up to the average. It may be observed that the average rates of produce of the various crops in the electoral divisions of Tiscoffin, [illegible], and [illegible] are in general low, but this is owing to the inferior quality of the soil—the district is bleak and hilly. No special injury has been caused to crops by insects or fungi. *Johnstown D.*—The crops in general have been very good this year, owing principally to the weather being generally favourable, and also to the using of good seed, &c. New hay was a rather light crop, owing to want of rain in the early growth. No special injury to crops from insects or fungi reported. *Kilkenny D.*—All the crops were good this year, chiefly owing to the favourable season. The first crop of hay was somewhat light, owing to the drought in the early summer, but the hay of the old meadows is well up to the standard of former years. There has been no special injury done to any of the crops by insects or fungi during the year. *Piltown D.*—The yield appears to have been somewhat above the average of previous years. Potatoes, however, in some parts have suffered a rather severe check through blight, but on the whole the yield was better than in former seasons, and the quality was also improved. In the lowland portion of the district the return of meadow new and old is good, but in the uplands a perceptible falling off is shown, due wholly to the very dry summer. This latter has principally affected most of the crops. No sign of any injury from insects or fungi. *Thomastown D.*—The good yield of crops is attributable to the fine summer, with a certain amount of rain-fall, larger than in neighbouring counties, I believe. There were no special injuries to crops from insects or fungi during the past season.

KING'S COUNTY. *Banagher D.*—This year the crops have been very fair all round. Hay plentiful, but in some instances light. Oats, barley and turnips good. In some instances the latter crop have a dry rot, but on the whole farmers are very pleased with the yield. Mangolds are a very good crop. There is very little wheat grown in this district, but what there is of it is good. Potatoes have been exceptionally good in yield, and are a healthy crop. There has been no damage by insects or fungi. *Edenderry D.*—Hay this year was a very fair crop. In low-lying lands it was heavy; in hilly lands light, owing to dry season. Oats was fair, but affected by drought in same way as hay. Barley was fair. Wheat a fairly good crop; not much sown. Rye same as wheat. Potatoes a very good crop; in a few places where there was a heavy clay soil, more than the average quantity was rotten. Turnips a fair crop. Mangolds good. Other green crops were about the average. In a few places the turnip crop was damaged; the heart of the turnip turned black. Very little trouble was experienced from weeds owing to dry season. There was no attempt made to deal with fungi by artificial means. The surface of the district is nearly level, and the dry weather did not appear to affect it unfavourably to any great extent. *Parsonstown D.*—There was no appreciable injury to any crops from insects or fungi during the past season. All the crops were very fair owing to the very favourable weather that prevailed, and farmers generally appear very well satisfied with results. *Shinrone D.*—Although the yield this year was not beyond that of last year, the crops have been much better saved and are of better quality. Owing to the severe drought of the early summer hay was lighter in the average yield, but was of far better quality. Turnips and mangolds also suffered at first from the drought, but afterwards grew well, and consequently are up to the average. Having instituted inquiry through the district concerning any injury to crops from insects or fungi, I find that they have not suffered in any way therefrom. *Tullamore D.*—The yield of crops has been generally good. The turnip crop, on account of the dry weather, has not been so good as was expected. The hay, for same reason, was not a heavy crop, but the quality was good. There was no injury done to any crops from insects or fungi.

LONGFORD COUNTY. *Ballymahon D.*—The lightning in the months of July and August had a very damaging effect on the potato crop, which would otherwise have been far above the average, owing principally to the dry season, which has had a remarkably good effect on this locality, both as to the crops themselves and the manner in which they have been saved. The above is the only point requiring observation. The other crops generally are up to if not over the average. *Granard D.*—Although the weather appeared to favour the potato crop the yield is not so good this year as it was last season, owing, it is alleged, to the blight coming over the crop at an unusually early period. The oats, owing to the favourable weather, is a very good crop generally, so are turnips, and the hay crop has been fair considering the dry weather. There has been no special injury to crops from insects or fungi. *Longford D.*—The potato crop is considered not to be so good as in other years, the blight having appeared earlier in the season than usual; what remains is good for use owing to dry season. Hay is not so good as in other years, owing to the dry season, but is considered a very fair crop, being well saved. Grass is very good on some lands having good soil, but in dry sandy lands owing to the drought it was not so good. The various green crops (excepting those mentioned) were considered above the average; the dry season is attributed as the reason. No injury has been done by fungi nor by weeds during the season.

LOUTH COUNTY. *Ardee D.*—The yield of the various crops sown has been much in advance of that of any of the preceding years for a considerable time back. The cause to which this is attributed was the remarkably good seasons in spring and autumn. There have been no complaints of any injury to crops from insects or fungi during the past season. *Collon D.*—Oats has been a fair crop, and is also

[illegible]

PROVINCE OF LEINSTER.

principal one. Barley is not much worse, but wheat was suffered from a sort of blight about the time it commenced to ripen, and did not fill properly. Potatoes have been all round a good crop. Turnips looked well in the beginning of the season, but at the end of the season a second growth appeared and they are not so sound in consequence. Mangel wurzel was a fairly good crop the season seeming to suit it. Cabbage has been a very good crop, and hay a very fair average; the first crop being light owing to the dryness of the season, but the second was very good. *Drogheda D.*—The cereal crops consisting of barley, oats, and wheat have yielded a fair return of grain, but deficient straw owing to the very dry and hot weather all through. The dry season has been favourable to the potato crop but injurious to turnips, which latter will not come up to the average yield. Same remarks apply to mangolds and carrots. Early meadows were good, and though the quantity of hay is not as large as usual all was saved in excellent condition, and in many cases there was a good second crop. I have heard no complaints of injury to crops from insects or fungi. *Dundalk D.*—I cannot find that any injury has been done to crops this year. The yield generally is much above the average owing to the favourable season. No trace of insects or fungi has been noticed.

MEATH COUNTY. *Athboy D.*—The abundant yield which almost all crops have produced this year, is, in my opinion, due to the fine season, and the absence from injury by insects, weeds, &c., which in former years have proved so destructive to farm crops. Except in rare instances of early sown turnips I have not heard of any complaint being made of injury to crops by insects. *Dunshaughlin D.*—All the crops here are good—many very good—but the turnip crop though a very good one, causes some anxiety as the roots are getting bad, for which no reason can be given; they rot at the heart. *Kells D.*—The good yield of the various crops is attributed to the goodness of the past season. The crops suffered no injury from insects or fungi during the past season. *Navan D.*—The yield for the various crops (except hay) was good, owing to the dry season and absence of blight, except in some few instances where it was light. The dry season somewhat injured the hay crop. There was no special injury to crops in this district from insects or fungi during the past season. It has been a very good season for the farmers. *Slane D.*—Nearly all the crops are well above the average this year, which is principally due to the exceptionally fine season. There are exceptions in the case of (1) hay which in new meadows was light owing to the long dry weather; (2) barley, which ripened too quickly; and (3) cabbage. The wire-worm appeared here and there but had no appreciable effect. There are no complaints of any other injury from insects, fungi, &c. *Trim D.*—With the exception of hay, crops have been very fairly good owing to the weather. The hay crop was short as the necessary damp did not come.

QUEEN'S COUNTY. *Abbeyleix D.*—The injury to crops has been exceptionally small this year from insects and fungi; in fact I hear of no injury from the latter at all, and I ascribe this state of things to the exceptionally dry and warm summer which has been unfavourable to their growth and development. *Ballybrittas D.*—All the crops here have yielded very satisfactorily. Wheat is very little sown, oats and barley were very good crops. Potatoes above the average, though a considerable number of partially diseased tubers were found in most places. Mangolds were a good crop. Turnips were an indifferent crop. In a great many cases the leaves were covered with mildew, probably owing to the drought. Hay of both descriptions, upland and new, was very good in quality but rather short in quantity owing to the dry weather. Grass is now abundant. No insects nor fungi were observed except the mildew above referred to. *Mountmellick D.*—The crops have returned a fair average yield. The chief factor with regard to them has been the great dryness and warmth of the season. Potatoes have done well, the tubers being large and free from disease. Hay is good and well saved, though the earlier crop was rather light. Barley and oats were rather a poor crop, the yield being scarcely up to the average, and the grain small from want of moisture to swell it. Turnips have not done very well. No special injury has been observed from fungi or insects, and the land is generally well tilled and kept free from weeds. *Maryborough D.*—Hay—First and second crop much under average, say 20 per cent., but excellent quality and cheaply saved; old meadow hay also under average, but not more than 10 to 15 per cent., and owing to the protracted period of fine weather many very late meadows have been saved, which in previous years have invariably been lost, so that there is a fairly abundant crop of old meadow hay. Oats—A good crop, average in yield and quality. Barley—A very good crop as regards quality, but barely up to average in yield. Turnips—A splendid crop, best for several years past. Mangolds also a good crop. Potatoes—Undoubtedly a good crop, especially in quality, and somewhat over average in yield, no blight. It does not appear that any of the aforementioned crops were injured by noxious insects, &c. In this district all crops except hay benefited greatly by the unprecedentedly fine and dry weather, especially as, although abnormally warm and dry, rain fell on several occasions over district when I am aware there was no rainfall in or about Dublin.

COUNTY WESTMEATH. *Ballymacarrigy D.*—In general, there was a fair average yield all round, and in the case of failures in any particular crop no special cause can be mentioned. The turnip crop suffered much in its early growth from the ravages of the "fly." *Castlepollard D.*—I would attribute the generally good yield of the different crops to the seasonable weather both in spring and summer in this county. I am not aware that any special injury to crops was caused from insects or fungi. *Delvin D.*—The crops have been exceptionally good for the season just closed owing to the favourable and open weather which prevailed. Early meadows were somewhat light in some places owing to dryness of season, but the general hay crop was abundant and well saved. No injuries from insects or fungi have been reported. *Kilbeggan D.*—The various crops are excellent. This is attributable to the fact that the dry, fine season has admirably suited the low-lying, and often marshy, nature of the soil. I do not think there is a single exception but that all crops are over average this year, though in a few localities where dry lands prevail the potatoes are small owing to the continued drought. Even in these places there is a good average crop. *Moate D.*—The good yield of the past season may be attributed to the fine dry season, which seems to suit this locality, the absence of rain being compensated by copious dews. I have not heard any special complaints of insects, but I never observed wasps and the caterpillar of the white butterfly more numerous. As for weeds, no attempt is made to eradicate them. *Mullingar D.*—The rates of produce of the several crops are exceptionally good this year. The good yield may be attributed to the dry and warm season. None of the crops have been injured by insects or fungi.

WEXFORD COUNTY. *Enniscorthy D.*—The hay crop which opened scarce became rather plentiful later on. It is a large crop in this part of the county. Though oats are very fair in quantity the straw will be scarce. Rain came too late to greatly affect turnips, and that crop may be said to be a failure. There has been no special injury from insects. *Gorey D.*—The poor hay crop was of course due to absence of rain in the early part of the season. *New Ross D.*—The crops, taken all round, are unusually good, owing to the very fine season we have had. The hay crop is light owing to so little rain during the summer, but is better than was expected. *Enniscorthy D.*—The crops in general are very light, owing to the unusually dry season, more especially hay and straw, which are very scarce, and a considerable amount of the potato crops are very much diseased. There are no complaints in district as to injury from insects, &c. *Wexford D.*—Owing to the continuous dry season which prevailed in this district the quantity of hay was not up to the average, the same remark may be applied to grain crops. Grain fairly good, but straw was short. Potatoes were well up to the average of former years. There have been no complaints of injury done to the crops by fungi, insects, or weeds.

WICKLOW COUNTY. *Arklow D.*—The crops generally this year are somewhere near the average, except hay, which is much below the average in consequence of the dry spring and early summer, but what hay there is is of better quality than usual, being well saved. Corn, although short in the straw, has borne good grain. Oats is the principal corn crop; wheat and barley are not much grown here. Potatoes are above the average, the dry spring and summer seems to have suited them well. It is noticed that lands artificially manured have been particularly productive this year. No special injury has been done by insects or fungi. *Bray D.*—The general crops for this year have been excellent, particularly potatoes, owing to the favourable dry season since April last, which was favourable for them in this part of the country, the hay crop being the exception, particularly in light soil, and in the hilly and mountainous parts where the continued drought [illegible] growth, and consequently in most places a light crop was the result; on the other hand what was there to cut was easily saved, and no loss resulted, and such has been stacked and ricked under favourable circumstances, and in the markets brings a highly remunerative price to the farmers. *Dunlavin D.*—The crops generally this season are good, and above the average yield. Owing to the exceptionally dry season, in some few instances the hay and oat crops are light. There is no injury reported as being caused to crops by insects. *Wicklow D.*—By far the worst crop this year was hay, which only yielded about half, owing to the prolonged drought. The same cause injured the turnips very much, and I look on them as the second worst this season. Oats and wheat are below the average, the same reason being assigned. Mangold in some places is up to the average, but taken all round is inferior to last year. The dry season favoured the potatoes which were abundant, but they are now considerably injured by blight.

PROVINCE OF LEINSTER.

PROVINCE OF MUNSTER.

PROVINCE OF MUNSTER.

CLARE COUNTY. *Ballyvaughan D.*—The hay crop was rather short, but this has been compensated for by the plentiful growth of aftergrass, due to the rainfall of the last two months. *Corofin D.*—Hay and all grain crops have been light here, owing to the long drought in the early summer and the nature of the soil, which is limestone, and requires much rain. Potatoes have not been so good as last year's crop for the same reasons. Turnips and other root crops are good, owing to the heavy rainfall which occurred in autumn. There has been no injury to crops in this district from fungi or insects. *Ennis D.*—In marshy and boggy lands the yield of potatoes was better, and in dry lands not quite so good as last year. The corn crop in some cases was deficient, all owing to the very dry season. The crops did not suffer from insects, weeds, or fungi. *Ennistimon D.*—The produce of the several crops was exceptionally good. The oats crop was not so abundant as last year, owing to the dryness of the weather at the end of spring. The crops did not suffer here from insects or fungi during the past season. *Kildysart D.*—The case of the potato crop hardly good enough, as the year was a favourable one, and there was little blight. The turnip and mangold crops seem to have suffered by wire worm to a noticeable extent, and the oat crop in some places appears also to have been affected when coming over the ground. The cabbage crop was also injured by caterpillars, of which there were great numbers this year. *Killaloe D.*—Crops of all kinds are very good this year, in fact some of them are above the average of previous years. For instance, turnips and mangolds are, in my opinion, above the average of other years. The season has been very favourable to which I attribute the good yield of the various crops. I have heard no complaints of any special injury to crops from insects or fungi. *Kilrush D.*—I think the good potato crop is attributable to good seed having been used, and the dry season. The oat crop was short, owing to want of rain. No particular injury occurred to any crop from insects or fungi, except to carrots, which between the great drought and insects failed. *Sixmilebridge D.*—On the whole there is this season a fair average yield of the several crops. There has been no special injury to crops, arising from insects or fungi. *Tulla D.*—In consequence of the very dry season, the hay and oat crops were not so good as in the previous year, the hay was lighter and the straw shorter. The potatoes, where planting was early, were good, but in cases of late planting, the crop suffered from blight a good deal before coming to maturity. The season turned out favourable to the turnip crop, which was good. Insects caused no special injury in this district to the crops.

CORK COUNTY, E.R. *Ballincollig D.*—Owing to the very dry summer the hay crop is said to have been short in produce. In low and limestone lands this remark also applies to all crops in general, but in hilly lands the crops, with the exception of the hay crop, are said to have been above the average yield this season. *Charleville D.*—The various crops grown have produced a fair average yield this year—except that on high dry lands hay was rather light; and in similar localities the oat crop was rather short in straw, and the grain not very well developed. This is attributable to the dry season. As far as can be ascertained no special injury has been caused by insects or fungi. *Cork North D.*—The crops have been well up to the average of former years. The grain crop was fairly good but might have been heavier had more rain fallen. The root crops, especially turnips, were very good, having got a fair quantity of rain in latter end of season. On the whole, the season was fair, which caused the good yield. No injury done as far as I can learn from insects, fungi, or weeds. *Cork South D.*—All grain crops have produced a good yield this year except barley which was somewhat light owing to the continued dry season. The old and new hay crops were also light, the result of dry weather. All root crops are very good, and no injury has been done them by insects, fungi, or weeds. Your special report of 10th October, 1893, has proved most useful when instituting inquiries. *Fermoy D.*—(1.) The good yield of the various crops is chiefly due to the dry season. (2.) No injury was done to the crops by insects, &c., during the past autumn. *Kanturk D.*—The various crops have yielded average crops

Province of Munster.

this year, except hay and oats, which are something below the average of former years, in consequence of the drought early in the season. This dry weather favoured the potato crop, which is above the average. Turnips were looked upon as a failure almost early in the season, but later on derived much benefit from occasional showers, and are now considered a fair crop. No complaint was received of any injury to crops from insects or fungi. *Kinsale D.*—I believe the average produce on the whole is better than last year, this is owing to the very favourable season; the grain crop is much better in quality, also, than it was last year, owing to same cause. Hay was a light crop, but the quality was good, and it was well saved; this is owing to the commencement of the season being very dry. There was no special injury to crops in this district from insects or fungi during the past season. *Mallow D.*—There was a good average yield of all kinds of crops this year, and farmers are well satisfied with the harvest returns. The potato crop has been unusually good, and there has been little or no damage done by insects. The cause of the excellence in this crop is believed to be the long dry weather, and its freedom from insects and disease is due to the dry weather and change of seed, as well as early sowing. The hay crop was light owing to the long period of dry weather, but for the same cause it is believed that it was well saved, and the quality is very good. The farmers realised large prices for their hay in the months of July and August, as owing to the scarcity of forage in England the price of hay was extremely high. Turnips and mangolds were a good crop. The only crop which was below the average is wheat. *Middleton D.*—With the exception of hay the crops generally were above the average yield, and were well saved. The drought of summer was not so continuous in this district as in many other parts of the country. Rain came several times during the summer, which did vast good. The weather was more or less fine from the end of February to the middle of September. The yield of hay has been about two-thirds the average yield, and sells now at £5 a ton, though quantities have been pressed and shipped to England. From inquiry made insects and fungi don't seem to be doing any serious damage. Potato crops suffer from the same seed being used year after year. *Mitchelstown D.*—The good potato crop is attributable to the dry season, and the absence of disease (potato blight) until the crop had fully matured. The cause of the hay crop being under the average is the long drought, but the quality is excellent owing to the fine harvest. All the other crops are good, and call for no special remarks. None of these have suffered any special injury from insects or fungi. *Newmarket D.*—All crops sown have produced a good yield. The turnip crop, which suffered early in the season from the want of rain has made very fair progress, and an average good crop is expected. The oat grain is small and firm. There have been no complaints respecting any crop, as the result is favourable. *Queenstown D.*—In this district the yield of wheat oats and barley has been above the average—the potato crop though abundant, is not as dry as that of last year, and hay, as a rule, is a thinner crop, but better saved than last year. Turnips good. There has been no injury to crops from insects or fungi. *Youghal D.*—It appears that with the exception of hay, turnips, and mangolds, the crops generally this year are above the average. This is due to the fine weather during spring and summer, and as the harvest season was fine crops are well saved. The hay crop and roots generally are below the average owing to want of rain. As far as I can ascertain no special damage has been done to crops by insects, fungi, or injurious weeds.

Cork County, W.R. *Bandon D.*—All the crops this season are good, with the exception of hay, which in high dry land was light. All the other crops are good, potatoes particularly so. The corn crop was light in dry sandy land in consequence of the dry spring, and it was injured in some places by the wire-worm. Mangolds and turnips are a fairly good crop, although the seed had to be put in twice, and suffered from the fly and drought in the early part of the season. I have not heard of any serious damage done by either insects or fungi. *Bantry D.*—The generally favourable yield of the crops for present season is owing to an unprecedentedly dry summer. The land here is as a rule wet, and the weather not sufficiently dry, so that several of these conditions favour these parts of Ireland. No special injury has been done to the crops by insects or fungi. *Castletown Bere D.*—So far as I can ascertain, the crops generally are below the average of preceding years, owing to the prolonged drought of summer. And to same cause is attributed the absence of insects or fungi (also weeds), which have only appeared to a very small extent this season. *Clonakilty D.*—The harvest on the whole has been good, excepting hay which is rather light, owing to the dry season. Barley, rather below an average crop, having been affected by the rains late in the season. Oats, a fair crop. Potatoes, a very good crop, owing to the favourable season, and the sulphate of copper and lime mixture having been used extensively in this district to prevent disease. Turnips, a good crop. Wheat, very little grown here, fair. No special injury done by insects or fungi. *Dunmanway D.*—The yield of the several crops was good this year, caused, I should say, by having had so fine a season. No special injury to crops from insects or fungi. *Macroom D.*—From personal observation as well as from inquiries made, the following are the reasons to which may be attributed the good or bad yield of the various crops:—Potatoes, the staple crop, were a good yield, and much over the average of previous years, owing to the absence of cold and rain, and the prevalence of sunshine from time of planting the same until full maturity. Hay was rather a light crop, owing to the absence of moisture, but what it lacked in quantity was made up for its excellent quality, being in nearly every instance saved without rain. Turnips and mangolds were a fair crop, especially those planted early, the seeds having well struck root before drought set in. The various other crops were a good average, being favourably influenced by the fineness of the weather. Careful inquiry amongst the farmers does not disclose any instance of special injury to crops from insects or fungi. *Millstreet D.*—The dry season suited the crops of the various kinds in this mountainous district. The potatoes are generally good. The oat crop suffered in the early part of the season from a "wire-worm," which cut the young blades of the oats. The crops did not suffer from weeds or fungi. *Skibbereen D.*—With the exception, perhaps, of the oat crop, all the crops have been equal to, and to great extent over the average. It is years since there has been such a fine yield in all descriptions of root crops. There may have been a slight decrease in the hay crop, but the farmers have been fully compensated by the very high price obtained, which was at least £1 per ton more than last year. The good yield is no doubt attributable to the very fine weather in the early part of the season, and the light rains later on. *Skull D.*—The good crop of potatoes is attributable to the unusual dryness of the past season, and the almost phenomenal success of sunshine. The hay crop was of good quality, but light in yield, owing to same causes. The other crops were fairly good in quality and quantity, but did not exhibit such a divergence from the average yield as to call for special remark. No special injury to crops was noticed from insects or fungi.

Kerry County. *Cahersiveen D.*—The bad yield of the several green crops may be attributable to the bad tillage and insufficient manuring, not sowing those crops in time, and their after cultivation being

PROVINCE OF MUNSTER.

[illegible] neglected (generally speaking). Potatoes were a good average yield in this district, better than former years; this is attributable to the dry summer, and the blight had little or no effect in consequence, neither had insects or fungi. Weeds were most injurious to the potatoes and other green crops in this district, as the farmers (with very few exceptions) will not go to the bother or trouble of weeding green crops. Their neglect in this respect is most observable, as when passing through the various localities in the harvesting time I see the farmers endeavouring to clear away the weeds (when it is too late) to enable them to get out the potatoes and other crops. Oats, hay, cabbages, were a fair average crop in this locality, the last suffered very much from the caterpillar, but fungi or other insects did not do much harm to the crops. This is attributable to the exceptionally dry season that this entire district has been favoured with. If the farmers of this district could be induced to sow their crops by rotation, and procure strange seeds from time to time from other places, better results in the average returns would follow. However, grazing and butter making is the chief industry of the inhabitants of this district. *Castleisland D.*—There is a good yield in the various crops, except the turnips. Owing to the very dry season the potato crop is exceptionally good. The hay crop is something under the average yield of last year, but is of a superior quality. The good yield in each case is attributable to the dry season we have had. So far as can be ascertained there has not been any special injury to the crops from insects or fungi. *Dingle D.*—The excellent yield of potatoes is to be attributed solely to the long continuance of dry weather. To the same cause also must be attributed a somewhat short hay crop and dearth of straw. In some cases the turnip crop has been much ravaged by insects, in some instances to such an extent as to necessitate a re-sowing. Little damage seems to have been done by fungi. *Kenmare D.*—The yield of the various crops is considered good, and is attributed to the dry, warm, season. There was no special injury to crops from insects or fungi during the season. *Killarney D.*—The potato crop is much above the average. The yield is good and is to be attributed to the fine dry season. The hay and oat crops for a similar reason are much under the average, and I may say the same as regards turnips and mangolds. There is no wheat or barley grown in this district. There has been no damage done to any crops by insects or fungi. *Killorglin D.*—All crops are good this season. No special injury to any of the crops this year has been done by insects, fungi, or weeds. *Listowel D.*—In general the various crops are good, on account of the very good season. *Tralee D.*—The crops were not injured this season by fungi, &c. Wheat, oats, and barley.—The yield in these crops was a good deal under the average of former years owing to the very dry summer. Potatoes.—The yield in the potato crop was excellent and far beyond the average for many years past, owing to the favourable spring for early sowing, and escaping frost and blight. Turnips.—With very few exceptions there was a fairly good yield of turnips, even where they failed at first the second sowing will give a fair return. Mangolds.—To this crop the same remarks apply as above. Cabbage—generally speaking, was a good crop. Hay.—The early hay was not as heavy as usual owing to the very dry season, but there was a fair average crop on the old meadows. These are the only crops sown in this district to any extent.

LIMERICK COUNTY. *Abbeyfeale D.*—The land is very wet and boggy, the good yield is owing to dry season. A dry season is invariably favourable to crops here. No damage done by insects or fungi. *Adare D.*—No special injury has been done to crops from insects, fungi, or weeds. The cabbage crop was a good deal ravaged by the caterpillar. There was a fair all round yield from the other crops. *Bruff D.*—There is not much tillage in this district. The greater portion of the land is grass land. There was a very fair yield of wheat and oats. Very little barley, bere or rye was sown. The potatoes are, as a rule, sound, which I believe is chiefly attributable to the dry season; the yield is fair, in one portion of the district they suffered from a sort of dry rot, especially in lowland. Hay is a light crop owing to the dry season, and cabbages have been affected from same cause. In one locality cabbages were injured by caterpillars. Turnips and mangolds yielded well. The late rains improved the grass in pasture lands. This should lead to a considerable saving of hay. No special injury from insects or fungi except as stated. *Kilfinane D.*—All the crops in this district were good, except turnips and mangolds, which suffered from the dry season. The hay also suffered from the same cause, but the quality is excellent owing to the exceptionally fine weather they had in saving it. *Limerick D.*—The crops have been about the average, except hay, which did not produce the usual yield owing to the exceptionally dry season. Oats fairly good, but straw short owing to same reason as hay. Turnips and mangolds, good average crops. Potatoes also good, and up to present have escaped disease. Very little wheat grown, and barley about an average. Cabbages good. Beans and peas not grown in any quantity. No complaints of injury by insects or fungi. *Newcastle D.*—The yield of all grain crops in this year much above average, the weather having been throughout favourable to these crops. Straw, however, is short. Green crops, owing to the same cause, are exceptionally good. Potatoes were an abundant crop, everywhere plentiful and dry. No instance of special injury from insects or fungi has come under notice. *[illegible] D.*—With the exception of hay and potatoes the crops were a fair average yield. The bad yield of hay and potatoes is attributable to the very dry summer which, in the case of hay, parched the land before the crop had come to maturity. Potatoes grown on light land suffered from a like cause, but where the soil was deep and rich, as well as in cold mountainous land, the warm summer proved beneficial to this crop. As far as I can learn there was no special injury to crops in this district from insects or fungi during the past season. *[illegible] D.*—The wheat crop is considered good owing to favourable weather received when ripening. Oats and barley considered a fairly good produce. Straw short, particularly the oaten straw, in consequence of dry weather in the early part of the season. Hay has been a fairly good average crop. The potato crop is considered a fairly good average yield, owing to good weather. Turnips, mangold wurzel, and cabbage, a fairly good yield. From inquiry I have made I have been informed that there has been no special injury done to crops by insects, fungi, or weeds injurious to farm crops.

TIPPERARY COUNTY, N.R. *Borrisokane D.*—The damage in the hay crop was due to the great drought which continued so long. However, what hay there was, was well saved, and none of it lost through bad weather. Corn and root crops were generally very good as the weather was suitable for them. Straw was short, and though the grain was rather deficient in quantity, the quality was very superior. The seasonable showers which have prevailed since August last have done great service to turnips and other root crops. There was absolutely no damage whatever from insects or fungi, and potatoes are of good quality, and quite free from disease. *[illegible] D.*—Crops generally have been good, but light, owing to the long and continued drought. No insects or fungi appear to have injuriously affected any crop, with the exception of oats in the [illegible] sub-district, where a worm called the "red worm" appears to have done damage to that crop. The blight attacked the potato crop, but

[illegible] [illegible]

too late to seriously injure it. Turnip and other root crops were sound and good, though light from want of rain. Barley is exceptionally good this season. *Newport D.*—The crops this year were good average crops, with the exception of hay, which owing to the long continued dry season was very light, except in low-lying lands. The dry weather favoured other crops. *Roscrea D.*—All the crops are exceptionally good, except the hay crop, which is slightly below the average, which may be attributed to the very dry season. There has been no appearance this year of insects or fungi, and weeds did not appear to affect the crops to such an extent as in former years. *Templemore D.*—The good yield of each crop is entirely due to the very fine weather which prevailed throughout the whole year. There has been no special injuries to any crop from either insects or fungi. *Thurles D.*—The yield of most crops shows but small change from last year. Exceptions:—*Force grass* hay is below the average owing to the dryness of the summer. In the Electoral Divisions of Two-Mile-Borris, Moycarky, Ballymurreen, and Littleton, there has been an increase of about two barrels per statute acre in the oat crop. There have been no injuries done to crops by insects, fungi, or weeds.

TIPPERARY COUNTY, S.R. *Cahir D.*—Wheat has been a fair crop, but not quite average, owing to the exceptionally dry weather. The same remark applies to oats. The grain did not fill properly, and straw is somewhat short. Barley is not much sown, and is hardly up to the average as the grain did not fill properly for want of rain. Bere and rye only sown in small patches here and there, and fairly good. Beans and peas only sown in private gardens—yield good. Potatoes are a very good crop, yielding well, and of good quality, owing to absence of blight, except in a few places. Turnips, a good crop. Mangold wurzel, a very good crop, above the average. Cabbage is a good crop. Vetches and rape not much sown, but fairly good where they are. Carrots are an exceptionally good crop. Meadowing generally was very light, owing to the continuance of dry weather. First crop hay was very light, but of good quality. Rain came in time to improve old meadows, but, on the whole, the hay crop is below the average, and is realising high prices. There are now good pastures owing to the recent rain. No complaints have been heard of injury to crops from insects or fungi. *Clogheen D.*—No very material injury was caused to crops by insects or fungi, and, on the whole, the past season must be looked on as a very healthy one for crops, not only in the rich moist lowlands, but on the wet mountain sides. The only injuries which can be ascertained are those caused to turnips in a few spots by large excrescences or fungi growing on the bulb, and sometimes exceeding it in size; and, in a few cases, the oat crop was injured by being attacked in the early spring by the "red worm" or wire worm. Flax, rye, turnips, mangel wurzel, and corn must be put down as very good crops. Potatoes are of medium size, healthy, and very dry. The "Champion" is especially dry. The "Early Puritan" variety yielded a magnificent crop, as also did the "Beauty of Hebron," but little of these varieties were grown. Carrots, red variety, were in many cases split, either from the weather or the nature of the soil. The white carrots were large and healthy. Parsnips are a fair crop. Cabbages in some fields suffered much, especially in sheltered places, from the attacks of caterpillars. *Carrick-on-Suir D.*—The good yield of crops is due to an exceptionally fine season. To some extent, injury was done from want of moisture. No special injury was caused from insects or fungi, and weeds, owing to dry season, were fewer than usual. *Cashel D.*—The grain crops were good, the season being favourable for ripening. Root crops are also good, having got rain in the proper time. Meadowing was light in consequence of the dry season. *Clonmel D.*—Owing to the excessive dryness of the season, cereals, as a rule, were a poor crop. The head did not fill properly, and straw was short. Potatoes, fair crop, but there is a good deal of disease. Hay, a very light crop for want of early rains, but of good quality. Roots, except in dry lands, a fair crop. *Killenaule D.*—All crops have been very good, and this applies specially to potatoes, which are, in quality, far better than they have been for many years past. The hay crop, owing to the dry summer, has been a rather light one—but, owing to the same cause, the quality is so good that it more than compensates for any loss sustained in the yield. There has been no injury done to crops by insects or fungi in this district this season. *Tipperary D.*—I attribute the good yield in crops to the favourable weather of the past season. I have not heard of any special injury to crops.

WATERFORD COUNTY. *Cappoquin D.*—The position of the several crops was very favourable. The corn crop was, generally speaking, good, and the yield in straw was of a fair average, except in high light ground, where the straw was very short. The hay crop was rather light, but otherwise very good. The potato crop has been fairly good, but there would be a better crop if the ground was kept clean from weeds, etc., which is not usually attended to. All the other green crops which were sown in proper time are fairly good. I have had no reports of insects or fungi having injured the crops this season. *Dungarvan D.*—The good yield of the various crops (except hay) is attributable to the dry spring and summer, as well as the favourable harvest weather that ensued. The bad yield of hay is attributed to the drought. There was no special injury to crops by insects or fungi in this district. *Portlaw D.*—All the crops are good with the exception of hay, which is of good quality, but light in consequence of the dry spring. The first sowing of turnips failed in many places, in consequence of the fly, but the second sowing did well. *Waterford D.*—The crops appear to be up to the average of recent years, with the exception of the hay crop, which is much under the average, owing to the unusually dry summer. The same cause operated in rendering the straw of oats and wheat very short. The turnip crop also suffered, to some extent, from the great drought. Potatoes are good, both in quality and quantity, but about one sixth of the crop is reported to be lost through disease. No injury was done by insects or fungi.

consequence, in dust. Potatoes are a splendid crop, and the quality excellent. *Belfast North D.*—From careful inquiry, I have learned from the farmers the reason why crops in general are good this season. They say it is chiefly owing to the dry and warm summer, and total absence of noxious insects. The special report of October, 1890 has given general satisfaction, and is much prized by the farmers. *Belfast South D.*—There is a consensus of opinion to the following effect:—The potato crop has been a signal success, owing to the dry spring and very warm summer, which suits the locality, possessing, as it does, a cold and stiff sub-soil. All the other crops are fairly good. The incessant drought affected them, but more particularly the hay, and in some cases the oat crop. There has been no special injury done by either insects or fungi. The special report on insects, fungi, and weeds, proved useful in facilitating inquiries on this subject. *Belfast West D.*—There is very little tillage in this district—a few acres, also a few acres of meadow and grassland. The meadow being "bottom" land, was fairly good, and was not much affected by the very dry season. Potatoes were very good, Champions being most productive. There was no special injury to crops from insects or fungi. *Larne D.*—The average yield of the several crops is considered good, and this is largely accounted for by the past dry season. The oat crop is, however, considered to have been somewhat light in maritime districts, caused by the dry season and light soil. No special injury has been caused to any crop (so far as can be observed) from insects or fungi during the past season. *Lisburn D.*—The yield of potatoes was better than last year, owing to the fine dry weather. The oat and wheat crop was somewhat lighter, owing to the prolonged drought; the grain was good but straw, &c., light. Turnips, &c.—The yield was unsatisfactory, owing to dry weather. No special injury was done to crops by insects, fungi, &c. *Lurgan D.*—The oat crop was a good yield, and may be attributed to the dry season, though the "wire-worm" made its appearance in the beginning of the season, but the damage done by it was of no consequence. The good yield of potatoes was caused by the dry season. The turnip crop which turned out fairly well was much interfered with by the "fly," and in some cases the drought caused this crop to make very little growth after sowing. Hay, which yielded well, was benefited much during the time of saving, by dry weather, but would have been much better had there been more rain in the early part of the season. Upland showed particularly the want of rain in the early part of the year. There has not been any case of special injury from insects or fungi, except as noted in the case of oats and turnips, which was, on the whole, slight.

ARMAGH COUNTY.—*Armagh D.*—The crops of all kinds have been good. This is to be attributed entirely to the dry season. In some instances the hay crop has been light, particularly owing to want of rain in early part of season. However, in the mountainous area extending from Keady to Newtownhamilton, and thence round to near Armagh, the dry weather was most beneficial. Potatoes, turnips, and roots are over an average. Corn, a good average. Hay, though in some instances light, is everywhere well saved. Flax has not been very much cultivated, and was injured less than in former years. There has been no injury to crops from insects or fungi, the dry season not being in favour of such. *Newry D.*—The rates of produce were on the whole, greater than last year, except upland hay, this crop was rather light, owing to the prolonged drought. The season was favourable for the other crops. On some dry sandy hills the potato crop was light, but of a good quality. There was no complaint about weeds, fungi, &c. *Portadown D.*—The good yield of the various crops is, so far as I can learn, attributable to the good season. There was no injury to the crops from fungi or insects.

CAVAN COUNTY.—*Bailieborough D.*—The crops generally were, so far as I can ascertain, very good, though the potato crop, I believe, is not so good as last year. This is attributable to the exceptionally dry season. I have no reason to think that the crops suffered from insects or fungi. In high light land they suffered less or more from the long drought. *Cavan D.*—The several crops have yielded a fair average generally, and have not been injured by insects or fungi to any considerable extent. *Killeshandra D.*—The crops are on the whole much above the average, which is attributable to the very dry season. The heavy dews at night during the summer supplied the place of rain. The potato crop was not up to the average of former years in this district, owing to a kind of blight which struck it. All the other crops were above the average, generally speaking. *Swanlinbar D.*—The various crops have been very good, and much over the average of recent years. The probable cause of this year's good yield is on account of the very dry season which so much benefited the cold, damp land in this side of the country. There has been no special injury to crops in this district this year from insects or fungi, and this is also attributed to the good dry season. *Virginia D.*—The yield of the several crops has been good this season, which may be attributed to the favourable season. There has been no special injury reported from insects or fungi. There is a general carelessness regarding weeds by the farmers. I have observed in many cases crops, especially the potato, from which weeds were never removed.

DONEGAL COUNTY. *Ardara D.*—The crops have been all good in consequence of the fine summer. Such a summer is always favourable to the peaty soil of this district. Cabbage in sheltered gardens suffered from caterpillars, but escaped in the open fields. Weeds are the great bane of the farming, such as it is. The meadow land is grazed far into the autumn. The crop is short in consequence, and left to grow till about the beginning of October, when the weather is generally unfavourable. It is cut close, and there is no after-grass to protect the roots from the frost. The growth is late next year, and so on. *Ballyshannon D.*—The very good crops of potatoes, oats, roots, hay, and aftergrass were undoubtedly caused by the unusually favourable season. No special injury to crops from insects or fungi or other cause came under notice during past season. *Buncrana D.*—The yield was somewhat over the yield of past years in the various crops, and attributable to the good seasonable weather in the spring and autumn. Some crops suffered a little from drought in the summer season. It was not observed that any crops suffered from insects or fungi. *Dunfanaghy D.*—Potatoes, oats, and hay are the principal crops grown, and all in my opinion are well above the average this year. Potatoes were never better—very large crops—and free from blight. In dry, light soil, oats and hay did not do so well in consequence of the drought, but as so much of this district is mountainous and boggy, the dry summer suited all crops, hay and oats especially. *Dunglow D.*—The crops are exceptionally good this season—the potato crop especially has not been so good for many years past, due I believe to the favourable weather in the early part of the season. Cabbages have suffered slightly from caterpillars, especially where planted too thickly, and in some cases turnips on coming to the surface of the ground were damaged by insects. *Letterkenny D.*—The yield of the several crops is above the average—this is attributed to the very favourable weather. The County Donegal being a cold and wet county, this year being dry and warm, the yield of the crops is much

[illegible]

better than in former years. No injury to crops in this district has occurred from insects or fungi. *Manor* [illegible] *D.*—The good yield of all crops may be attributed to the dry season. There was no injury to crops due to insects or fungi. *Raphoe D.*—The crops are all good, but the green crops may be somewhat (but not much) below the average, owing to the long-continued dry weather. *Rathmullen D.*—The crops in general are good. This is due principally to the early spring, dry summer, and timely harvest, all the crops having been safely gathered. The oat crop, meadow, and pasture grass suffered, however, a little from the drought during the summer. The same applies to the turnip crop, cabbage and vetches. Potatoes.—This crop is very good throughout this district. The cause given in all cases being the early spring and dry summer. Flax is a very fair crop, and the same remarks apply as in the case of the oat crop. The other crops in districts are grown in such small quantities that their good or bad yield cannot be attributed to any general cause. No special injury was done (as far as can be ascertained) to crops from insects of any kind.

DOWN COUNTY. *Banbridge D.*—The yield of all crops is very good—hay excepted—owing to the exceptionally fine summer and autumn. Hay crop is light owing to want of rain. No injury done by insects or fungi. *Downpatrick D.*—The crops are up to the average of former years with exception of hay and straw, which are light owing to the dry season. The quality of the grain is superior to that of previous years. Turnips suffered a good deal from the fly in early part of the season, but fungi have done very little injury in this locality of recent years. *Newtownards D.*—There has been a bad yield of corn, hay and flax owing to the season being too dry. The hay crop is principally lea-grass, and was cut and won before the rain came, hence a bad light crop. Mangel-wurzel and turnips have given a good yield, as they are a late crop, and got the rain in the latter part of the season. So far as I can ascertain crops do not suffer from insects or fungi. *Rathfryland D.*—The harvest was, speaking generally, most satisfactory. In particular, most crops are good in quality and most abundant. Cereals were thoroughly saved, though a little short in straw owing to the continued dry weather. Flax was a splendid crop, and prices far in excess of those obtainable during recent years. On the whole the farmer has every reason to feel satisfied. There has been no injury caused by insects, fungi, &c.

FERMANAGH COUNTY. *Derrygonnelly D.*—No special injury from insects or fungi is reported. Crops generally were very good and plentiful, especially corn and hay. The cause of this was that light-dropping rains fell just when wanted, and though the season was very dry for this neighbourhood, where the rainfall is generally excessive, there was nothing like a drought, as in other parts. *Enniskillen D.*—The crops are very good, which is attributed to the dry season. There has been no injury of much importance from insects, &c. *Kesh D.*—I attribute the good yield in most of the various crops this season to the exceptionally fine weather experienced during the spring, summer, and early harvest. No special injury resulted to any crop from insects or fungi during the past season. The special Report on Insects, Fungi and Weeds received in October, '93, is very useful and interesting. *Lisnaskea D.*—The crops all round were excellent and plentiful this year, due to exceptionally fine weather. No injuries to crops from destructive insects came under my observation, nor was any such reported to me. In two cases I observed "Eau Bordelaise" used on potatoes, I believe with good effect, to stop disease.

LONDONDERRY COUNTY. *Coleraine D.*—The crops generally are a good yield, which is attributed to the dry spring and favourable autumn. There has been no special injury to crops from insects or fungi. *Limavady D.*—Generally speaking, this has been a most favourable year for the crops. The oat, flax, and potato crops have been both excellent in quality and above the average yield of late years. The hay crop, though of good quality, was short and light, owing to the extremely dry spring and summer. Straw is also a little shorter than usual for the same reason. The turnip and mangold crop has been abundant. No complaints have been made of any injury to crops from insects or fungi during the past season. *Londonderry D.*—The rates of produce have been much above the average this year, and the good yield of the various crops is attributed to the very favourable season. In some instances I find that Aberdeen turnips were attacked by insects, the leaves fell off and the crop was rendered useless. This, however, was not general, and it is attributed in most cases to early sowing. *Magherafelt D.*—A very abundant harvest in this extensive district has been all secured. Flax has seldom been so abundant in fibre as this season. Potatoes are very good and are almost free from disease. Meadow, or hay, has been, perhaps, not so much in bulk as usual, but in material, and having been particularly well saved, make up for this, and may be said to be a good crop. Green crops are very promising. All round, this harvest's crops will go a long way to recruit farmers and put them in a much better position financially than heretofore. In my opinion, the abundant harvest is entirely owing to the great amount of sunshine we have had this summer and the absence of frosts at night in May.

MONAGHAN COUNTY. *Carrickmacross D.*—All crops have been good; no doubt the cause is due to the exceptionally good season and good weather. I have heard of no injury to crops in the district from insects or fungi during the past season. The land throughout is generally good. *Clones D.*—Crops of all kinds have been above the average, except late-sown turnips, which were affected by insects in the dry season, and lea grass and meadow on dry, sandy land was also affected by the dry season. *Monaghan D.*—I beg to report that the various crops have been very good, which are as follows:—Wheat, not much sown—it is a good crop; oats, a good crop; barley, a good crop, but very little sown in district; bere, none in district; rye, a good crop, but very little; beans, a good crop—very little in district; peas, none; potatoes, a good crop of all kinds; turnips, a good crop; mangel-wurzel, a good crop; carrots, a good crop—very little in district; cabbage, a good crop, which is generally planted on the side of the potato ridges; vetches, a good crop—very little sown; rape, a good crop—very little in district; flax, a very good crop this year; hay, a light crop, owing to the dry season. The springtime was very favourable for getting in all kinds of crops, which continued, and there was no frost in May, like other seasons, which injured the potato crop. The harvest weather was very good this year, which benefited the ripening and gathering into the haggards of all kinds of crops safe, and with much less trouble and expense than other years. I have received no reports from the enumerators relative to the crops in any case having been injured by insects or fungi.

TYRONE COUNTY. *Aughnacloy D.*—In nearly all cases the yield is above the average, which is attributed to the favourable weather in spring and throughout the whole season. The hay crop was somewhat light owing to the dry weather. No special injury from insects or fungi, has been reported. *Clogher D.*—The crops have been very much above the usual average. This is mainly attributable to the very dry season. There have not been any cases of injury to crops from insects. *Dungannon D.*—Wheat is but little sown. There is, however, a fair crop in isolated instances. Oats—This crop is above the average, the yield has been very good in wet mountainous districts. Potatoes—The early crops did not do very well, but the later crops were good. The "Irish whites" seem best suited for this locality. Turnips and mangel wurzel are good crops above the average. Cabbage.—This crop has been fairly good. Flax.—This has been a good crop, better than any crop for the last few years. It commands a high price, owing to failure of continental crop. Rye is little grown, but is a fairly good crop. Hay—This crop is not up to the average. The quality is also bad. On the whole the crops are better than usual. Chemical treatment has been found useful in preventing the potato blight. It has been restricted to less tropical years. *Newtownstewart D.*—All crops were up to the average. Flax, turnips, and potatoes were above the average owing to the suitable weather. Hay was not good—having suffered from the long drought. None of the crops were injured by insects, fungi, or weeds. *Omagh D.*—The crops generally were very good owing to the fine summer and mild autumn. The farmers generally were well pleased with the yield of farm produce. There was no special injury to crops. *Strabane D.*—The crops generally throughout this district have been very good this year. The season on the whole has been very favourable to the farmers. In corn crops the straw was somewhat short, owing to the dry season, but the yield of grain is excellent. In my experience I have never seen such fine root crops, turnips being particularly good. Potatoes are above the average, cabbages also. Flax was a splendid crop. I have heard of no injury having been done by insects or fungi.

Province of Ulster.

PROVINCE OF CONNAUGHT.

Province of Connaught.

Galway County. *Athenry D.*—The average rate of produce of all crops is considered fair, save oats and hay, which crops were light owing to the dry summer. The land too is of a light description, hence only a fair yield could be expected. I can find no complaints as to insects. *Ballinasloe D.*—The crops, generally, have been exceptionally good during past season owing to its extraordinary warmth. No special injury seems to have occurred from insects or fungi. *Clifden D.*—The crops are above the average. There has been no sign of disease, fungi, or injurious weeds. Potatoes are a good crop, there being very little blackness among them. The grain crop is good enough, the straw is a little short owing to the dry weather. The turnips, &c., are good. The good yield is due to the dry season. In this district a very little rain suffices the crops. *Clonbur D.*—The potato crop is good, there is little disease, probably owing to the dry season; other crops are good for the same reason. *Dunmore D.*—I find the crops, generally, have been a good average yield. It is considered, on account of the dry season, very little injury, if any, has been done by insects, fungi, or weeds. To the dry season also is attributed the good crop of potatoes, corn, &c., in fact all the crops are good this year. The rain came a little late for the hay, but on old meadow land the yield is very good. *Galway D.*—The good yield of the various crops may be attributed to the favourable season. I am not aware of any special injury to the crops from insects or fungi during the past season. *Gort D.*—The crops are fair. The grain crops and meadows were much affected by the long drought. The potatoes are a good crop. The green crops, turnips, mangolds (although having to be sown twice in some instances) are a fairly good crop, as is also cabbage. There are no complaints of any special injury to any of the crops by insects, fungi, &c. *Loughrea D.*—Wheat, a good return obtained, the season being exceptionally favourable; oats, not so good, owing, it is believed, to want of moisture, straw short, and grain did not fill properly, but, on the whole, the farmers are well satisfied; barley, bere, rye, beans, peas, not sown; potatoes, this crop has done remarkably well, giving a return much above the average, attributable to the dry harvest and absence of blight; turnips, a fair average crop, but in light limestone and sandy soils the dry season materially interfered with the growth; mangolds, same remarks as on turnip crop apply; carrots, none sown; cabbage, a good crop, chiefly confined to rich garden soils, and cultivated carefully; vetches, none sown; rape, good crop, the rain in August and September having improved it; hay, clover, &c., average not so good as in previous years, owing to the very dry spring and summer; insects, fungi, &c., had no material effect on the crops. *Moylough D.*—The crops have been good, which is attributable, in my opinion, to the favourable season. The yield of potatoes was good, but the oat crop was light owing to the dry weather. Hay is a fairly good crop, and turnips a very good one. No special injury has been caused by either insects or fungi. *Oughterard D.*—The crops call for no special mention. They are a very fair crop all round. There has been no special injury from insects or fungi. *Portumna D.*—The yield all round of the various crops is good. The potato crop is very good. There is no special injury to crops from insects or fungi during the past season. *Roundstone D.*—Regarding the crops there is little to say. The main crops are potatoes, grain, and hay. Potatoes are very good owing to the dry weather. Grain crops not very good, especially on light land, from the same cause, and, similarly hay on light land has been short, but late cut meadows have given a fair yield. Turnips have been generally poor, enough owing to dry weather. In one part of the district it is reported that this crop was injured by insects in the dry weather, the name of the insect is not known. *Spiddle D.*—On the whole the crops were very good, though, of course, light, owing to the excessively dry season. There is very little depth of soil, and consequently the ground requires a great deal of moisture. *Tuam D.*—All the crops grown are well up to the average produce of former years, the oat crop excepted being light and under the average yield in consequence of the dry season. *Woodford D.*—The wheat crop was good this year owing to the dry weather. The oat crop was also fairly good, but straw rather short for same reason. Potatoes are rather an uneven crop. Crops cut early turned out very well, but others withered rather soon, and the tubers had scarcely sufficient time to come to proper maturity. There are few bad potatoes. Turnips looked bad at end of June, but since then they have done splendidly and are an excellent crop. There was some rain early in July, and the end of the month being so favourable were probably the causes of the improvement. Hay cut early was light, but late meadows turned out very fairly, there was so much late growth.

Leitrim County. *Ballinamore D.*—The yield of the various crops grown in this district is fair. Oats is about the average; and would be better but for the dry season. Wheat, barley, bere, rye, beans and peas, not sown. Potatoes are a fairly good crop, would be well above the average had the blight not set in somewhat early. Turnips and mangold wurzel middling. Carrots, not sown. Very little cabbage grown; what is, appears fair. Vetches, rape, and flax, not cultivated. Hay, good in quality; but a

M 2

PROVINCE OF CONNAUGHT.

light crop, owing to prolonged drought. Pasture, hardly up to the average. No special injury to crops from insects or fungi. *Carrick-on-Shannon D.*—In my judgment, all crops have been good this year, the hay crop has been a larger crop than last year, and it has all been exceptionally well saved, and secured in ricks in good weather, and very early in the season. The oat crop was also exceptionally good. I have never known the harvest in these parts so early as this year. The crop was cut, saved, and secured very early, and there is positively no inferior oats this year. The straw is also exceptionally sound and good; no other corn crop is grown in any quantity in the district. All green crops are good. Mangolds, particularly so, these, with turnips and cabbages, are the only crops of this class grown. Grass was good this year, and for many years I have not seen cattle in such forward condition. Potatoes are a fairly average crop and fairly sound. In new ground, such as upland lea, where the crop was sown early, the potatoes are extremely good. The blight set in earlier than usual this year, and on this account, the potatoes are in late sown lands not quite so big as they might be. The crops generally round here did not suffer any special injury from weeds or fungi, though I must say the people are very careless about eradicating weeds, and do not till the land sufficiently well, both before putting in the crop and during its growth, where practicable. The furrows of turnips and mangolds are not sufficiently grubbed, and potatoes are not sufficiently weeded. They are also too sparing of manure, and have very little idea of the suitability of the manure they use to some soil, often using the same kind of manure for heavy, strong upland, than they use for light moory ground; and they do not pay sufficient attention to changing their seed oats and seed potatoes, sowing the land with the produce of the previous year instead of using imported seed. They are also too fond of sowing potatoes too frequently in the same ground. The cabbage crop suffered somewhat from the ravages of caterpillars, but the growth was so good that the plants could not be checked so as to materially damage them. *Drumshanbo D.*—The good yield of the different crops is attributed to the exceptionally fine weather which prevailed during the spring and summer. Perhaps more damage than usual was done by caterpillars to cabbage plants, &c., this year, but further, there is nothing special to report with regard to insects, fungi, &c. *Manorhamilton D.*—The good yield of the various crops is attributed to the dryness of the season, as the soil is of a sterile, cold nature. No injury has been caused to crops from insects or fungi during the past season in this district. *Mohill D.*—The potato crop in some cases is not good, but this is owing to late sowing, and having been cut away by the blight much earlier this year than years past.

MAYO COUNTY. *Ballaghaderreen D.*—The crops raised are good. The potato crop was not so good for many years past. Oats are also good, but the straw is shorter than in former years, owing to the dry season. Hay is fairly good and well saved, but the yield is not so good as in former years owing to the dry summer. The other crops raised in this district, viz.:—Turnips, cabbage, clover, rye, and mangold wurzel are fairly good, none of the crops have suffered from insects or fungi. *Ballina D.*—The prevailing crops are potatoes, oats, turnips, and mangolds, all of which are, owing to the dry season, a high average this year. The land about here is for the most part cold and damp, and a dry season suits it particularly well. There has not been such a satisfactory harvest all round for many years, with the result that farmers are well satisfied with the quality and quantity of their crops. Hay was rather light, but of good quality, and where a low average appears it is owing to bad cultivation, and too much reliance being placed upon artificial manures. The dry season prevented much injury from weeds or fungi, on the whole this may be regarded as an exceptionally favourable season. *Ballinrobe D.*—There appears to have been no special injury done to crops by insects or fungi. The yield of the several crops, which is good, is I believe to be attributed to the exceptionally fine season and the absence of disease. *Belmullet D.*—There were no special features worth reporting, except that from the situation of the district, we enjoyed a more humid summer than other parts of Ireland. *Castlebar D.*—The yield of the several crops is (with the exception of the hay crop) somewhat better than in the past few years, and this is attributed to a dry season, and absence of frost last spring, but the drought had a severe effect on the hay crop, which caused the yield to be lower than in former years. There has been no injury done to crops in this district by either insects, fungi, or weeds during the past season. *Claremorris D.*—All the crops are up to the average, owing to the good summer. The hay and straw crops are short as the season was so dry. There has been no injury to crops from insects or fungi during this season. *Newport D.*—Owing to the very dry summer we had, the crops this year were excellent all round. The potato crop was the best for years, also hay. Even in Achill there was a wonderfully good yield all round. *Swinford D.*—All the crops were excellent, and matured a month in advance of other years, which may be accounted for by the exceptionally dry spring and summer. I have not heard that any of the crops suffered from insects or fungi. *Westport D.*—In general the crops are good, and above the average, owing, it is believed to the very dry season, which suits this locality. The potato crop especially is very abundant, and good for food. In some localities, however, the tubers are discoloured through them with dark spots, and conspicuous rings which renders them unfit for human food. The farmers cannot account for this, as they never saw them similarly affected before. The crops have not been injured to any extent by insects or fungi, except the cabbage which suffered very much from the caterpillar, especially in close kitchen gardens. The ravages of these insects were due to the very dry summer.

ROSCOMMON COUNTY.—*Athlone D.*—The good yield of the various crops may be attributed to the excellent weather we have had during the season. There was no injury done to the crops by insects, fungi, or weeds injurious to farm crops. *Boyle D.*—The crops have been very good and generally above the average, which is attributable to the exceptionally good season. No special injury to crops in this district has been caused from insects or fungi. It is a very weedy district, and farmers take no trouble to destroy weeds. *Castlerea D.*—The yield of crops was good, this is attributed to the good dry season we had throughout. There has been no complaint of any special injury to crops from insects or fungi during past season. *Roscommon D.*—There is no doubt but that the good yield of all crops, which I believe there was in this district this year, is due to the exceptionally fine and dry season we had. *Strokestown D.*—All round the average is very fair. In some instances the potato crop has been much injured by the early blight, but with these exceptions the yield is fair, and in a few cases owing to suitability of soil, &c., this crop is very good. Cereals are also a very fair crop, except in light and hilly soils, where the yield was not good owing to dry season. Good in rich low-lying lands. Very little, if any, injury has been caused by insects or fungi.

SLIGO COUNTY.—*Ballymote D.*—There is no particular cause to which the good or bad yield of the crops in this district may be attributed. Heavy loamy land produced the best yield; light dry land did not do so well, the season being dry. There has been no special injury to the crops in this district. *Galway D.*—The several crops grown are much above the average of past years. This pleasing fact is almost in all cases attributed to the beautiful spring, summer, and harvest we have had this year. The potato crop was put in much earlier this year than any year for a long time past, and as a consequence they were full-grown and healthy before the blight set in, except in some rare cases of bad farming. In some dry upland the meadows were somewhat light in consequence of continued fine weather; but what the hay lost in quantity in such cases, it has gained in quality, being much superior to past years. Oats in some few cases suffered from sterility [illegible], but the grain is generally very sound in all cases. All the other crops did very well. With regard to any special injury done to crops from insects or fungi, I have to inform you that if any injury has occurred it has been very small, as no farmers have complained, which has not been the case in previous years; and in some manner as regards the potato crop. The farmers believe that the fine dry season has had the effect of keeping away such troublesome visitors from their farms, a blessing which they ardently hope for in the future also. *Easky D.*—The crops are generally good, owing to the dry season being favourable to the nature of the soil, except oats, the yield of which is rather under the average, and the straw short. As far as I can ascertain, there are no complaints of injury to crops from insects. *Sligo D.*—The generally good average produce of the several crops sown is due entirely to the fine season. This district being close to the coast suffered much in past years from excessive rain. There was no special injury to crops from insects or fungi. *Tubbercurry D.*—I consider the generally good average of crops this year due to the warm summer and favourable harvest weather.

PROVINCE OF CONNAUGHT.

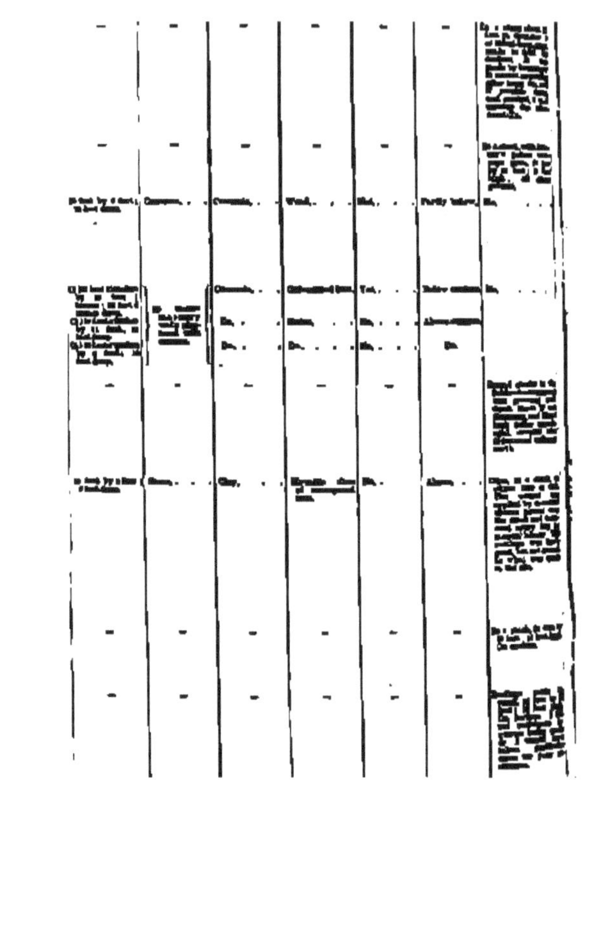

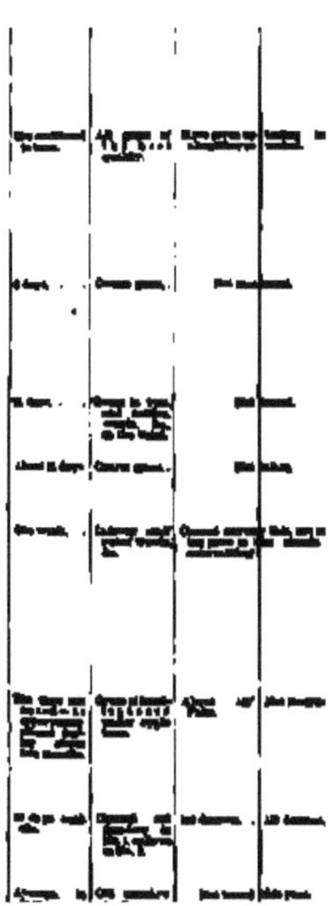

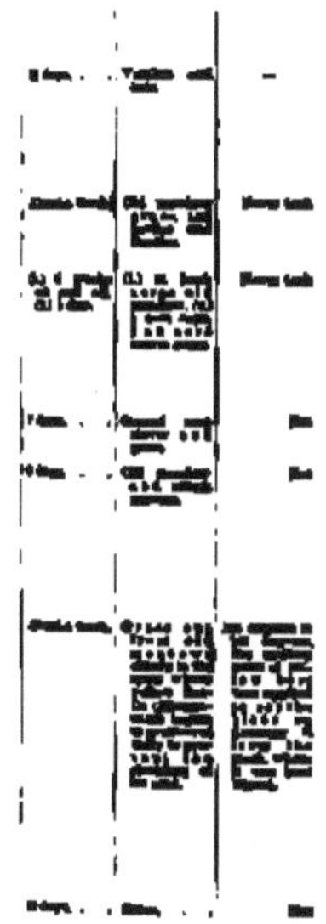

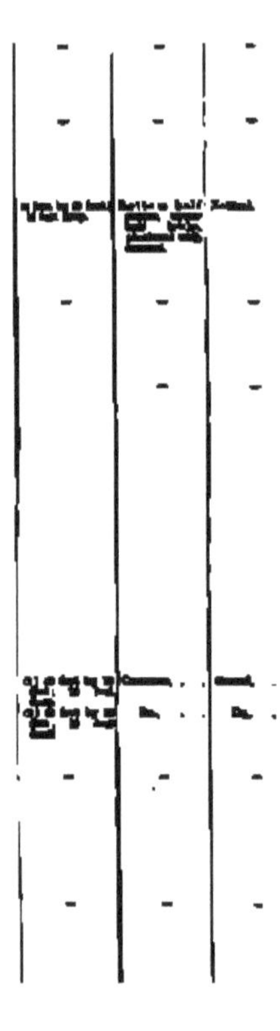

LEICESTER—continued.

[illegible]	[illegible]	Compensation.		[illegible]	[illegible]	Remarks.
		[illegible]	[illegible]			
[illegible]	[illegible]	[illegible]		[illegible]	[illegible]	[illegible]
[illegible]	[illegible]	[illegible]		[illegible]	[illegible]	[illegible]
—	[illegible]	[illegible]	[illegible]	—	[illegible]	—
[illegible]	[illegible]	[illegible]	[illegible]	[illegible]	[illegible]	—

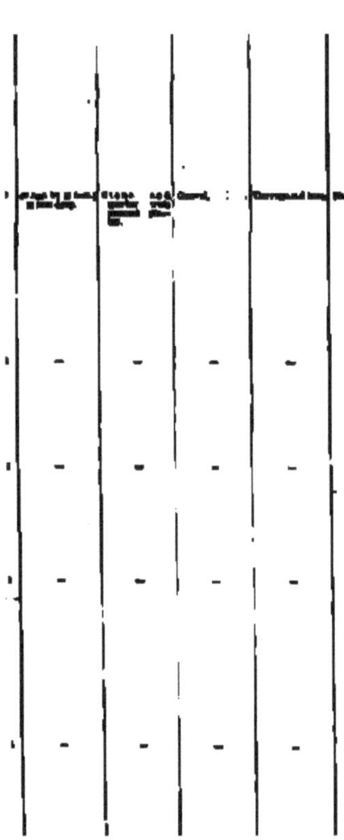

LEINSTER—continued.

[illegible]	[illegible]	[illegible]		[illegible]	[illegible]
		[illegible]	[illegible]		
[illegible]	[illegible]	[illegible]		[illegible]	[illegible]
[illegible]	[illegible]	[illegible]	[illegible]	[illegible]	[illegible]
[illegible]	[illegible]	[illegible]		[illegible]	[illegible]
[illegible]	[illegible]	[illegible]	[illegible]	[illegible]	[illegible]

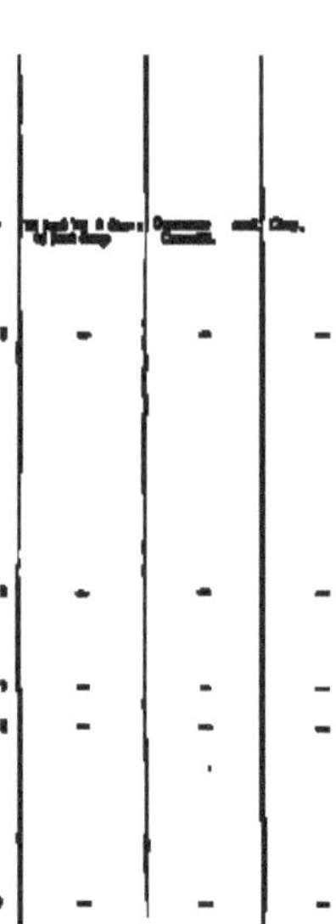

LEINSTER—continued.

[illegible]	[illegible]	[illegible]
		[illegible]

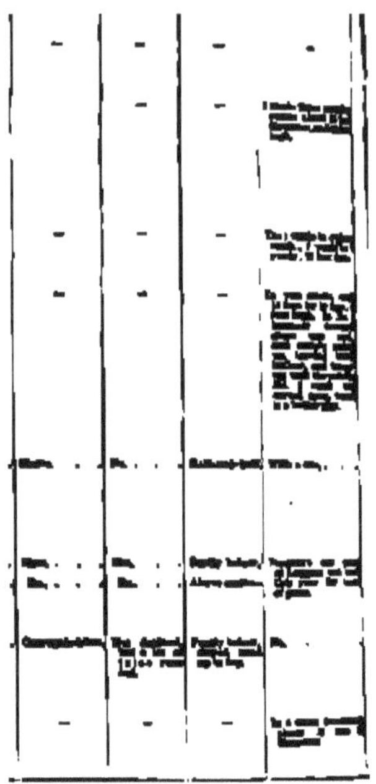

PROVINCE OF

LEINSTER—*continued.*

[illegible]	[illegible]	Temperature		[illegible]	[illegible]	[illegible]
		[illegible]	[illegible]			
[illegible]	[illegible]	[illegible]	[illegible]	[illegible]	Store cattle.	[illegible]
[illegible]	Ordinary meadow grass.	Not tested.		[illegible]	[illegible]	[illegible]
[illegible]	Crops.	[illegible]	[illegible]	[illegible]	Store cattle.	[illegible]

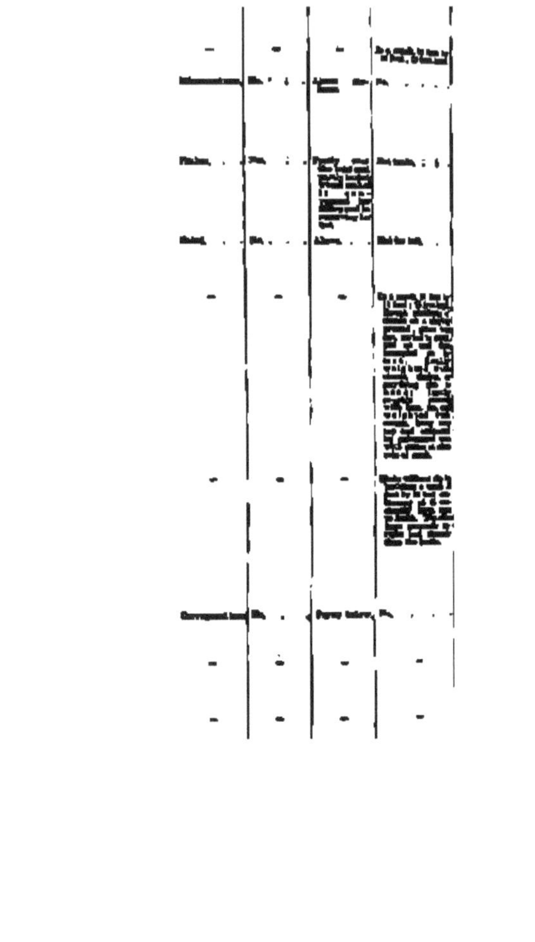

[illegible]—continued.

[illegible]	[illegible]	Temperature.		[illegible]	[illegible]	Remarks.
		[illegible]	[illegible]			
—	—	—	—	—	—	[illegible]
—	[illegible]	—	—	—	[illegible]	[illegible]
[illegible]	—	[illegible]	[illegible]	[illegible]	[illegible]	[illegible]
[illegible]	[illegible]	[illegible]		[illegible]	[illegible]	[illegible]
—	[illegible]	[illegible]		[illegible]	[illegible]	[illegible]
[illegible]	[illegible]	[illegible]	[illegible]	[illegible]	—	[illegible]
—	[illegible]	[illegible]		[illegible]	[illegible]	—
—	—	—	—	—	—	[illegible]
[illegible]	[illegible]	Can't say.	—	—	[illegible]	[illegible]
[illegible]	[illegible]	[illegible]	—	[illegible]	[illegible]	[illegible]

PROVINCE OF

[illegible]	[illegible]	[illegible]	[illegible]	Materials of Silos: Walls	Floors	Roof	[illegible]	[illegible]	[illegible]
[illegible] COUNTY—continued.									
[illegible]	–	[illegible]	–	–	–	–	–	–	[illegible]
[illegible]	[illegible]	–	[illegible]	[illegible]	[illegible]	[illegible]	[illegible]	[illegible]	[illegible]
[illegible]	–	[illegible]	–	–	–	–	–	–	[illegible]
[illegible]	–	[illegible]	–	–	–	–	–	–	[illegible]
[illegible]	–	[illegible]	–	–	–	–	–	–	[illegible]
TIPPERARY COUNTY.									
[illegible]	[illegible]	[illegible]	[illegible]	[illegible]	Clay.	[illegible]	[illegible]	[illegible]	[illegible]
			[illegible]	Do.	Do.	Do.	Do.	Do.	
[illegible]	[illegible]	[illegible]	[illegible]	[illegible]	[illegible]	[illegible]	[illegible]	[illegible]	[illegible]
[illegible]	[illegible]	–	[illegible]	[illegible]	[illegible]	[illegible]	[illegible]	[illegible]	Do.
[illegible]	–	[illegible]	–	–	–	–	–	–	[illegible]

[illegible]	[illegible]	[illegible]
[illegible]	[illegible]	[illegible]
[illegible]	[illegible]	[illegible]
[illegible]	[illegible]	[illegible]
[illegible]	[illegible]	[illegible]
[illegible]	[illegible]	[illegible]
[illegible]	[illegible]	[illegible]
[illegible]	[illegible]	[illegible]

[illegible]	[illegible]	[illegible]			[illegible]	[illegible]	[illegible]
		Walls.	Floor.	Roof.			
[illegible]	—	—	—	—	—	—	[illegible]
[illegible]	—	—	—	—	—		[illegible]
[illegible]	[illegible]	[illegible]	[illegible]	[illegible]	[illegible]	[illegible]	[illegible]
[illegible]	—	—	—	—	—	—	[illegible]
[illegible]	—	—	—	—	—	—	[illegible]

[illegible]	[illegible]	Stone and Lime,	Paved,	Slates,	Wet,	Above,	—
[illegible]	[illegible]	Stone and Lime.	[illegible]	Corrugated iron	[illegible]	Below,	—
[illegible]	—	—	—	—	—	—	[illegible]
[illegible]	—	—	—	—	—	—	[illegible]
[illegible]	[illegible]	[illegible]	[illegible]	[illegible]	—	[illegible]	[illegible]
[illegible]	—	—	—	—	—	—	[illegible]

AGRICULTURAL STATISTICS FOR THE YEAR 18[illegible].

PROVINCE OF

[illegible]	[illegible]	[illegible]	[illegible]			[illegible]	[illegible]	[illegible]
			[illegible]	[illegible]	[illegible]			
[illegible]	[illegible]	—	—	—	—	—	—	[illegible]
[illegible]	[illegible]	—	—	—	—	—	—	[illegible]
[illegible]	—	—	[illegible]	[illegible]	—	—	[illegible]	[illegible]
[illegible]	[illegible]	—	—	—	—	—	—	[illegible]
[illegible]	—	[illegible]	[illegible]	[illegible]	[illegible]	[illegible]	[illegible]	[illegible]
[illegible]	[illegible]	—	—	—	—	—	—	[illegible]
[illegible]	[illegible]	—	—	—	—	—	—	[illegible]

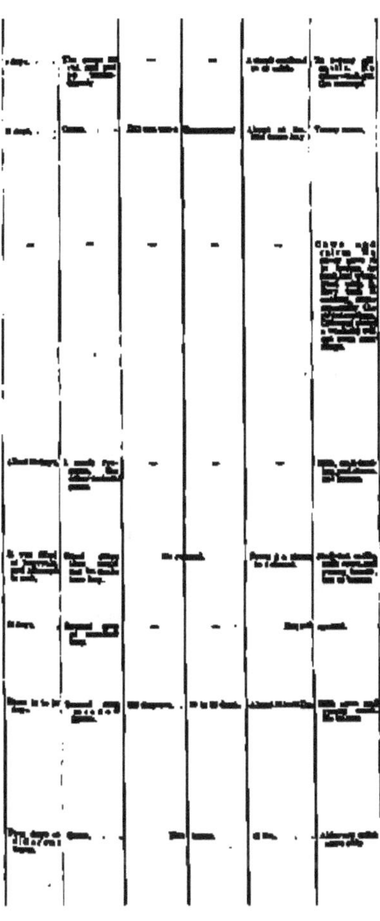

[illegible]	No. of [illegible]	[illegible]	Materials of Mine.			[illegible]	[illegible]	[illegible]
			Walls.	Floors.	Roof.			
[illegible]	—	[illegible]	[illegible]	[illegible]	[illegible]	[illegible]	[illegible]	[illegible]
		[illegible]	Do.	[illegible]	[illegible]	[illegible]	[illegible]	
—	[illegible]	—	—	—	—	—	—	[illegible]
[illegible]	—	[illegible]	[illegible]	[illegible]	[illegible]	[illegible]	[illegible]	Do.
[illegible]	—	[illegible]	[illegible]	[illegible]	[illegible]	[illegible]	[illegible]	Do.
—	[illegible]	—	—	—	—	—	—	[illegible]
[illegible]	—	[illegible]	—	—	—	[illegible]	[illegible]	[illegible]
[illegible]	—	[illegible]	[illegible]	[illegible]	[illegible]	[illegible]	[illegible]	Do.
[illegible]	—	[illegible]	[illegible]	—	—	[illegible]	[illegible]	—
—	[illegible]	—	—	—	—	—	—	[illegible]
—	[illegible]	—	—	—	—	—	—	[illegible]
—	[illegible]	—	—	—	—	—	—	[illegible]
—	[illegible]	—	—	—	—	—	—	[illegible]
[illegible]	—	[illegible]	[illegible]	[illegible]	[illegible]	Do.	[illegible]	—
[illegible]	—	[illegible]	[illegible]	[illegible]	[illegible]	[illegible]	[illegible]	Do.

ULSTER—*continued.*

[illegible]	[illegible]	Temperature.		[illegible]	[illegible]	Remarks.
		[illegible]	[illegible]			
[illegible]	[illegible]	[illegible]	[illegible]	[illegible]	[illegible]	[illegible]
—	[illegible]	[illegible]	[illegible]	[illegible]	[illegible]	[illegible]
—	[illegible]	[illegible]	[illegible]	[illegible]	[illegible]	[illegible]
[illegible]	[illegible]	[illegible]	[illegible]	[illegible]	[illegible]	[illegible]
[illegible]	[illegible]	[illegible]	[illegible]	[illegible]	[illegible]	[illegible]
[illegible]	[illegible]	[illegible]	[illegible]	[illegible]	[illegible]	[illegible]
[illegible]	[illegible]	[illegible]	[illegible]	[illegible]	[illegible]	[illegible]
[illegible]	[illegible]	—	—	[illegible]	[illegible]	[illegible]
[illegible]	[illegible]	[illegible]	[illegible]	[illegible]	[illegible]	[illegible]
[illegible]	[illegible]	[illegible]	[illegible]	[illegible]	[illegible]	[illegible]
—	[illegible]	—	—	[illegible]	[illegible]	[illegible]
[illegible]	[illegible]	[illegible]	[illegible]	[illegible]	[illegible]	[illegible]
—	[illegible]	[illegible]		[illegible]	[illegible]	[illegible]
[illegible]	[illegible]	[illegible]		[illegible]	[illegible]	

[illegible]	[illegible]			[illegible]	[illegible]	[illegible]
	[illegible]	[illegible]	[illegible]			
[illegible]	[illegible]	[illegible]	[illegible]	[illegible]	[illegible]	[illegible]
[illegible]	[illegible]	[illegible]	[illegible]	[illegible]	[illegible]	[illegible]
—	—	—	—	—	—	[illegible]
—	—	—	—	—	—	[illegible]
—	—	—	—	—	—	[illegible]
—	—	—	—	—	—	[illegible]
[illegible]	Do.	[illegible]	Do.	Do.	[illegible]	[illegible]
[illegible]	[illegible]	[illegible]	[illegible]	—	[illegible]	[illegible]
[illegible]	Do.	Do.	[illegible]	—	Do.	
—	—	—	—	—	—	[illegible]

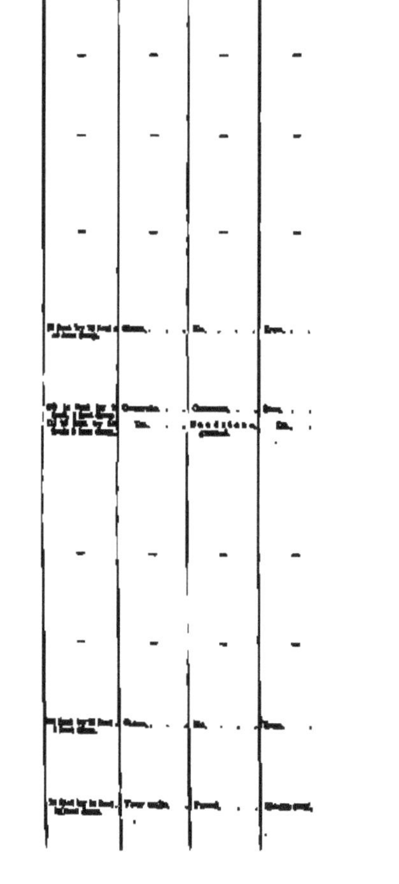

—	—	—	—
—	—	—	—
—	—	—	—
[illegible]	[illegible]	Do.	[illegible]
[illegible]	Concrete	Cement	[illegible]
[illegible]	Do.	Sandstone, [illegible]	Do.
—	—	—	—
—	—	—	—
[illegible]	[illegible]	Do.	[illegible]
[illegible]	[illegible]	[illegible]	[illegible]

[illegible]—continued.

[illegible]	[illegible]	Temperature.		[illegible]	[illegible]	
		[illegible]	[illegible]			
[illegible]	[illegible]	Not ascertained.		[illegible]	[illegible]	
[illegible]	[illegible]	[illegible]		[illegible]	[illegible]	[illegible]
[illegible]	[illegible]	Not taken.		[illegible]	[illegible]	[illegible]
[illegible]	[illegible]	Not taken.		[illegible]	[illegible]	
[illegible]	[illegible]	—	—	[illegible]	[illegible]	[illegible]
[illegible]	[illegible]	[illegible]	[illegible]	[illegible]	[illegible]	[illegible]
[illegible]	—	[illegible]		[illegible]	[illegible]	[illegible]
[illegible]	[illegible]	[illegible]		[illegible]	[illegible]	
[illegible]	[illegible]	—	—	[illegible]	[illegible]	
[illegible]	[illegible]	—	—	[illegible]	[illegible]	[illegible]

[illegible]	[illegible]	[illegible]	[illegible]	[illegible]
[illegible]	Do.	Do.	Do.	Do.
[illegible]	Do.	Do.	Do.	Do.
[illegible]	Do.	Do.	Do.	Do.
[illegible]	[illegible]	[illegible]	[illegible]	[illegible]

THE WEATHER.

Abstract of Meteorological Observations registered at the Ordnance Survey Office (Height above the Sea 155·3 Feet) Phœnix Park, Dublin, during the year 1892:—

The barometer stood highest in 1892, on the 30th December, at 9 A.M., wind calm, when it was 30·718 inches; it was lowest at 9 A.M. on 12th December, when it was 28·443 inches. The highest temperature of the air during the year was 82·0 degrees of Fahrenheit on 16th August, and the lowest 18·6 degrees on 3rd January. The greatest quantity of rain which fell in a day (24 hours) was 1·120 inches on 12th July, with wind N.N.E. The point from which the wind chiefly prevailed was the W.; it blew from that direction on 148 days, at 9 A.M. The strongest wind was from the N. on the 18th November, when the pressure was 8·00 lbs. per square foot.

1892.	Barometer. Corrected for Altitude and reduced to 32° Fah. Mean. 9 A.M.	9 P.M.	Mean.	Range.	Highest in Month.	Lowest in Month.	Range.	Thermometer. Self-Registering Thermometers. Highest in Month.	Lowest in Month.	Range.	Mean. Of all Highest.	Of all Lowest.	Temp.	Range.	Hygrometer. 9 A.M. Mean. Dry Bulb.	Wet Bulb.	Dew Point.	Elastic Force of Vapour.	Humidity.
January,	[illegible]	[illegible]	[illegible]	[illegible]	[illegible]	[illegible]	[illegible]	[illegible]	[illegible]	[illegible]	[illegible]	[illegible]	[illegible]	[illegible]	[illegible]	[illegible]	[illegible]	[illegible]	[illegible]
February,	[illegible]	[illegible]	[illegible]	[illegible]	[illegible]	[illegible]	[illegible]	[illegible]	[illegible]	[illegible]	[illegible]	[illegible]	[illegible]	[illegible]	[illegible]	[illegible]	[illegible]	[illegible]	[illegible]
March,	[illegible]	[illegible]	[illegible]	[illegible]	[illegible]	[illegible]	[illegible]	[illegible]	[illegible]	[illegible]	[illegible]	[illegible]	[illegible]	[illegible]	[illegible]	[illegible]	[illegible]	[illegible]	[illegible]
April,	[illegible]	[illegible]	[illegible]	[illegible]	[illegible]	[illegible]	[illegible]	[illegible]	[illegible]	[illegible]	[illegible]	[illegible]	[illegible]	[illegible]	[illegible]	[illegible]	[illegible]	[illegible]	[illegible]
May,	[illegible]	[illegible]	[illegible]	[illegible]	[illegible]	[illegible]	[illegible]	[illegible]	[illegible]	[illegible]	[illegible]	[illegible]	[illegible]	[illegible]	[illegible]	[illegible]	[illegible]	[illegible]	[illegible]
June,	[illegible]	[illegible]	[illegible]	[illegible]	[illegible]	[illegible]	[illegible]	[illegible]	[illegible]	[illegible]	[illegible]	[illegible]	[illegible]	[illegible]	[illegible]	[illegible]	[illegible]	[illegible]	[illegible]
July,	[illegible]	[illegible]	[illegible]	[illegible]	[illegible]	[illegible]	[illegible]	[illegible]	[illegible]	[illegible]	[illegible]	[illegible]	[illegible]	[illegible]	[illegible]	[illegible]	[illegible]	[illegible]	[illegible]
August,	[illegible]	[illegible]	[illegible]	[illegible]	[illegible]	[illegible]	[illegible]	[illegible]	[illegible]	[illegible]	[illegible]	[illegible]	[illegible]	[illegible]	[illegible]	[illegible]	[illegible]	[illegible]	[illegible]
September,	[illegible]	[illegible]	[illegible]	[illegible]	[illegible]	[illegible]	[illegible]	[illegible]	[illegible]	[illegible]	[illegible]	[illegible]	[illegible]	[illegible]	[illegible]	[illegible]	[illegible]	[illegible]	[illegible]
October,	[illegible]	[illegible]	[illegible]	[illegible]	[illegible]	[illegible]	[illegible]	[illegible]	[illegible]	[illegible]	[illegible]	[illegible]	[illegible]	[illegible]	[illegible]	[illegible]	[illegible]	[illegible]	[illegible]
November,	[illegible]	[illegible]	[illegible]	[illegible]	[illegible]	[illegible]	[illegible]	[illegible]	[illegible]	[illegible]	[illegible]	[illegible]	[illegible]	[illegible]	[illegible]	[illegible]	[illegible]	[illegible]	[illegible]
December,	[illegible]	[illegible]	[illegible]	[illegible]	[illegible]	[illegible]	[illegible]	[illegible]	[illegible]	[illegible]	[illegible]	[illegible]	[illegible]	[illegible]	[illegible]	[illegible]	[illegible]	[illegible]	[illegible]
Total,	[illegible]	[illegible]	[illegible]	-	-	-	-	-	-	-	[illegible]	[illegible]	[illegible]	-	[illegible]	[illegible]	[illegible]	[illegible]	[illegible]
Mean,	[illegible]	[illegible]	[illegible]	-	-	-	-	-	-	-	[illegible]	[illegible]	[illegible]	-	[illegible]	[illegible]	[illegible]	[illegible]	[illegible]

1892.	Rain. Number of Days on which Rain fell.	Total Amount for Month.	Greatest Amount in 24 hours.	Ozone. 9 A.M.	Cloud. Monthly Total.	Daily Mean.	Wind. Number of days in Wind in certain directions at 9 A.M. and the total pressure in lbs. per Square Foot. N.	Pressure.	N.E.	Pressure.	E.	Pressure.	S.E.	Pressure.	S.	Pressure.	S.W.	Pressure.	W.	Pressure.	N.W.	Pressure.	Calm.
January,	[illegible]	[illegible]	[illegible]	[illegible]	[illegible]	[illegible]	[illegible]	[illegible]	[illegible]	[illegible]	[illegible]	[illegible]	[illegible]	[illegible]	[illegible]	[illegible]	[illegible]	[illegible]	[illegible]	[illegible]	[illegible]	[illegible]	[illegible]
February,	[illegible]	[illegible]	[illegible]	[illegible]	[illegible]	[illegible]	[illegible]	[illegible]	[illegible]	[illegible]	[illegible]	[illegible]	[illegible]	[illegible]	[illegible]	[illegible]	[illegible]	[illegible]	[illegible]	[illegible]	[illegible]	[illegible]	[illegible]
March,	[illegible]	[illegible]	[illegible]	[illegible]	[illegible]	[illegible]	[illegible]	[illegible]	[illegible]	[illegible]	[illegible]	[illegible]	[illegible]	[illegible]	[illegible]	[illegible]	[illegible]	[illegible]	[illegible]	[illegible]	[illegible]	[illegible]	[illegible]
April,	[illegible]	[illegible]	[illegible]	[illegible]	[illegible]	[illegible]	[illegible]	[illegible]	[illegible]	[illegible]	[illegible]	[illegible]	[illegible]	[illegible]	[illegible]	[illegible]	[illegible]	[illegible]	[illegible]	[illegible]	[illegible]	[illegible]	[illegible]
May,	[illegible]	[illegible]	[illegible]	[illegible]	[illegible]	[illegible]	[illegible]	[illegible]	[illegible]	[illegible]	[illegible]	[illegible]	[illegible]	[illegible]	[illegible]	[illegible]	[illegible]	[illegible]	[illegible]	[illegible]	[illegible]	[illegible]	[illegible]
June,	[illegible]	[illegible]	[illegible]	[illegible]	[illegible]	[illegible]	[illegible]	[illegible]	[illegible]	[illegible]	[illegible]	[illegible]	[illegible]	[illegible]	[illegible]	[illegible]	[illegible]	[illegible]	[illegible]	[illegible]	[illegible]	[illegible]	[illegible]
July,	[illegible]	[illegible]	[illegible]	[illegible]	[illegible]	[illegible]	[illegible]	[illegible]	[illegible]	[illegible]	[illegible]	[illegible]	[illegible]	[illegible]	[illegible]	[illegible]	[illegible]	[illegible]	[illegible]	[illegible]	[illegible]	[illegible]	[illegible]
August,	[illegible]	[illegible]	[illegible]	[illegible]	[illegible]	[illegible]	[illegible]	[illegible]	[illegible]	[illegible]	[illegible]	[illegible]	[illegible]	[illegible]	[illegible]	[illegible]	[illegible]	[illegible]	[illegible]	[illegible]	[illegible]	[illegible]	[illegible]
September,	[illegible]	[illegible]	[illegible]	[illegible]	[illegible]	[illegible]	[illegible]	[illegible]	[illegible]	[illegible]	[illegible]	[illegible]	[illegible]	[illegible]	[illegible]	[illegible]	[illegible]	[illegible]	[illegible]	[illegible]	[illegible]	[illegible]	[illegible]
October,	[illegible]	[illegible]	[illegible]	[illegible]	[illegible]	[illegible]	[illegible]	[illegible]	[illegible]	[illegible]	[illegible]	[illegible]	[illegible]	[illegible]	[illegible]	[illegible]	[illegible]	[illegible]	[illegible]	[illegible]	[illegible]	[illegible]	[illegible]
November,	[illegible]	[illegible]	[illegible]	[illegible]	[illegible]	[illegible]	[illegible]	[illegible]	[illegible]	[illegible]	[illegible]	[illegible]	[illegible]	[illegible]	[illegible]	[illegible]	[illegible]	[illegible]	[illegible]	[illegible]	[illegible]	[illegible]	[illegible]
December,	[illegible]	[illegible]	[illegible]	[illegible]	[illegible]	[illegible]	[illegible]	[illegible]	[illegible]	[illegible]	[illegible]	[illegible]	[illegible]	[illegible]	[illegible]	[illegible]	[illegible]	[illegible]	[illegible]	[illegible]	[illegible]	[illegible]	[illegible]
Total,	[illegible]	[illegible]	-	[illegible]	[illegible]	[illegible]	[illegible]	[illegible]	[illegible]	[illegible]	[illegible]	[illegible]	[illegible]	[illegible]	[illegible]	[illegible]	[illegible]	[illegible]	[illegible]	[illegible]	[illegible]	[illegible]	[illegible]
Mean,	[illegible]	[illegible]	-	[illegible]	[illegible]	[illegible]	[illegible]	[illegible]	[illegible]	[illegible]	[illegible]	[illegible]	[illegible]	[illegible]	[illegible]	[illegible]	[illegible]	[illegible]	[illegible]	[illegible]	[illegible]	[illegible]	[illegible]

METEOROLOGICAL OBSERVATIONS

FOR EACH MONTH OF THE YEAR 1893.

By J. W. MOORE, Esq., M.D., F.R.C.P.I., F.R. MET. SOC.

(Extracted from the Dublin Journal of Medical Science.)

JANUARY.—The promise of a cold month afforded by very severe weather during the first ten days or a fortnight was not fulfilled. So decided was the recovery of temperature after the 15th, that the mean temperature of the whole month scarcely fell below the average. The mean temperature of the 1st–14th, inclusive, was 35·0°; that of the 15th–31st, inclusive, was 44·3°. Ireland escaped to a remarkable extent, the Siberian cold which prevailed on the Continent of Europe, and to a less degree in Great Britain throughout a large portion of the month. In Dublin the cloudiness of the sky was one of the chief features of the weather. Another interesting point was the singular mildness, which the northerly and north-westerly winds of an Atlantic anticyclone brought to Ireland in the period between the 15th and the 24th.

In Dublin the arithmetical mean temperature (40·8°) was slightly below the average (41·4°); the mean dry bulb readings at 9 a.m. and 9 p.m. were 40·1°. In the twenty-eight years ending with 1892, January was coldest in 1881 (M. T. = 32·2°), and warmest in 1876 (M. T. = 46·6°). In 1867 the M. T. was 34·7°, and in 1868 it was 37·6°. In 1871 and in 1888 the M. T. was 37·9°; in 1879 (the "cold year") it was 33·3°. In 1888 the M. T. was 41·1°; in 1889, 41·1°; in 1890, 44·5°; in 1891, 40·1°; and in 1892, 38·6°. As a general rule, January in Dublin is not colder, but a shade warmer, than December. This is owing to the full development in January of a winter area of low pressure over the Atlantic to the north-westward of the British Isles, and to a resulting prevalence of S.W. winds in their vicinity. January, 1892, proved an exception to this rule, the M. T. being 4·2° below that of December, 1891 (42·0°). But January, 1893, conformed to the rule, the M. T. being above that of December, 1892.

The mean height of the barometer was 30·033 inches, or 0·176 inch above the corrected average value for January—namely, 29·857 inches. The mercury rose to 30·559 inches at 7 30 a.m. of the 31st, and fell to 29·178 inches at 9 p.m. of the 24th. The observed range of atmospherical pressure was, therefore, as much as 1·381 inches—that is, a little less than one inch and four-tenths.

The mean temperature deduced from daily readings of the dry bulb thermometer at 9 a.m. and 9 p.m. was 40·1°, or 1·2° above the value for December, 1892. Using the formula, *Mean Temp.* = *min.* + (*max.*—*min.* × ·52), the M. T. becomes 41·0°, compared with a twenty-five years' average of 41·3°. The arithmetical mean of the maximal and minimal readings was 40·8°, compared with a twenty-five years' average of 41·4°. On the 20th the thermometer in the screen rose to 54·9°—wind, W.S.W.; on the 3rd the temperature fell to 20·3°—wind, W.N.W. The minimum on the grass was 14·4°, also on the 3rd.

The rainfall was 2·239 inches, distributed over 19 days. The average rainfall for January in the twenty-five years, 1865–89, inclusive, was 2·200 inches, and the average number of rainy days was 17·2. The rainfall, therefore, was very slightly above the average, while the number of rainy days was more decidedly above it. In 1877 the rainfall in January was very large—4·322 inches on 25 days; in 1866, also, 4·158 inches fell—on, however, only 18 days. On the other hand, in 1874, only ·408 of an inch was measured on but 9 days; and in 1880, the rainfall was only ·488 of an inch on but 8 days. In January, 1888, only 2·244 inches of rain were measured on as many as 20 days; in 1887 ("the dry year"), 1·918 inches fell on 16 days; in 1888, 1·747 inches on 9 days; in 1889, 2·213 inches on 16 days; in 1890, 3·873 inches on 21 days; in 1891, only ·673 of an inch on 14 days; and in 1892, 1·638 inches on 20 days.

Solar halos were seen on the 16th and 25th. A Lunar halo was seen on the 28th. The atmosphere was foggy on the 2nd, 4th, 12th and 29th. High winds were noted on not less than 18 days, reaching the force of a gale, however, on only 4 days—the 7th, 8th, 16th, and 29th. Hail fell on the 3rd, 7th, 14th, and 31st, and snow or sleet on the 1st, 2nd, 7th, and 14th. Temperature exceeded 50° in the screen on 7 days, compared with 6 days in 1892, only 3 days in 1891, 17 days in 1890, and 8 days in 1889; while it fell to or below 32° in the screen on only 4 nights, compared with 14 nights in 1892, 7 nights in 1891, and 1 night in 1890, and 3 nights in 1889. The minima on the grass were 32°, or less, on 16 nights, compared with 23 nights in 1892, 31 nights in 1891, 15 nights in 1890, and 16 nights in 1889.

The first week of 1893 will long be remembered for the intensity of the cold which prevailed in both Northern Hemispheres, and for the remarkable height reached by the barometer in Northern and Eastern Europe—31·28 inches at Archangel on Tuesday, the 3rd, 31·12 inches at Haparanda, on the Gulf of Bothnia, on Wednesday, and 31·27 inches at Moscow on Thursday. At 8 a.m. of Sunday, the 1st, the thermometer stood at minus 37° Fahr. at Haparanda, or 69° below freezing point. During the ensuing night the minimal reading at this station was —43°, or 75° of frost. At the beginning of the month a vast anticyclone stretched from the extreme North of Europe to the westward of the British Islands. Strong S.E. winds blew in Ireland, and on Monday morning a fall of snow occurred in Dublin. This was followed by severe frost, the thermometer falling to 20·3° in the screen, and to 14·4° on the ground during Monday night, even in the heart of the city. On Wednesday the 4th, a decided change of weather set in over Ireland, where the sky became densely overcast, with freshening S.E. winds and rising temperature. In Great Britain at this time the frost only "stiffened," and fog prevailed. By the end of the week, however, strong S.E. or E. winds, with falls of cold rain and sleet or snow had become general, and the weather was most inclement in all parts. In Dublin the mean height of the barometer was 30·110 inches, pressure ranging from 30·369 inches, at 9 a.m. of Wednesday (wind calm), to 29·76[illegible] inches at 9 p.m. of Saturday (wind, E., blowing a moderate gale). The corrected mean temperature was 33·[illegible]°. The mean dry bulb readings at 9 a.m. and 9 p.m. were 33·6°. The screened thermometers rose to [illegible]° on Friday, having fallen to [illegible]° on Tuesday. The rainfall amounted to ·[illegible] inch on five days, ·[illegible] inch being registered on Saturday. The precipitation consisted largely of snow or sleet and hail. The prevalent wind was S.E. A noteworthy feature was the relatively high temperature which accompanied this wind in the south-western parts of England and Ireland, and in Brittany.

Although the cold in Ireland and in Great Britain also was much less intense during the week ended Saturday, the 14th, than in the two previous weeks, the record is again one of wintery weather. At the beginning of the period a large area of low atmospherical pressure was found over the Atlantic south-westward of the British Isles. Strong E. and S.E. winds or gales were blowing in Ireland, where also cold rain or sleet fell heavily. During the next two days the depression made its way across the Bay of Biscay and France to Germany, bringing with it to those countries higher temperatures and a thaw. Meanwhile an area of high pressure formed in the far North, causing easterly to northerly winds, and cloudy, cold weather generally. This system subsequently retreated in a south-westerly direction, and disappeared off the S.W. of Ireland on Friday, when a series of depressions was preparing to travel southwards across the British Isles and North Sea. In front of these disturbances a transitory rise of temperature took place on Friday, and rain fell at night. On Saturday, however, rain gave place to frequent showers of sleet, snow, and hail, as the wind veered to N. and N.E. in the rear of the depressions, which continued their southerly course. In Dublin the mean height of the barometer was 30·090 inches, pressure ranging from 29·616 inches, at 9 p.m. of Sunday (wind, E.), to 30·440 inches, at 9 a.m. of Wednesday (wind, E.N.E.). From this high reading it receded to 29·764 inches, at 9 a.m. of Saturday (wind, W.N.W.). The corrected mean temperature was 38·6°. The mean dry bulb readings at 9 a.m. and 9 p.m. were 38·[illegible]°. On Friday the screened thermometers rose to 44·4°; on Saturday they fell to 33·0°. The rainfall was ·[illegible] inch on four days, ·[illegible] inch being measured on Sunday. The prevailing winds were—first, easterly, then north-westerly.

The most marked characteristic feature in the weather of the week ended Saturday, the 21st, was a decided advance in temperature all over the British Islands, but especially in Ireland, Scotland, and the West of England (including Wales). In France and Germany, on the contrary, the cold "stiffened" daily until Friday, when warmer weather spread in from the Atlantic over the Continent also. A very interesting circumstance is that the milder weather came with N.W. and N. winds, which formed part of the circulation round an anticyclone found generally over the Atlantic to the westward or south-westward of Ireland. On Tuesday morning also a southerly wind carried cold weather from the frozen Continent to the S.E. of England, where the thermometer remained all day below the freezing point. Not for many years has such extreme cold been felt in Germany and France as during the greater part of this week—at Munich the minima have been −11°, −15°, −15°, −5°, −6°, +1°, and +12°; at Lyons the corresponding values have been +11°, −3°, −1°, (?), 6°, +3°, +6° (?), and +17°. During all this time temperatures as high as from 48° to 53° were being recorded on the Atlantic coasts of both the United Kingdom and France. In the interval between Wednesday and Friday a vast depression crossed the extreme northern parts of Scandinavia, bringing with it a thaw even to those high latitudes at a time when intense frost held as far south as Lyons and Munich. On Saturday cold weather was re-established in Scotland and Scandinavia. In Dublin the mean height of the barometer was 30·[illegible] inches, pressure ranging from 29·616 inches at 2 p.m. of Monday (wind, N.W.) to 30·539 inches at 7.30 a.m. of Saturday, (wind, W.N.W.). The corrected mean temperature was 42·0°. The mean dry bulb readings at 9 a.m. and 9 p.m. were 42·6°. On Sunday the thermometers in the screen fell to 29·5°; on Thursday they rose to 50·6°. Rain was measured on four days to the amount of ·341 inch, of which ·277 inch fell on Sunday. The prevailing winds were W.N.W. and W.

A further advance in temperature occurred during the week ended Saturday, the 28th, which proved open, changeable, and breezy, with prevalent westerly to southerly winds. At first an anticyclone lay to the southward of Ireland—on the morning of Sunday, the 22nd, the barometer stood as high as 30·[illegible] inches at Corunna, in the N.W. of Spain—while several shallow depressions were found over the North Sea, Germany, and the Baltic. The winds curved from S.W. in the west of Ireland, through W. in the east of this country to N.W. in the S.E. of England, and to N. in parts of France. The weather was mild and damp, and light rain fell at many stations. On Wednesday morning a depression appeared off the south of Ireland, ultimately forming portion of a complex V-shaped depression, which caused southerly gales, and in places heavy rains during the ensuing 24 hours. As this disturbance passed off to the northward a sharp but temporary dip in temperature took place. On Friday another and more serious depression advanced over Ireland from S.S.W., bringing with it southerly gales, a renewed rainfall, and generally broken weather, which lasted to the close of the week. In Dublin the mean height of the barometer was 29·916 inches, pressure ranging from 30·412 inches, at 9 a.m. of Sunday (wind, W.), to 29·176 inches, at 9 p.m. of Saturday (wind, S.). The corrected mean temperature was 45·7°. The mean dry bulb temperature at 9 a.m. and 9 p.m. was 44·4°. On Tuesday the screened thermometers rose to 53·0°; on Friday they fell to 37·4°. The rainfall was ·383 inch on five days, ·124 inch being measured on Friday, and ·240 inch on Saturday. The prevailing winds were W. and S. to S.S.E. A lunar halo was visible at 9 p.m. of Saturday.

Sunday, the 29th, was a fine mild day. The 30th was very mild, but changeable. On the 31st the heaviest rainfall of the month occurred at night, and hail fell in places in the afternoon.

In Dublin, the rainfall up to January 31, 189[illegible], amounted to 2·229 inches on 16 days, compared with a twenty-five years' (18[illegible]–18[illegible]) average of 1·[illegible] inches on 17·[illegible] days.

At Knockdolian, Greystones, Co. Wicklow, 3·[illegible] inches of rain fell on 16 days. The heaviest falls in 24 hours were ·510 inch on the 7th, and ·675 inch on the 25th.

The rainfall in January at Cloneevin, Killiney, Co. Dublin, amounted to 2·98 inches, on 10 days. The average rainfall for January at this station is 1·73 inches on 13·5 days. Both rainfall and rainy days were, therefore, considerably in excess this year. The greatest rainfall in 24 hours was ·58 of an inch on the 25th.

FEBRUARY.—The month now under review was, like February, 1892, wet, cold, stormy, and cloudy. Rain or snow fell in measurable quantity on 22 out of 28 days, and on 4 days the wind reached the force of a gale in Dublin. On the 9th, 14th, 21st, and 26th, atmospherical depressions with minima much below 29 inches were found crossing the British Islands. On the 21st and 26th the centres passed over the north of England.

In Dublin the mean temperature (41·7°) was 0·1° below the average (42·8°); the mean dry bulb readings at 9 a.m. and 9 p.m. were 41·7°. In the twenty-eight years ending with 1892, February was coldest in 1873 (M.T.=37·9°), and warmest in 1869 (M.T. = 46·7°). In 1886 the M.T. was 39·7°. In the year 1879 (the "cold year") it was 40·1°. In 1888 it was as low as 38·6°; in 1889 it was 40·2; in 1890 it was 41·3°; in 1891 it was as high as 44·7°; and in 1892 it was 41·2°.

The mean height of the barometer was 29·604 inches, or 0·251 inch below the average value for February—namely, 29·855 inches, and ·794 inch below the mean pressure in February, 1891. The mercury rose to 30·218 inches at 9 p.m. of the 4th, and fell to 28·780 inches at 7.30 a.m. of the 14th. The observed range of atmospherical pressure was, therefore, 1·438 inches—that is, a little less than an inch and a half.

The mean temperature deduced from daily readings of the dry bulb thermometer at 9 a.m. and 9 p.m. was 41·7°, or 1·6° above the value for January, 1893. Using the formula, *Mean Temp.* = *Min.* + (*max.*—*min.* × ·50), the M.T. becomes 42·7°, compared with a twenty-five years' average of 42·6°. On the 16th the thermometer in the screen rose to 56·4°—wind, S.W.; on the 25th the temperature fell to 28·0—wind, W.S.W. The minimum on the grass was 23·6°, on the 25th.

The rainfall was 2·669 inches, distributed over 22 days. The average rainfall for February in the twenty-five years, 1865–89, inclusive, was 2·150 inches, and the average number of rainy days was 17·2. The rainfall, therefore, was decidedly above the average, while the rainy days were also much above it. In 1883 the rainfall in February was large—3·752 inches on 17 days; in 1879, also, 3·706 inches fell on 23 days. On the other hand, in 1873, only ·925 of an inch was measured on but 8 days; in 1890, only ·802 of an inch fell on but 7 days; and in 1887 only ·611 of an inch fell on 11 days. The rainfall in 1887 was much the smallest record in February for very many years. But the record for 1891 is probably unparalleled—·043 inch on 2 days. The nearest approach to this drought was in September, 1865, when only ·056 of an inch of rain was measured on but 2 days. In 1892, the rainfall was 2·119 inches, on 19 days.

There was no snow, sleet, or hail in Dublin in February, 1891, but in the present month snow or sleet fell on 7 days—the 11th, 12th, 22nd, 23rd, 24th, 25th, and 26th; while hail was observed on 6 days—the 7th, 20th, 21st, 22nd, 23rd, and 25th.

The atmosphere was foggy on 3 days—namely, the 26th, 27th, and 28th. The amount of cloud—68·2 per cent.—was in excess of the average—66 per cent. High winds were noted on 11 days, reaching the force of a gale on 4 occasions—namely, the 7th, 9th, 10th, and 14th.

The temperature reached or exceeded 50° in the screen on 16 days, compared with 6 days in 1892, and as many as 16 days in 1891; while it fell to or below 32° in the screen on 5 days, compared with 5 days in 1892, and with 2 days in 1891. The minima on the grass were 32°, or less, on 16 nights, compared with 16 nights in 1892, and 17 nights in 1891. On 3 days the thermometer failed to rise to or above 40° in the screen.

Lightning was seen on the night of the 7th. There was an aurora on the night of the 18th. Solar halos were seen on the 15th and 26th, a lunar halo was seen on the evening of the 28th.

During the first four days of the month open but changeable and often rainy weather prevailed in the British Islands. At first it was mild also in France and Germany, but intense frost prevailed in the Gulf of Bothnia, whence a high pressure system with its accompanying cold spread southwards and westwards from Northern over Western Europe before the close of the period. On the night of Wednesday, the 1st, thunder and lightning occurred at Belmullet, Co. Mayo, and rain fell heavily at many Irish stations—·440 inch in Dublin and ·480 inch in the Phœnix Park. As the cold spread from the Baltic over Norway in one direction, and to Denmark, Germany, and England in another, the weather became finer and drier. In Dublin, the 3rd and 4th were quite spring-like days.

During the week ended Saturday, the 11th, open but blustering, rainy, and generally unsettled weather prevailed in Western Europe. At the beginning, no doubt, it was cold in England, very cold on the continent, owing to the presence of an anticyclone in those parts; but even at that time mild southerly winds swept over Ireland and Scotland, keeping the thermometer well above freezing point. On Sunday night the shade thermometer fell to 26° at Loughborough, 24° in London, and 21° at Cambridge. At 8 a.m. of Tuesday temperature exceeded 40° at all British Stations, and touched 50° at Valentia Island, in Kerry. A series of depressions, each deeper than its predecessor, now began to approach the N.W. of Europe from the Atlantic. They caused S.W. to W. gales of considerable violence and frequent and sometimes heavy rains. On Tuesday night severe squalls, with thunder and lightning, hail and rain, occurred over Ireland. The most serious disturbance of the week however, came in on Thursday afternoon. Its centre lay between the N.E. of Scotland and the S.W. of Norway on Friday morning—the barometer falling below 28·70 inches over that portion of the North Sea. Sleet and snow fell in Scotland, hail in Ireland, and thunder and lightning were again reported from several stations. On Saturday a general reduction of temperature took place, and cold rain and sleet fell in the afternoon. Very intense frost prevailed in the Baltic, over Finland and the North of Russia, all through this week—at Haparanda, on the Gulf of Bothnia, the 8 a.m. readings of the thermometer were + 1°, + 6°, − 1°, − 6°, − 33°, − 37°, and

–19° respectively. In Dublin the mean height of the barometer was 29·628 inches, pressure ranging between 29·928 inches at 8 a.m. of Sunday (wind, S.S.E.) and 29·340 inches at 9 p.m. of Thursday (wind, W.). The corrected mean temperature was 43·0°. The mean dry bulb temperature at 9 a.m. and 9 p.m. was 44·3°. On Monday and Tuesday the shade thermometer rose to 52·8°, falling on Saturday to 34·9°. The rainfall equalled ·762 inch on six days—·420 inch being measured on Thursday. The prevailing winds were—first, S., then W. Lightning was seen on Tuesday night, and sleet fell on Saturday.

The striking features in the meteorological conditions during the week ended Saturday, the 18th, were—first, the persistence of severe cold in the north of Europe (Scandinavia, Finland, and Northern Russia); second, the very disturbed state of the atmosphere over the North Atlantic to the west and north of the British Islands—four definite barometrical depressions of prime importance having skirted our Atlantic coasts within the period. These cyclonic systems caused, as is usual, very unsettled weather; severe gales were felt at times, rain or hail and sleet fell frequently, and the changes in temperature were sudden, fitful, and large. Sunday was cold and chiefly fine, but some local showers of sleet and hail fell. Monday was mild and changeable. At night a very deep depression approached Ireland, and at 8 a.m. of Tuesday the barometer was down to 28·63 inches at Mullaghmore, near Sligo, and to 28·79 inches even in Dublin. In the course of this day a violent S.E. gale was felt on the east coast of Scotland, while it blew hard from N.W. in Ireland, and from W. and S.W. in England. Aurora Borealis was seen on the nights of Wednesday and Thursday. On Friday afternoon a sudden rise of temperature took place. This high temperature was more than maintained on Saturday, which was spring-like in its mildness—dull, however, in England, although bright in Ireland. In Dublin the mean atmospherical pressure was only 29·324 inches, the barometer ranging from 29·848 inches at 9 p.m. of Sunday (wind, W.) to 28·780 inches at 7.10 a.m. of Tuesday (wind, W.). The mean temperature was 44·0°—highest, 56·4° on Saturday; lowest, 34·1° on Sunday. The mean dry bulb readings at 8 a.m. and 9 p.m. were 43·4°. Rain fell on five days, but only to the amount of ·257 inch, of which more than one-half (·143 inch) fell on Wednesday. The prevailing winds were W. and S.S.W.

Winter reasserted its sway in the British Islands in the course of the week ended Saturday, the 25th, which began with mild, spring-like weather, and closed with frost and a snow-covered country. The most striking feature in the meteorological record for the period was the passage across the south of England in an east-north-easterly direction of a deep atmospherical depression in the interval between Monday night and Wednesday morning. In the South-east of England the barometer fell below 28·7 inches—to 28·65 inches at the mouth of the Thames—on Tuesday afternoon. The winds accompanying this system were not strong, but large quantities of rain, hail, and sleet fell in most districts. This inclement weather was all the more felt, as Sunday—while dull and rainy, though mild in Ireland—had been a spring-like day in most parts of England, except the S.W. Bright sunshine was enjoyed for many hours, and the thermometer rose to 58° and even 60° (at Loughborough) in the shade all over the central and south-eastern counties. During the following night temperature gave way quickly and never recovered itself during the remainder of the week, except in the S. of England for a few hours in front of the deep depression already referred to. In Dublin hail, or sleet and snow, fell daily on and after Monday; and on Saturday evening there was a considerable fall of unusually light and powdery crystalline snow at a temperature varying from 27° to 31°. On the night of Saturday a violent snowstorm occurred, followed by rain. The weather was extremely cloudy and dull, except on Monday, Friday, and Saturday. In Dublin the mean height of the barometer was only 29·313 inches. Atmospherical pressure ranged between 29·657 inches at 9 a.m. of Sunday (wind S.), and 28·916 inches at 7.30 a.m. of Tuesday (wind, N.N.E.). The mean temperature was 39·2°. The mean dry bulb temperature at 8 a.m. and 9 p.m. was 38·1°. On Sunday the thermometers in the screen rose to 52·6°. On Saturday they fell to 28·0°. The rainfall (which largely consisted of hail, snow, and sleet) measured ·893 inch, ·390 inch being referred to Wednesday. The prevailing winds were S.S.E. and E.

The last three days of the month were cold, changeable, but for the most part dry. There were sharp night frosts, and a solar halo was seen on the afternoon of the 28th, followed by a lunar halo at 8 p.m.

In Dublin, the rainfall up to February 28, 1893, amounted to 4·606 inches on 41 days, compared with 6·617 inches on 39 days in the same period in 1892, ·714 inch on 16 days in 1891, and a twenty-five years' (1865–1889) average of 4·330 inches on 34·6 days.

At Knockdolian, Greystones, Co. Wicklow, 3·650 inches of rain fell in February on 25 days; and 3·620 inches in January on 18 days. The total fall to February 28th inclusive was 7·270 inches on 43 days.

The rainfall in February at Cloneevin, Killiney, Co. Dublin, amounted to 3·60 inches on 22 days. The average rainfall for February at this station is 1·543 inches, on 11·6 days. Both rainfall and rainy days were, therefore, considerably in excess this year—in fact it was a very wet month. The greatest rainfall in 24 hours was ·48 of an inch on the 1st. Since January 1, the rainfall was 5·49 inches, on 42 days.

MARCH.—A singularly dry, warm, sunny month—more like May than March. It broke the record as regards height of temperature, deficiency of rainfall, and clearness of the sky and bright sunshine. The arithmetical mean temperature was 5·0° above the average for the month and no less than 9·0° above that of March, 1892 (39·1°). It was even 0·8 above the mean temperature of March, 1868 (47·2°), which had proved the warmest March since these records began in 1865 up to the present year. The deficiency in the rainfall was equally striking, the only comparable year for drought in March being 1871, when, however, ·615 inch of rain fell on 12 days against ·298 inch on 6 days in 1893. Not one-half of the sky was on the average covered with clouds, and the air was often very dry; consequently, the diurnal range of temperature was large—hot sunshine by day being followed by sharp nights. This was markedly the case in central England, where on more than one occasion during the latter half of the month the thermometer in the shade traversed more than 40° within a few hours.

In Dublin the arithmetical mean temperature (46·1°) was considerably above the average (42·1°); the mean dry bulb readings at 9 a.m. and 9 p.m. were 45·5°. In the twenty-eight years ending with 1892, March was coldest in 1867 and 1883 (M. T. = 39·0°), and warmest in 1868 (M. T. = 47·3°). In 1878 the M. T. was 41·1°, in 1879 (the "cold year") it was 42·5°, in 1888 it was as low as 39·6°, in 1889 it was 44·0°, and in 1890 it was as high as 45·1°. In 1891, it was only 41·7°; and in 1892 it was as low as 39·1°. As a general rule, February in Dublin is only a shade colder than March. This is due to the fact that the Continental anticyclone usually embraces the British Isles and Scandinavia in March, causing easterly winds. In 1882 February was actually 2·4° warmer than March, but in the present year March was 5·5° warmer than February.

The mean height of the barometer was 30·085 inches, or 0·169 inch above the corrected average value for March—namely, 29·916 inches. The mercury rose to 30·411 inches at 9 a.m. of the 19th, having fallen to 29·267 inches at 9 a.m. of the 1st. The observed range of atmospherical pressure was, therefore, 1·144 inches—that is, more than an inch and one-tenth.

The mean temperature deduced from daily readings of the dry bulb thermometer at 9 a.m. and 9 p.m. was 45·5°, or 4·8° above the value for February, 1893. Using the formula, *Mean Temp.* = *min.* + (*max.*—*min.* × ·465), the M.T. becomes 47·0°. The arithmetical mean of the maximal and minimal readings was 46·1°, compared with a twenty-five years' average of 42·1°. On the 29th the thermometer in the screen rose to 64·8°—wind, W.S.W.; on the 17th the temperature fell to 34·0°—wind, W.N.W. The minimum on the grass was 29·0° on the 17th, and also on the 31st.

The rainfall was only ·238 inch, distributed over 8 days. The average rainfall for March in the twenty-five years, 1865–89, inclusive, was 2·081 inches, and the average number of rainy days was 16·8. The rainfall, therefore, was much below the average, while the rainy days were also much below it. In 1867 the rainfall in March was very large—4·972 inches on 22 days; in 1888, 3·753 inches fell on 18 days; in 1866, also, 3·629 inches fell on 21 days. On the other hand, in 1871, only ·815 of an inch was measured on 13 days, and in 1876 only ·953 of an inch fell on 13 days. In 1887 (the "dry year"), 1·485 inches of rain fell on 15 days; in 1889, 1·076 inches fell on, however, as many as 17 days; in 1890 the fall was as much as 2·533 inches on 17 days; but in 1891 only ·938 of an inch fell on 18 days, and in 1892 only ·931 of an inch on but 8 days.

The atmosphere was thick with dry smoke fog in the city on 8 days, viz., the 2nd, 3rd, 13th, 19th, 20th, 24th, 25th, and 27th. High winds were noted on 11 days, reaching the force of a gale, however, on only one occasion, the 1st. Snow or sleet occurred on the 16th and 17th; and hail fell on the 1st and 16th. The temperature exceeded 50° in the screen on as many as 22 days, compared with only 7 days in 1892, 9 days in 1891, and 19 days in 1890; while it never fell to 32° in the screen, whereas in March, 1892, frost occurred in the shade on as many as 16 nights. The minima on the grass were 32°, or less, on 13 nights, compared with 25 nights in 1892, 20 nights in 1891, and 16 nights in 1890. On 4 days the thermometer rose above 60° in the screen, while it never failed to reach 40°. In March, 1892, the thermometer did not rise to 40° in the screen on 9 days.

The first four days of the month were warm and changeable, with frequent rain or showers and variable, chiefly westerly, winds. As compared with the closing days of February a marked increase of atmospherical pressure occurred after Wednesday, the 1st. On that day a depression passed by the North of Ireland across Scotland towards Denmark. Temperature rose fast, and a considerable rainfall was reported from most British stations. A ridge of high pressure followed this disturbance, but on Friday, the 3rd, a shallower depression in the N., with a "secondary" in the S. again threw the weather into a cloudy, showery condition. Saturday, the 4th, however, proved fine and for the most part bright in Ireland. On the 3rd the thermometer rose to 56·7° in the screen in Dublin.

Singularly favourable and mild weather for the time of year held over the British Islands throughout the week ended Saturday the 11th. The rainfall also was but slight except at some exposed stations in the N.W. of Ireland and N. of Scotland. In Scandinavia, however, conditions were far otherwise—severe cold and excessive gales and snow-storms being experienced. This state of things was brought about by the persistence of an anticyclone, in which at one time (Friday morning) the barometer touched 30·60 inches off the S.W. and S. of Ireland; while a series of atmospherical depressions of ever increasing intensity swept eastwards across Northern Europe. Of these disturbances the most serious was observed on Friday, at 8 a.m. of which day the barometer was down to 28·78 inches at Hernösand in Sweden as compared with the reading 30·60 inches recorded at the same time at Valentia Island, in Kerry. Fresh to strong westerly to north-westerly winds prevailed generally in the United Kingdom. At first the sky was very cloudy, but towards the close of the week the clouds dispersed and the air became very dry, so that the diurnal range of temperature was large—at Cambridge, on Wednesday, the maximum was 65°, the minimum was 37°. In Dublin the mean height of the barometer was 30·287 inches, pressure ranging between 30·402 inches at 9 p.m. of Wednesday (wind W.) and 29·996 inches at 9 p.m. of Saturday (wind S.W.). The corrected mean temperature was 48·4°. The mean dry bulb readings at 9 a.m. and 9 p.m. were 46·9°. On Sunday and again on Tuesday the thermometer rose to 56·8° in the screen; on Friday it fell to 37·0° in the screen, and 31·4° on the grass. The rainfall was ·034 inch on one day—Monday. The prevalent winds were westerly and north-westerly.

The most striking feature in the meteorology of the week ended Saturday, the 18th, was the continued depression of the barometer over the Norwegian Sea and the North of Europe generally. At first temperature was high for the time of year in all parts of the British Islands; but in England the diurnal range was extremely large—amounting to 30° or upwards between Sunday afternoon and Monday morning—at Loughborough the extreme thermometer readings at 8 a.m. of Monday were: Max. 65°, Min. 32°, range 33°. As the disturbances in the far North drew after them subsidiary depressions across the United Kingdom, temperature gave way and the weather fell into an unsettled, showery, squally condition. On both Thursday and Friday hail, sleet, and snow

B

occurred in many parts, and electrical phenomena were observed along a track extending from the N. of Ireland across the S. of Scotland to the mouth of the Elbe. On Tuesday night bright aurora borealis had been seen in Scotland and the S. of Ireland. At 8 a.m. of Thursday the barometer stood as low as 28·34 inches at Christiansund on the W. coast of Norway, while it read 30·06 inches at Nice. Needless to say that strong S.W. to N.W. winds and gales swept over Western Europe. In Dublin the mean height of the barometer was 29·643 inches, pressure being observed to range from 29·075 inches at 7.15 a.m. of Thursday (wind, W.N.W.) to 30·230 inches at 9 p.m. of Saturday (wind, E.S.E.). The corrected mean temperature was 44·6°. The mean dry bulb readings at 9 a.m. and 9 p.m. were 43·6°. On Sunday the screened thermometers rose to 55·9°, on Friday they fell to 34·0°. The rainfall measured ·118 inch on four days. The heaviest rainfall in 24 hours was ·066 inch on Saturday. Snow or sleet fell on Thursday and Friday; hail on Thursday. There was a slight fog on Monday night.

Many years have passed since a spell of more beautiful weather than that enjoyed during the week ended Saturday, the 25th, has been recorded in March. After Sunday, which was a cloudy day, very little cloud appeared by day or night, and warm sunny days were followed by calm, sharp nights. Throughout the week, conditions were anticyclonic in Western Europe. The centre of highest atmospherical pressure was generally found over the south of England, France, Belgium, and Holland, and in these regions, under the combined influence of a clear sky and dry air, the diurnal range of temperature was almost phenomenal. For example, at Loughborough, in Leicestershire, on Monday night the screened thermometer sank to 23°, while it rose to 65° in the course of Tuesday—a range of 42° in a few hours. A similar excessive range was observed on Saturday at the same station. In Ireland the extremes of temperature were of the same character, though much less marked. At the very beginning of the week severe frost occurred in Great Britain, the minima in the screen on Sunday being 25° at Leith, Shields, and Dungeness; 23° at York, and in London; 24° at Nairn; 22° at Oxford, and Cambridge; and 20° at Loughborough. The morning of this day in Ireland broke dull and damp, but the weather improved as the day wore on. In Dublin light easterly sea breezes by day alternated with calms by night. The mean height of the barometer was 30·318 inches, pressure ranging from 30·411 inches at 9 a.m. of Sunday (wind, E.S.E.) to 30·185 inches at 9 a.m. of Thursday (wind, calm), and again rising to 30·409 inches at 9 a.m. of Saturday (wind, E.). The corrected mean temperature was 48·2°. The mean dry bulb readings at 9 a.m. and 9 p.m. were 46·2°. On Thursday, the screened thermometers rose to 61·9°; on Tuesday, they fell to 35·3°. There was no measurable rainfall after 9 a.m. of Sunday. Bright sunshine was unusually prevalent and greatly exceeded the mean during this week. At the Ordnance Survey Office, Phœnix Park, the sun shone brightly for 64·3 hours, being 76 per cent. of the possible duration of sunshine. In Guernsey the percentage was 90, in Jersey it was 91. These values in the Channel Islands are higher than any hitherto obtained during any period since the sunshine recorders were established in 1881. In nearly all British and Irish districts the percentages of bright sunshine recorded this week are far higher than any previously observed in the month of March.

The weather was by no means so settled during the closing period (26th–31st inclusive) as it had been during the preceding week. Clouds increased at times, and both atmospherical pressure and temperature became unsteady. Rainfall however, was again markedly deficient in all parts of the United Kingdom, although in parts of Spain, Portugal, and the extreme south of France there were some heavy downpours—for example, ·67 inch fell at Lisbon on Tuesday, the 28th, and 1·50 inches at Perpignan on Wednesday, the 29th. Until this last-named day an anticyclone stretched northwestwards across the North Sea, while pressure was low and conditions were cyclonic over the Iberian Peninsula. Light to moderate easterly winds prevailed in the British Islands. The first two days of the period were cool and at times cloudy in Dublin. Tuesday proved brilliant, and on Wednesday (with the displacement of the easterly wind by a S.W. and W. current) the thermometer rose in this city to 64·6°. Thursday was cooler. On Good Friday, the 31st, a depression came in from the Atlantic causing squally S.W. winds and a slight rainfall in the evening. The diurnal range of temperature was again excessive at some inland English stations—thus on Tuesday, the thermometer fell from 67° to 25° at Cambridge and from 64° to 24° at Loughborough. In Dublin the barometer ranged from 30·299 inches at 9 a.m. of Sunday (wind, N.E.) to 29·924 inches at 3 p.m. of Friday (wind, S.W.). On Monday the screened thermometers fell to 37·0°, on Wednesday they rose to 64·6. Rain fell on Friday to the amount of ·022 inch only.

The rainfall in Dublin during the three months ending March 31st has amounted to 6·106 inches on 49 days, compared with 4·806 inches on 48 days in 1892, only 1·650 inches on but 32 days in 1891, 7·970 inches on 45 days in 1890, 5·728 inches on 53 days in 1889, 6·097 inches on 41 days in 1888, and a twenty-five years' average of 6·411 inches on 51·0 days (1866–1890, inclusive).

At Knockdolian, Greystones, Co. Wicklow, only ·305 inch of rain fell on 6 days during March; and the total rainfall since January 1, 1893, equals 7·878 inches on 49 days. The corresponding figures for 1892 are ·986 inch on 9 days, the total rainfall since January 1 being 4·203 inches on 40 days.

The rainfall in March at Clonsevin, Killiney, Co. Dublin, was ·26 inch on 9 days, as against ·98 inch on 10 days in 1892, and an eight years' average of 1·90 inches on 14·6 days. The maximum in the 8 years was 3·69 inches in 1888, the minimum was ·74 inch in 1891.

APRIL.—April proved a fitting sequel to the record-breaking March of 1893. Like its predecessor, the month was characterised by drought, bright sunshine, and a high temperature. The mean amount of cloud was only 40 per cent., falling at 9 p.m. to 33·3 per cent. So powerful was the heating power of the sun by day that, notwithstanding free radiation by night, the thermometer did not fall below 36·[illegible]° in the screen, and 3[illegible]° on the grass in the city of Dublin. The drought was happily interrupted in Ireland by copious falls of rain on the 16th and 17th, and again on the 29th and 30th.

In the matter of temperature, however, April 1893 breaks the record, the mean being 3·7° above average, and also 1·0° above the mean of the Aprils of 1865 and 1874, which had been the warmest since the present records began up to 1893. Unwonted drought held throughout the month in south-eastern England, the rainfall in London, for example, being only one-tenth of an inch on only 4 days.

In Dublin the arithmetical mean temperature (51·4°) was 3·7° above the average (47·7°); the mean dry bulb readings at 9 a.m. and 9 p.m. were 50·3°. In the twenty-eight years ending with 1893, April was coldest in 1879 (the cold year), (M. T. = 44·5°), and warmest in 1865 and 1874 (M. T. = 50·4°). In 1886, the M. T. was 46·5°, in 1887 it was as low as 45·1°, in 1888 it was (as also in 1891) only 45·7°, in 1889, 45·1°, in 1890, 47·5°; and in 1892, 46·[illegible]°. The month now under discussion thus proves to have been the warmest April for at least 30 years.

The mean height of the barometer was 30·171 inches, or 0·231 inch above the average value for April—namely, 29·850 inches. The mercury was as high as 30·575 inches at 9 a.m. of the 8th, and fell to 29·793 inches at 4 p.m. of the 19th. The observed range of atmospherical pressure was, therefore, 0·782 inch—that is, a little more than three-quarters of an inch.

The mean temperature deduced from daily readings of the dry bulb thermometer at 9 a.m. and 9 p.m. was 50·3°, or 6·6° above the value for March, 1893. Using the formula, *Mean Temp.* = *min.* + (*max.* — *min.* × ·476), the value becomes 51·1°, or 3·7° above the average mean temperature for April, calculated in the same way, in the twenty-five years, 1865–89, inclusive (47·4°). The arithmetical mean of the maximal and minimal readings was 51·4°, compared with a twenty-five years' (1865–1889 inclusive) average of 47·7°. On the 22nd, the thermometer in the screen rose to 68·6°—wind, S.E.; on the 14th the temperature fell to 36·2°—wind, W.S.W. The minimum on the grass was 29·[illegible]°, also on the 14th.

The rainfall was only 1·046 inches, distributed over 7 days. The average rainfall for April in the twenty-five years, 1865–89, inclusive, was 2·055 inches, and the average number of rainy days was 16·2. The rainfall, therefore, was considerably below the average, while the rainy days were also very deficient. In 1877 the rainfall in April was very large—4·707 inches on 21 days; in 1882 also 3·526 inches fell on 20 days. On the other hand, in 1873, only ·466 of an inch was measured on 8 days; and in 1870 only ·638 of an inch fell, also on 8 days. The fall in 1890 was 1·475 inches on 14 days, in 1891, 1·853 inches fell on 16 days, and in 1892, 1·114 inches on 12 days.

There was a lunar halo on the 22nd. The atmosphere was more or less foggy on the 8th and 17th. High winds were noted on only 4 days, and did not reach the force of a gale on any occasion. No snow or sleet was seen, but hail fell on the 29th. The temperature exceeded 50° in the screen on every day compared with only 25 days in April, 1892, and 18 days in April, 1891. It rose above 60° on 11 days, but never fell to 32° in the screen. The minimum on the grass was 32°, or less, on 6 nights, compared with 13 nights in March, 18 in February, and 16 in January. The mean lowest temperature on the grass was 39·2°, compared with 38·4° in 1892, 34·1° in 1891 and 1890, 34·4° in 1888, 34·6° in 1886, and 31·6° in 1887.

The first day of the month was cloudy and cool, but dry.

The drought, which set in at the beginning of March, continued through the week ended Saturday, the 8th. Temperature showed a decided tendency to fall, particularly on the eastern coasts of both Ireland and Great Britain, in which parts much sea-fog was prevalent. At the beginning of the week an anticyclone lay over Ireland and England, while an extensive and deep depression, with central barometrical readings below 29·30 inches, swept eastwards across the extreme North of Europe. Beautiful, bright weather prevailed, except in the far north, where clouds gathered and rain fell. Shallow depressions formed over the S.W. of Europe on and after Tuesday, so that a decided easterly air-current set in and fogs and low temperatures prevailed on the east coasts of the British Isles, while bright sunshine and warmth held inland. The most striking example of these conditions was presented on Thursday, when the thermometer rose to 63° at Loughborough, Oxford, and Cambridge—all inland stations, whereas the maximum was only 44° at Yarmouth and 46° at Spurn Head. On Friday the maximum was 68° in London, but only 47° at Shields and Spurn Head. After Thursday a new and much larger anticyclone formed in the N.W. and N., causing N.E. winds, clouds, and low temperatures on Friday and Saturday. In Dublin the mean pressure was 30·303 inches, the barometer falling to 30·051 inches at 4·30 p.m. of Wednesday (wind, S.), and rising to 30·575 inches, at 9 a.m. of Saturday (wind, N.E.). The corrected mean temperature was 49·6°. The mean dry bulb readings at 9 a.m. and 9 p.m. were 48·0°. On Sunday the screened thermometers fell to 36·6°, on Wednesday they rose to 61·4°. A very slight shower fell at 6 p.m. of Thursday, but yielded no measurable rainfall. The prevailing wind was easterly.

With the exception of a general decrease of temperature, the weather of the week ended Saturday, the 15th, resembled that of its immediate predecessors, being singularly fine, dry, and quiet. Anticyclonic areas were found lying over one or another portion of the British Islands on every day of the week. At the same time shallow atmospherical depressions lay over southern Europe and the Mediterranean Basin, producing easterly winds and lower temperature in England and Ireland; while deeper cyclonic systems passed eastwards or south-eastwards across northern Europe, where frost and snow resumed their sway as the week advanced. Towards the close of the period the anticyclone began to move southwards, its centre on Thursday lying over the South of Scotland, on Friday over the midland counties of England, and on Saturday over the east of France. Sharp night frosts were felt at many stations during the week—the sharpest of all occurred on Thursday night, when the thermometer fell to 24° in the screen at Loughborough and Cambridge, and to

57° at Oxford. In Dublin, Sunday, Tuesday, and Thursday were rather cloudy and very cool. Wednesday, also, was cold, but the air was dry and bright sunshine prevailed. In this city the mean height of the barometer was 30·231 inches, pressure ranging from 30·479 inches at 9 a.m. of Wednesday (wind, E.N.E.), to 30·183 inches at 9 p.m. of Saturday (wind, W. by S.). The corrected mean temperature was 47·6°. The mean dry bulb temperature at 9 a.m. and 9 p.m. was 47·6°. On Friday, the screened thermometers fell to 36·8°, on Saturday they rose to 60·6°. There was no rainfall until the early morning of Sunday, the 16th, when two-thousandths of an inch (·002) fell. The prevailing winds were, at first, E.N.E., afterwards W. and W.S.W.

While the general character of the weather during the week ended Saturday, the 22nd, was favourable, conditions were less stable than of late, and at the beginning of the week a grateful and copious rainfall in Ireland and Scotland gave a marvellous impetus to vegetation. On Sunday morning a shallow depression was found off the N.W. of Ireland, and a much deeper depression—with central readings of the barometer as low as 28·75 inches at Haparanda on the Gulf of Bothnia—was travelling eastwards across Lapland. In the course of the day rain fell in abundance at many Irish and several British stations, the downpour being renewed on Monday evening. At this time a well-defined anticyclone lay over the North Sea, influencing the English stations and causing fine and cooler weather. On Thursday morning the distribution of atmospherical pressure was very irregular, and several local and shallow depressions caused thunder showers in parts of Great Britain. Temperature had previously risen to an unusual height for the time of year at inland stations—to 68° at Parsonstown, 75° at Holyhead, 73° in London and at Oxford, 76° at Loughborough, and 78° at Cambridge on Wednesday. In Dublin the maximum next day (Thursday) was 66·6°, but in London it was 83° and at Cambridge 81°. Friday was very fine, but at night thunderstorms occurred at Roche's Point and Scilly. Saturday proved very warm but changeable in Ireland. In Dublin the mean height of the barometer was 30·014 inches, pressure varying between 30·161 inches at 9 p.m. of Thursday (wind, N.) and 29·793 inches at 4 p.m. of Wednesday (wind, E.S.E.). The corrected mean temperature was 53·3°. The mean dry bulb readings at 9 a.m. and 9 p.m. were 54·5°. On Friday the minimal temperature was 46·0°, on Saturday the maximum was 68·8°. Rain fell on five days to the total amount of ·762 inch, ·370 inch being measured on Monday. The prevalent winds were first S.W., afterwards E.S.E.

The record is once more one of most favourable weather during the week ended Saturday, the 29th. Bright, sunny, warm days were followed by quiet, clear, cool nights until Saturday, when copious showers fell at intervals, refreshing the face of nature and aiding vegetation. Areas of relatively high atmospherical pressure (anti-cyclonic systems) were found lying over the greater part of the British Islands until Saturday, when an extensive and definite depression travelled eastwards across the northern half of the United Kingdom, causing squally W. to N.W. winds and the grateful showers already mentioned. Throughout the week the barometer was comparatively low over the Iberian Peninsula, the Bay of Biscay, and France. Except at Lisbon, however, where 3·46 inches of rain fell on five days up to Friday morning, the weather was at first generally dry within the area of low pressure. On Thursday there was a downpour all over the south of France, ·83 inch being measured at Nice, ·87 inch at Biarritz, and 1·24 inches at Perpignan on Friday morning. Thunderstorms occurred at Prawle Point during the night of the 22nd–23rd, and at Holyhead on Monday night. In Dublin the mean height of the barometer was 30·087 inches, pressure varying from 30·127 inches at 9 a.m. of Monday (wind, N.) to 29·847 inches at 3 p.m. of Saturday (wind, W.S.W.). The corrected mean temperature was 52·6°. The mean dry bulb readings at 9 a.m. and 9 p.m. were 52·5°. On Tuesday temperature rose to 65·7° in the shade; on Saturday it fell to 43·0°. Rain and hail fell on Saturday in heavy showers to the amount of ·158 inch. The prevailing winds were N. and N.W.

Sunday, the 30th, was changeable, but favourable.

The rainfall in Dublin during the four months ending April 30th amounted to 6·363 inches on 35 days, compared with 3·923 inches on 47 days during the same period in 1892, only 2·252 inches on 46 days in 1891, 9·043 inches on 53 days in 1890, 8·341 inches on 74 days in 1889, 6·050 inches on 48 days in 1888, and a twenty-five years' average of 8·486 inches on 66·1 days.

At Ballinacor, Greystones, Co. Wicklow, the rainfall during April, 1893, amounted to only 1·653 inches, distributed over only 5 days—·730 inch falling on the 16th. The total fall since January 1st, 1893, equalled 6·630 inches on 34 days.

The rainfall in April at Cloneevin, Killiney, Co. Dublin, was 1·15 inches on 6 days, as against an eight years' average of 1·46 inches on 13·6 days. The maximal fall in 24 hours was ·63 inch on the 16th.

May.—Like March and April of the present year, this month was singularly fine—warm and for the most part dry. Unlike March and April, however, the amount of cloud was considerable—61·8 per cent. compared with only 49·1 per cent. in March, and only 40·0 per cent. in April. Nor was the drought at all so severe as in the two previous months. In Dublin rain fell abundantly at the beginning and in the middle of the month, the total fall being 1·930 inches, against only ·829 inch in March and 1·040 inches in April. As regards temperature, this was a "record month," the mean being 0·9° above that for May, 1868—namely, 56·7° against 55·8°.

In Dublin the arithmetical mean temperature (56·7°) was decidedly above the average (52·0°); the mean dry bulb readings at 9 a.m. and 9 p.m. were 55·3°. In the twenty-eight years ending with 1892, May was coldest in 1869 (M. T. = 46·3°), in 1885 (M. T. = 48·7°), and in 1879 (the "cold year") (M. T. = 49·8°). It was warmest in 1868 (the "warm year") (M. T. = 55·8°), and 1875 (M. T. = 54·9°). In 1886 the M. T. was 50·5°; in 1887, 51·3°; in 1888, 53·5°; in 1889, 54·6°; in 1890, 53·2°; in 1891, only 49·6°; and in 1892, 53·6°.

The mean height of the barometer was 30·038 inches, or 0·049 inch above the corrected average value for May—namely, 29·959 inches. The mercury rose to 30·453 inches at 9 a.m. of the 10th, and fell to 29·407 inches at 4 p.m. of the 19th. The observed range of atmospherical pressure was, therefore, 1·046 inches.

The mean temperature deduced from daily readings of the dry bulb thermometer at 9 a.m. and 9 p.m. was 55·3°, or 5·0° above the value for April, 1892. Using the formula, *Mean Temp.* = *Min.* + (*max.*—*min.* × ·47), the value was 56·8°, or 3·7° above the average mean temperature for May, calculated in the same way, in the twenty-five years, 1865–89, inclusive (51·6°). The arithmetical mean of the maximal and minimal readings was 56·7°, compared with a twenty-five years' average of 52·0°. On the 11th the thermometer in the screen rose to 70·9°—wind, W.N.W.; on the 31st the temperature fell to 42·8°—wind, N.N.E. The minimum on the grass was 39·6°, also on the 31st.

The rainfall amounted to 1·668 inches, distributed over 10 days. The average rainfall for May in the twenty-five years, 1865–89, inclusive, was 2·030 inches, and the average number of rainy days was 15·6. The rainfall and the rainy days, therefore, were much below the average. In 1868 the rainfall in May was very large—5·473 inches on 21 days; in 1869 also 5·414 inches fell on 19 days. On the other hand, in 1871, only ·378 of an inch was measured on 9 days; in 1876 only ·798 of an inch fell on 6 days; in 1887 only ·683 of an inch on 10 days; and in 1884 only ·074 of an inch on 11 days. In 1890, 2·438 inches fell on 17 days. In 1891 May was the first month in which the rainfall exceeded the average. It amounted to 2·792 inches on 17 days. In 1883 the large amount of 4·177 inches fell on 19 days.

Solar halos were seen on the 8th and 10th. High winds were noted on only 4 days, never attaining the force of a gale. Thunder was heard on the 15th, 20th, and 25th. No hail, sleet, or snow fell.

During the month the thermometer did not fall below 32°, either in the screen or on the grass. The mean minimal temperature on the grass was 43·5°, compared with 41·9° in May, 1892, 37·7° in 1891, 43·8° in 1890, 43·4° in 1889, 37·3° in 1888, and 37·9° in 1887.

During the period ended Saturday, the 6th, the weather was most favourable. Rain fell in copious showers on Monday and Tuesday, the 1st and 2nd, after which came a succession of fine, dry days, with intervals of hot sunshine. On Sunday, April 30th, a "hollow" of low atmospherical pressure stretched south-eastwards from Iceland to Denmark, so that N.W. winds, low temperatures, and changeable showery weather were experienced in the British Islands. During the next two days the barometer was unsteady, especially over Ireland and Scotland, in which countries rain fell pretty freely. In the South of England and the neighbourhood of London, however, the drought continued almost uninterruptedly. On Thursday a large anticyclone began to form over Norway, the North Sea, and Great Britain, and the weather became once more fine, brighter, and warmer. Over Ireland much cirriform cloud was at this time daily observed travelling in an upper air-current from S.W., while the surface wind was S.E. or E. In Dublin the air-pressure ranged from 29·773 inches, at 4 p.m. of Tuesday (wind, S.W.) to 30·254 inches at 9 a.m. of Saturday (wind, E.S.E.). On Monday the shade minimum was 46·1°, on Friday the shade maximum was 69·7°. Rain fell on the first two days to the amount of ·403 inch, ·352 inch being measured on Monday, the 1st. The prevalent winds were first westerly, then east-south easterly. A solar halo was seen on Saturday forenoon.

The weather was exceedingly fine and dry throughout the week ended Saturday, the 13th—at least in England and Ireland—in Scotland refreshing rains fell on Wednesday and the two following days. At the beginning of the period a vast anticyclone stretched south-westwards from Sweden, where the barometer stood above 30·9 inches (30·95 inches at Hernösand at 8 a.m. of Sunday), across the North Sea to the British Isles. The wind was rather squally from E. and S.E. and temperature was low—night frosts occurring in parts of England as well as on the Continent. By Wednesday a great change was in progress—the barometer was falling in the N. and rising in the S., while a tongue of high pressure still stretched across England and Ireland. The change was attended by a copious rainfall in many parts of France on Tuesday; and was followed by the setting in of westerly winds over the northern half of the British Isles, where also clouds increased and rain fell as above mentioned. After a sharp night on Wednesday, temperature rose considerably in England on Thursday, when also the thermometer exceeded 70° in the shade in Dublin for the first time this season. Friday was at first cloudy, but afterwards fair; and Saturday proved a brilliant summerlike day. In Dublin the mean height of the barometer was 30·317 inches, pressure ranging from 30·453 inches at 9 a.m. of Wednesday (wind, E.N.E.) to 30·070 inches at 9 p.m. of Saturday (wind, calm). The corrected mean temperature was 53·9°. The mean dry bulb readings at 9 a.m. and 9 p.m. were 53·5°. On Thursday the thermometer rose to 70·9° in the shade, having fallen to 47·1° on Wednesday. There was no rainfall. The prevailing winds were E. and W.N.W.

The week ended Saturday, the 20th, may be said to have witnessed the break-up of the drought, which—with slight and transitory interruptions—had held in Western Europe since the end of February. At the beginning the barometer was falling over England, Ireland, and the West of France, as a large, but not deep, depression formed over the Bay of Biscay and the Atlantic off our S.W. coasts. On Sunday the weather remained dry in most places, but much lofty cirriform stratus cloud came up from the southward, causing the sky to assume an unsettled, thundery appearance. On Monday thunder storms occurred in the West of England and in Wales, and from that time onwards to the close of the week thunder and lightning were daily reported from one part or another of the British Islands. Some very heavy rainfalls occurred—for example, 1·03 inches at Roche's Point on Tuesday, 1·60 inches at Loughborough on Wednesday, ·71 inch at Parsonstown on Friday, and ·73 inch in the City of Dublin on Saturday. On this day 1·[illegible] inches of rain fell at the Ordnance Survey Office, Phoenix Park, and 1·030 inches at the Botanic Gardens, Glasnevin. As temperature remained fairly high throughout, the beneficial effects of the rainfall on vegetation became instantly apparent. In Dublin the mean height of the barometer was 29·834 inches, or as much as ·[illegible] inch below the mean for the preceding week. The barometer read 30·010 inches at 9 a.m. of Sunday (wind, E.S.E.), and fell to 29·407 inches at 4 p.m. of Friday (wind, E.S.E.). The corrected mean temperature was 57·1°. The mean dry bulb temperature at 9 a.m. and 9 p.m. was 55·4°. On Sunday the screened thermometers rose to 68·7°, on Saturday they fell to 46·2°. Distant thunder was heard on Monday and Saturday. Rain fell on three days to the amount of ·947 inch, ·780 inch being measured on Saturday. The prevailing winds were E. and S.E.

Changeable, but favourable weather prevailed during the week ended Saturday, the 27th. At first showery, it afterwards became dry and fine, although the amount of cloud remained considerable to the end. The period began with a high pressure system lying over the Baltic and Scandinavia, and depressions to the westward and northwestward of the British Islands. As the week advanced these conditions became reversed—the depressions travelled northeastward, and a new area of high pressure (anticyclone) came in over Ireland from the Atlantic. At the close of the period a low pressure system was found over the Baltic and Sweden, while the anticyclone remained almost stationary over, and off the west coast of Ireland. In Dublin Sunday forenoon was rainy; light showers fell in the afternoon, but the evening proved fair. Monday was cloudy but fine. Tuesday was cloudy, showery, and squally. Some rain fell on Wednesday morning, after which the weather remained chiefly dry, but very cloudy to the close of the week. The mean height of the barometer in Dublin was 30·016 inches, pressure ranging from 29·543 inches at 9 a.m. of Sunday (wind, W.) to 30·287 inches at 9 p.m. of Friday (wind, N.N.W.). The corrected mean temperature was 56·6°. The mean dry bulb temperature at 9 a.m. and 9 p.m. was 55·7°. On Sunday the screened thermometers fell to 46·9°; on Saturday they rose to 64·8°. Rain was measured on four days, the total amount being ·137 inch, of which ·059 inch fell on Sunday. The prevalent wind was first westerly, then northerly.

During the last four days the weather, which was chiefly fine but changeable, was governed by a depression over the south of Sweden and an anticyclone to the westward of Scotland. North-easterly winds prevailed, and a tendency to electrical disturbances existed on Sunday and Monday, the 28th and 29th. On the afternoon of the latter day thunder and heavy rain occurred in both London and Dublin. The weather on the 30th and 31st was bright and bracing—hot sunshine and a cold N.E. wind asserting themselves with alternate power.

The rainfall in Dublin during the five months ending May 31st amounted to 7·908 inches on 66 days, compared with 19·099 inches on 80 days in 1892, only 5·996 inches on 63 days in 1891, 11·469 inches on 78 days in 1890, 10·476 inches on 91 days in 1889, 9·043 inches on 69 days in 1888, 6·459 inches on 63 days in 1887, and a 25 years' average of 10·496 inches on 81·6 days.

It may be remembered that on Saturday, May 28th, 1892, 3·056 inches of rain were measured at this station, 1·900 inches having fallen within 6 hours, or at the rate of 7·6 inches in 24 hours. No such measurement had been recorded in Dublin since October 27, 1880, when 2·736 inches of rain fell. May 28, 1892, was only the third occasion within the past twenty-eight years on which the rainfall exceeded 2 inches within 24 hours in Dublin.

At Knockdolian, Greystones, Co. Wicklow, the rainfall in May, 1893, was 1·036 inches, distributed over 11 days. Of this quantity ·310 inch fell on the 18th, and ·290 inch on the 29th. The total fall since January 1st, 1893, equals 12·565 inches on 65 days.

At Clonsevin, Killiney, Co. Dublin, the rainfall in May was 1·11 inches on 10 days, compared with an eight years' average of 2·49 inches on 15·5 days. The total fall since January 1 at this station has been 8·06 inches on 67 days. The maximal fall on any one day in May was ·49 inch on the 29th.

JUNE.—June, 1893, was the fourth month in succession with a mean temperature above average and a rainfall below average. The month under review did not—it is true—"break the record" as regards either high temperature or scanty rainfall; but it was in all respects most favourable. In Dublin rain fell freely from the 3rd to the 6th inclusive (·331 inch) and again from the 22nd to the 28th inclusive (1·164 inches), but the weather was otherwise dry, except for local thunder-showers on the 15th.

In Dublin the arithmetical mean temperature (59·9°) was above the average (57·8°) by 2·1°; the mean dry bulb readings at 9 a.m. and 9 p.m. were also 59·9°. In the twenty-eight years ending with 1893, June was coldest in 1882 (M. T.=55·6°), and in 1879 (the "cold year") (M. T.=54·9°). It was warmest in 1887 (M. T.=62·2°), in 1865 (M. T.=61·0°), and in 1868 (the "warm year") (M. T.=60·6°). In 1888 the M. T. was 57·3°; in 1889, 58·2°; in 1889, 59·4°; in 1890, 55·1°; in 1891, 59·0°; and in 1892, 56·7°.

The mean height of the barometer was 30·002 inches, or 0·085 inch above the corrected average value for June—namely, 29·917 inches. The mercury rose to 30·236 inches at 9 a.m. of the 7th, and fell to 29·289 inches at 11 p.m. of the 27th. The observed range of atmospherical pressure was, therefore, 1·078 inches—that is, less than an inch and one-tenth.

The mean temperature deduced from daily readings of the dry bulb thermometer at 9 a.m. and 9 p.m. was 59·9°, or 4·5° above the value for May, 1893. Using the formula, *Mean Temp.*=*Min.*+(*max.*−*Min.*×·465), the value was 59·6°, or 2·2° above the average mean temperature for June, calculated in the same way, in the twenty-five years, 1865–89, inclusive (57·4°). The arithmetical mean of the maximal and minimal readings was 59·9°, compared with a twenty-five years' average of 57·8°. On the 19th the thermometer in the screen rose to 76·7°—wind, N.N.E.; on the 22nd the temperature fell to 46·9°—wind, N.N.W. The minimum on the grass was 42·6° also on the 22nd.

The rainfall amounted to 1·716 inches, distributed over 12 days. The average rainfall for June in the twenty-five years, 1865–89, inclusive, was 1·817 inches, and the average number of rainy days was 13·4. The rainfall was, therefore, slightly below, while the rainy days were also below the average. In 1878 the rainfall in June was very large—5·058 inches on 19 days; in 1879 also

1·046 inches fell on 24 days. On the other hand, in 1889, only ·100 of an inch was measured on 6 days; in 1887, the rainfall was only ·242 of an inch, distributed over only 5 days; in 1876 only ·403 of an inch was measured on 9 days; and in 1868 only ·677 of an inch fell on but 6 days. In 1886 the rainfall was as much as 3·045 inches, distributed over as many as 13 days. In 1890 it was 1·930 inches on 15 days, in 1891 2·753 inches on 14 days, and in 1892 1·671 inches on 17 days.

High winds were noted on 7 days, but the force of a gale was attained on only one occasion—the 24th. Temperature reached or exceeded 70° in the screen on 9 days, compared with 17 days in 1887, only 1 day in 1888, 10 days in 1889, only 2 days in 1890, 5 days in 1891, and 4 days in 1892. Thunder was heard on the 15th. A solar halo was seen on the 11th.

On Thursday, the 1st, a depression which had for several days lain almost motionless over the south of Sweden dispersed, and an irregular area of low pressure began to form over Ireland. The weather, however, remained dry until Saturday, the 3rd, when electrical showers fell heavily in places, particularly at Blackrock, Co. Dublin. Thunder was heard on this day at Glasnevin Botanic Gardens.

At the beginning of the week ended Saturday, the 10th, the weather was unsettled and showery, owing to the presence of shallow irregular depressions to the northward, while an anticyclone lay over the Bay of Biscay. In Dublin rain fell very freely on Monday and in smaller quantity on Tuesday. On Sunday thunderstorms occurred all along the east coast of Great Britain. During most of this changeable time the barometer rose steadily, so that by 8 a.m. of Wednesday readings were everywhere high and remarkably uniform. In fact, at the hour named, the extreme difference in atmospherical pressure all over the United Kingdom was only ·08 inch—the highest reading being 30·42 inches at Yarmouth, and the lowest 30·34 inches in the Scilly Islands. After Wednesday the anticyclone held to the close of the week, the area of highest pressure being found off the east coast of Scotland, where dense fogs and low temperature prevailed. In most other parts of the Kingdom summer warmth daily increased until Saturday—the thermometer rising to 79° at Loughborough on Wednesday, 78° at Liverpool on Thursday, and 74° at Parsonstown and in London on Friday. On the evening of this day a thunderstorm with heavy rain (1·18 inches) occurred at Parsonstown. In Dublin the mean height of the barometer was 30·313 inches, pressure ranging from 30·105 inches at 9 a.m. of Sunday (wind, W. by S.) and 30·393 inches at 9 a.m. of Wednesday (wind, N.E.). The corrected mean temperature was 55·6°. The mean dry bulb readings at 9 a.m. and 9 p.m. were 56·3°. On Thursday both maximal and minimal temperatures for the week were recorded—viz., 69·6° and 49·5°—range, 20·1°. Rain fell on the first three days to the amount of ·315 inch, ·139 inch being registered on Sunday and ·101 inch on Monday. The prevailing winds were at first W.S.W., afterwards E. Much fog and haze prevailed in the Irish Sea after Wednesday, so that the fog-gun at the Kish-bank lightship was frequently fired both by day and by night.

Splendid weather characterised the week ended Saturday, the 17th. Until Wednesday it was cool as well as dry, but on and after that day temperature was high and summerlike by night as well as by day. On Sunday local thunderstorms occurred in the N. and N.W. of Ireland, notwithstanding an anticyclonic distribution of atmospheric pressure. After Sunday a shallow depression advanced northwards across France. It caused thunderstorms and heavy rains over the greater part of that country, but in the British Isles only local thundershowers occurred, although thunder and lightning were very prevalent on Wednesday and Thursday. On the afternoon of the latter day thundershowers fell in Dublin, yielding ·051 inch of rain, the only rainfall of the week. In this city the influence of easterly sea-breezes in lowering day-temperature was well seen, particularly in the earlier part of the period—thus, the maxima of the first four days were 66°, 65°, 66°, and 67° in Dublin, compared with 75°, 76°, 71°, and 75° at Parsonstown. On the east coast of Great Britain, similarly, the thermometer failed to reach 60° at most stations on Sunday and Monday. In Dublin the mean height of the barometer was 30·104 inches, pressure decreasing from 30·330 inches at 9 a.m. of Sunday (wind, E.N.E.) to 29·853 inches at 9 a.m. of Wednesday (wind, E.), and then increasing to a maximum of 30·273 inches at 9 p.m. of Saturday (wind, E.). The corrected mean temperature was 61·4°. The mean dry bulb readings at 9 a.m. and 9 p.m. were 62·6°. On Tuesday the screened thermometers fell to 50·1°, on Saturday they rose to 75·9°. The mean direction of the wind was easterly.

As to the week ended Saturday, the 24th—at first summerlike in the extreme—very warm, calm and bright—the weather afterwards fell into a very unsettled state, becoming cold, squally, and showery after Wednesday, the 21st—the longest day. On Sunday, the anticyclonic isobar of 30·0 inches embraced nearly the whole of the British Islands—at 8 a.m. the extreme pressures at mainland stations differed by only one-tenth of an inch, the highest readings being 30·08 inches at Loughborough, Cambridge, Malin Head, and Belmullet; the lowest being 30·98 inches at Prawle Point in Devon. The weather was bright, calm, and hot—the thermometer rising to 86° in the shade at Cambridge and Loughborough, and to 80° even at Parsonstown and Valentia Island. In the evening a thunderstorm occurred at the last-named station. On Monday the heat was still more intense—88° in the shade being recorded in London and at Cambridge. Thunderstorms occurred towards evening in the South of Ireland, South Wales, and the eastern and south-eastern parts of England. After this a cold northerly current passed rapidly southwards, bringing heavy showers which became general during the last three days. On Thursday a depression formed over Scotland and moved slowly south-eastwards and finally eastwards, becoming deeper and larger as it travelled. At 8 a.m. of Friday the barometer was down to 29·24 inches at Shields, and below 29·60 inches all over the north of England and south of Scotland. In Dublin the mean pressure was 29·946 inches, the barometer falling from 30·260 inches at 9 a.m. of Sunday (wind, E.), to 29·467 inches at 9 a.m. of Friday (wind, N. by W.). The corrected mean temperature was 59·0°—that for Sunday and Monday having been 65·6°. The mean dry bulb temperature at 9 a.m. and 9 p.m. was 58·7°. On

Monday the thermometer in the screen rose to 74·7°: on Friday they fell to 46·9°. Rain fell on the last three days to the amount of ·310 inch, ·130 inch being measured on Thursday and ·100 inch on Saturday. The prevalent wind was northerly—N.N.E. to N.W.

During the closing period of the month—from the 25th to the 30th inclusive—the weather presented two distinct types. Unsettled, squally, and showery as well as cool at first, it improved after Wednesday, the 28th, and the month closed with fine, warm, and in all respects summerlike conditions. On Sunday, the 25th, the well-defined depression, which had travelled from Scotland in a south-easterly direction on the previous Friday (see above), lay with its centre over the south of Norway. N.W. winds and cool, showery weather prevailed in the British Islands. In Dublin heavy showers fell locally at 2.30 and 11 p.m. Next day (Monday) an irregularly-shaped depression passed northwards across Ireland, causing a heavy rainfall in the south of this country (1·10 inches at Roche's Point, Cork), and in Wales and parts of England. During Tuesday and Wednesday a well-marked cyclonic system travelled north-eastwards from the N. of Ireland and across Scotland to the Norwegian Sea, where it dispersed. This disturbance produced moderate to fresh S.W. and W. gales at some Irish stations, as well as in the English Channel and off the mouth of the Thames. The barometer now rose quickly, and at 8 a.m. of Friday, the 30th, atmospherical pressure was uniformly high all over the kingdom—pressure ranging only from 30·30 inches over Central England to 30·44 inches at Belmullet. Quiet, bright, summerlike weather was the consequence, and so the month closed. In Dublin, during this period, the barometer ranged from 29·580 inches at 11 p.m. of Tuesday (wind, S.S.W.) to 30·142 inches at 9 a.m. of Friday (wind, S.E.) As regards temperature, on Monday and Friday the minimum in the thermometer screen was 50·0°; on Tuesday the maximum was 69·6°. Rain fell on the first four days of the period to the amount of ·634 inch, ·432 inch being registered on Monday. This was the maximal fall in 24 hours recorded during the month. The prevailing winds were S.E. and S.W.

The rainfall in Dublin during the six months ending June 30th amounted to 9·624 inches on 78 days, compared with 11·770 inches on 97 days in 1892, 5·748 inches on 77 days in 1891, 12·412 inches on 94 days in 1890, 10·578 inches on 97 days in 1889, 12·113 inches on 87 days in 1888, 6·741 inches on 67 days in 1887, and a twenty-five years' average of 12·218 inches on 93·4 days.

At Knockdolian, Greystones, Co. Wicklow, the rainfall in June, 1893, was 2·311 inches, distributed over 10 days. Of this quantity ·750 inch fell on the 26th, and ·410 inch on the 5th. The total fall since January 1 has been 11·776 inches, on 75 days.

The rainfall at Cloneevin, Killiney, Co. Dublin, amounted to 1·63 inches on 10 days. The greatest fall in 24 hours was ·61 inch on the 26th. The average rainfall for June in eight years was 1·49 inches on 11·1 days. There was absolute drought from the 7th to the 21st, both days inclusive. Since January 1, 1893, 9·69 inches of rain have fallen on 77 days, the average rainfall for the six months ending June 30 having been in eight years 10·64 inches on 89 days.

JULY.—A changeable, rather showery, but warm month, of high mean temperature and almost average rainfall, with a decided prevalence of north-easterly and north-westerly winds.

In Dublin the arithmetical mean temperature (61·6°) was decidedly above the average (60·6°); the mean dry bulb readings at 9 a.m. and 9 p.m. were 60·5°. In the twenty-eight years ending with 1893, July was coldest in 1879 (the "cold year") (M. T. = 57·2°). It was warmest in 1887 (M. T. = 63·7°), and in 1868 (the "warm year") (M. T. = 63·6°). In 1888 the M. T. was 61·0°; in 1889 it was as low as 57·6°; in 1889 it was 58·7°; in 1890, 58·1°; in 1891, 59·0°; and in 1892, 57·6°. From this, July, 1887, proves to have been the warmest since the present records commenced, whilst July, 1879, was the coldest. In only 8 years since 1831 was July colder than in the year 1893.

The mean height of the barometer was 29·896 inches, or ·019 inch below the corrected average value for July—namely, 29·915 inches. The mercury marked 30·234 inches at 9 p.m. of the 27th, and fell to 29·429 inches at 7.15 p.m. of the 19th. The observed range of atmospherical pressure was, therefore, 0·805 inch—that is, a little more than eight-tenths of an inch.

The mean temperature deduced from daily readings of the dry bulb thermometer at 9 a.m. and 9 p.m. was 60·6°, or 0·6° above the value for June, 1893. Using the formula, *Mean Temp.* = min. + (max.—min. × ·465), the value was 61·1°, or 0·9° above the average mean temperature for July, calculated in the same way, in the twenty-five years, 1865–89, inclusive (60·2°). The arithmetical mean of the maximal and minimal readings was 61·6°, compared with a twenty-five years' average of 60·6°. On the 23rd, the thermometer in the screen rose to 74·5°—wind, S.W.; on the 22nd the temperature fell to 48·0°—wind, W.N.W. The minimum on the grass was 44·6° on the 21st and again on the 22nd.

The rainfall was 2·048 inches, distributed over 14 days. The average rainfall for July in the twenty-five years, 1865–89, inclusive, was 2·620 inches, and the average number of rainy days was 17·2. The rainfall, therefore, was considerably below the average, while the rainy days were also below it. In 1880 the rainfall in July was very large—6·087 inches on 24 days; in 1871 also 4·391 inches fell on 23 days. On the other hand, in 1870, only ·539 of an inch was measured on 8 days; in 1869, the fall was only ·739 of an inch on 9 days, and in 1868, only ·741 of an inch fell on but 5 days. In 1872, 1·248 inches fell on 12 days.

High winds were noted on 9 days, but did not attain the force of a gale on any occasion. Temperature reached or exceeded 70° in the screen on 5 days. In July, 1887, temperature reached or exceeded 70° in the screen on no fewer than 17 days. In July, 1889, the maximum was only 68·7°. In July, 1891, maxima of 70° were reached on only 3 days, and in July, 1892, on only 2 days. Severe thunderstorms occurred on the 18th, and distant thunder was heard on the 13th.

Saturday, the 1st, was very fine and warm, with beautiful cirro-cumuli travelling from S.

Warm and generally favourable weather held during the week ended Saturday, the 8th. In parts of England severe thunderstorms and heavy rains were felt in the beginning—on Sunday and

Monday in the N. and N.E. as well as in the North Midland Counties; on Tuesday, in the S.W. and S. of that country and in the English Channel. On Saturday electrical disturbances were again prevalent. On Monday the rainfall was 1·33 inches at York and 1·8 inches at Stoke-on-Trent; on Tuesday 3·05 inches of rain fell at Prawle Point in Devonshire, 1·15 inches at Jersey, ·91 inch at Hurst Castle, in Hants, and ·67 inch at Dungeness in Kent. The distribution of atmospherical pressure was irregular and shifting until Thursday, when the barometer began to give way steadily in the west, and freshening S.E. and S. winds sprang up on the Irish coasts, with heavy rain at Valentia Island (·68 inch at 8 a.m. of Friday). The heat in England was very great on Sunday, when the thermometer rose to 85° at Oxford, 84° in London and at Loughborough, and 86° at Cambridge; and also on Thursday, when the maxima were 81° at Loughborough, 83° at Oxford, 84° in London, and 86° at Cambridge. On Friday the thermometer rose to 90° at Cambridge, 85° at Loughborough, and 87° in London. At 8 a.m. of Saturday, temperature was 80° in London and 79° at Cambridge, and the thermometer subsequently rose to 87° in London, 88° at Cambridge, and 94° locally at Elsing in Norfolk. In Ireland the highest readings were about 10° to 15° lower—71° being touched at Belmullet, Co. Mayo, on Wednesday. In Dublin the maximum exceeded 70° on five days, the highest reading of all being 71·6° on Monday and Saturday. The minimum in the screen was 54·8° on Thursday. The mean height of the barometer was 29·960 inches, pressure falling from 30·201 inches at 9 a.m. of Monday (wind, N.E.) to 29·591 inches at 9 p.m. of Saturday (wind, S.E.). The corrected mean temperature was 63·8°. The mean dry bulb readings at 9 a.m. and 9 p.m. were 63·6°. The rainfall ·187 inch on one day—·184 inch of the amount fell on the morning of Sunday, July 9. The prevailing winds were first N.E., afterwards S.E.

Very unsettled, rainy, thundery weather held during the greater part of the week ended Saturday, the 15th, and temperature showed a decided falling off compared with the previous fortnight. At 8 a.m. of Sunday a depression lay over the British Islands, its centre stretching from Ulster to the Lowlands of Scotland. It caused heavy rains in many places—1·61 inches being measured at Malin Head on Monday morning. In Dublin rain fell in torrents from 11 to 11.30 a.m. of Sunday, and on this day as well as on Monday thunderstorms occurred over the greater part of England. On Tuesday a new depression appeared off the S.E. of Ireland, whence it travelled slowly eastwards and north-eastwards to the Kattegat, which it reached on Friday morning. This system was accompanied by severe thunderstorms in many places. On Wednesday two distinct storms passed over Dublin—the second causing torrents of rain (·650 inch) in an hour (3.15 to 4.15 p.m.). At the Ordnance Survey Office, Phœnix Park, the rainfall on this day was 1·120 inches. Next day also there were heavy thundershowers near this city. Friday proved cloudy and cool, but rainless. On Saturday, however, showers again set in, as a new and large but shallow depression advanced over our northern coasts. In Dublin the mean height of the barometer was 29·766 inches, pressure ranging from 29·483 inches at 9 a.m. of Sunday (wind, W.) to 30·015 inches at 9 p.m. of Friday (wind, N.). The corrected mean temperature was 58·0°, the mean dry bulb readings at 9 a.m. and 9 p.m. being 58·6°. On Wednesday temperature rose to 67·9° in the screen, on Friday it fell to 51·6°. The rainfall measured 1·359 inches, on five days, ·971 inch being registered on Wednesday and ·249 inch on Sunday. The wind was variable—S., N.E., N., and W. being the predominant directions.

Changeable, showery, but withal favourable weather held throughout the week ending Saturday, the 22nd. The general distribution of atmospherical pressure was cyclonic in and near the British Isles—primary systems of some depth passing eastwards across the North of Scotland, while numerous secondary systems brought rain and squalls to the southern half of the United Kingdom also. Owing to the amount of cloud and to the freshness of the S.W. to N.W. winds which prevailed, temperature never became very high and seldom exceeded 70° even in the S.E. and centre of England. On the Continent, where the barometer was higher and conditions were at times anticyclonic, much warmer weather was experienced—at least towards the close of the week. Thus on Thursday the thermometer rose in the shade to 82° in Paris and 85° in Berlin, while the maximum on this day in London was only 65°. At 8 a.m. of Friday temperature was as high as 78° at Stockholm. In Dublin the extremes of temperature for the week occurred on Saturday—the minimum being 50·0° and the maximum 65·9°. The mean height of the barometer in this city was 29·729 inches, pressure ranging from 30·031 inches at 9 p.m. of Monday (wind, N.N.W.) to 29·453 inches at 7.15 p.m. of Wednesday (wind, W.), from which low value it again increased to 30·057 inches at 9 p.m. of Saturday (wind, W.S.W.). The corrected mean temperature was 58·9°. The mean dry bulb readings at 9 a.m. and 9 p.m. were 58·1°. The rainfall amounted to ·350 inch on five days—·101 inch being registered on Tuesday. The prevailing winds were westerly (S.W. and N.W.).

While changeable and far from settled, the weather was chiefly fine and dry in the period ended Saturday, the 29th. The general distribution of pressure was cyclonic in the North, anticyclonic in France and Germany, as well as in the British Islands on Thursday, the 27th, when an area of high pressure passed eastwards across Ireland to England. The fine, quiet weather accompanying this system was of short duration, and on Friday a fresh depression appeared off the N.W. of Scotland, causing clouds to increase and a shift of wind to S.W., from which point it freshened at some stations. Before the anticyclonic period, thunderstorms occurred very generally over the midland, eastern and south-eastern parts of England on Wednesday, but the attendant rainfall was not large. In Manchester, however, ·610 inch fell. Showers fell in many places on the day named, and with the advent of northerly winds and a clearing sky, temperature fell fast in the succeeding night. In Dublin the mean height of the barometer was 30·036 inches—pressure ranging between 29·747 inches at 9 p.m. of Monday (wind, W.) and 30·234 inches at 9 p.m. of Thursday (wind, N.). The corrected mean temperature was 61·9°. The mean dry bulb readings at 9 a.m. and 9 p.m. were 61·9°. On Sunday the thermometer rose to 74·8° in the screen; on Thursday it fell to 50·2°. The rainfall amounted to ·069 inch, of which ·049 inch was measured on Saturday. The prevalent winds were between W. and N.

Sunday, the 30th, was bright and fair in Dublin, but heavy showers fell in Edinburgh and thunderstorms occurred along the east coast of England. Monday, the 31st, was changeable and showery in many places.

The rainfall in Dublin during the seven months ending July 31st amounted to 11·186 inches on 83 days compared with 13·783 inches on 108 days during the corresponding period in 1892, 10·425 inches on 97 days in 1891, 15·587 inches on 116 days in 1890, 13·146 inches on 112 days in 1889, 13·294 inches on 105 days in 1888, 7·935 inches on 80 days in 1887, and a 25 years' average of 14·739 inches on 112·6 days.

At Knockdolian, Greystones, Co. Wicklow, the rainfall in July was 1·290 inches on 15 days, compared with 3·928 inches on only 10 days in 1892, 1·325 inches on 18 days in 1891, and 1·489 inches, distributed over 14 days in 1890. Of the total rainfall ·300 inch fell on the 9th, and ·290 inch on the 13th. The total fall since January 1 has been 13·080 inches on 90 days, compared with 16·705 inches on 90 days in 1892.

At Clonsevin, Killiney, Co. Dublin, the rainfall in July was 1·36 inches on 17 days, compared with an eight years average of 1·854 inches on 15 days. On the 13th the rainfall was ·25 inch. Since January 1, 1893, 11·04 inches of rain have fallen at this station (Clonsevin).

AUGUST.—Although changeable, as in 1892, and forming no exception to the rule that August is characterised by heavy rains, this was a record month as regards high temperature. On no fewer than 15 days did the thermometer exceed 70° in the shade, and the mean temperature was one degree above that of August, 1871, when it reached 62°. The present month also is remarkable for the magnificent display of lightning which occurred on the evening and during the night of the 9th. The cyclonic depressions, which are periodic in the last week of August, arrived almost a week earlier than usual, the barometer falling to 28·80 inches off the west coast of Scotland on the 21st.

In Dublin the arithmetical mean temperature (63·0°) was much above the average (59·7°); the mean dry bulb readings at 9 a.m. and 9 p.m. were 61·8°. In the twenty-eight years ending with 1892, August was coldest in 1881 (M. T.—57·9°), and warmest in 1871 (M. T.—60·0°). In 1886, the M. T. was only 57·1°; in 1879 (the "cold year"), it was 57·7°; in 1887, 60·3°; in 1888, 58·5°; in 1889, 58·6°; in 1890, only 57·3°; in 1891, 58·1°; and in 1892, 60·0°.

The mean height of the barometer was 29·963 inches, or 0·066 inch above the corrected average value for August—namely, 29·897 inches. The mercury marked 30·306 inches at 9 a.m. of the 29th, and fell to 29·200 inches at 9 a.m. of the 21st. The observed range of atmospherical pressure was, therefore, 1·106 inches—that is, a little more than an inch and one-tenth.

The mean temperature deduced from daily readings of the dry bulb thermometer at 9 a.m. and 9 p.m. was 61·8°, or 3·7° above the value in August, 1888 and 1889, 3·0° above that in 1890, 4·1° above it in 1891, and 2·2° above it in 1892. It was also 0·6° above the value for July, 1893. Using the formula, *Mean Temp.* = *min.* + (*max.*—*min.* × ·47), the mean temperature was 62·6°, or 3·3° above the average mean temperature for August, calculated in the same way, in the twenty-five years, 1865–89, inclusive (59·3°). The arithmetical mean of the maximal and minimal readings was 63·0°, compared with a twenty-five years' average of 59·7°. On the 15th the thermometer in the screen rose to 79·6°—wind, light and variable; on the 26th the temperature fell to 47·9°—wind, N.W. The minimum on the grass was 41·8° on the 26th.

The rainfall was 2·713 inches, distributed over 16 days. The average rainfall for August in the twenty-five years, 1865–89, inclusive, was 2·835 inches, and the average number of rainy days was 15·5. The rainfall, therefore, was slightly below average, while the rainy days were slightly in excess of the average. In 1874, the rainfall in August was very large—4·940 inches on 18 days; and in 1868 also 4·748 inches fell on, however, only 13 days; but the heaviest downpour in August occurred in 1880, when 5·747 inches were registered on 23 days. On the other hand, in 1884, only ·777 inch was measured on 8 days. In 1887, 1·930 inches of rain fell on 18 days; in 1888, 1·870 inches on 12 days; in 1890, 2·799 inches on 19 days; in 1891, 4·849 inches on 25 days, and in 1892, 3·357 inches on 22 days.

High winds were noted on as many as 10 days, and attained the force of a gale on three occasions—namely, the 4th, 20th and 21st. A thunderstorm of great severity occurred on the 9th. Thunder was also heard on the 18th. Lightning was also seen on the 13nd and 16th. Temperature reached 70° in the screen on as many as 14 days. Hail fell on the 18th. It was foggy on the 12th, 16th, and 14th.

The weather remained changeable and showery, with fresh westerly (S.W. to N.W.) winds, throughout the period ended Saturday, the 5th. A new disturbance reached our northwest coasts on Tuesday, the 1st, leading to rain without much wind. On Wednesday afternoon, however, the barometer fell briskly and the wind backed to S.W. and freshened with a threatening appearance as a much more decided depression approached the N.W. of Ireland from the Atlantic. This system was quickly followed by another on Thursday night, so that by Friday the weather was thoroughly broken, squally and showery, in all parts of the United Kingdom. On the afternoon of this day thunderstorms and heavy rains occurred in London and many other places. A brisk recovery of pressure now took place and the wind drew towards N. and moderated, with fine dry weather on Saturday. In Dublin the mean height of the barometer for the week ended Saturday, the 5th was 29·691 inches, pressure ranging between 29·434 inches at 9 a.m. of Friday (wind, W. by S.) and 30·088 inches at 9 p.m. of Saturday (wind, N.). The corrected mean temperature was 60·4°. The mean dry bulb readings at 9 a.m. and 9 p.m. were 58·8°. The screened thermometers rose to 71·8° on Friday and fell to 53·4° on Tuesday. The rainfall was ·818 inch on five days, ·370 inch being measured on Wednesday. The prevailing wind was N.W. Changeable, but very warm and generally summerlike weather characterised the week ended Saturday, the 12th. On Wednesday and Thursday thunderstorms of quite exceptional intensity raged over many parts of England and

Ireland, extending subsequently to parts of Scotland also. In Ireland, the distribution of atmospherical pressure was cyclonic, except on Tuesday and Saturday, when a Continental anticyclone spread westwards as far this country. As the general direction of the wind in the British Islands was southerly, temperature ranged very high—the thermometer rising to 85° or 86° at the inland English stations on Tuesday and Wednesday—even at Holyhead a maximum of 83° was recorded on Wednesday. The highest in Paris on the same day was 91°. This tropical heat was the more remarkable, as the week commenced with very low temperatures, indeed, the minima recorded on Sunday morning were 46° in London and at Oxford, 44° at Leith, 43° at York, Loughborough, and Ardrossan; 42° at Bunbeg Head, 41° at Wick and Aberdeen, 40° at Stornoway, and 35° at Nairn! But the most striking phenomenon of the week was the violent thunderstorm of Wednesday night. In Dublin the lightning, which was almost incessant from dusk until after midnight, was extraordinarily vivid. The storm passed from S.S.E. to N.N.W. directly over the city between 10 and 11 p.m., in which time a quarter of an inch of rain fell. The mean height of the barometer was 29·[illegible] inches, pressure ranging between 29·806 inches at 4 p.m. of Thursday (wind, S.E.) and 30·128 inches at 9 p.m. of Saturday (wind, S.). The corrected mean temperature was 65·6°. The mean dry bulb temperature at 9 a.m. and 9 p.m. was 63·6°. On Friday the screened thermometers rose to 77·7°, having fallen to 52·0° on Sunday. The rainfall was ·460 inch on four days, ·250 inch being recorded on Wednesday. The prevalent winds were S.W. and S.E.

Many years have passed since such really tropical heat has been experienced in Spain, France, and the British Isles, as that which has made the week ended Saturday, the 19th, memorable in meteorological annals. At Rochefort, on the west coast of France, the daily maxima were 102°, 106°, 91°, 93°, 100°, 90°, and 81°. In London the corresponding values were 81°, 85°, 87°, 90°, 93°, 93°, and 78°. On Thursday night the thermometer did not sink below 72° in London, and by 8 a.m. of Friday it had already risen to 84°. Even in Dublin a maximum of 79·5° was recorded on Tuesday, the 15th—this being the highest shade temperature registered in the Irish capital since July 14, 1876, when the phenomenal reading 87·3 was attained. On Tuesday the maximum at the Ordnance Survey Office, Phoenix Park, was 82·0°; at Glasnevin Botanic Gardens it was 80·6°. Only on the nights of Tuesday and Friday did the minimum fall below 60°. On every day the maximum exceeded 70°. There was an anticyclonic distribution of atmospherical pressure over western Germany, France, England, and Ireland until Thursday, when isobars became cyclonic and decided gradients for southerly winds formed over all parts of the United Kingdom. Thunderstorms of some severity occurred in the North of Ireland and the northern half of Great Britain on Tuesday night, while drenching showers of rain and hail fell in and about Dublin on Friday, accompanied by thunder. It is noteworthy that the weather was quite cool in Scandinavia throughout the week. In Dublin the mean height of the barometer was 29·954 inches, pressure ranging from 30·170 inches at 9 a.m. of Monday (wind, S.S.E.), to a minimum of 29·687 inches at 9 p.m. of Saturday (wind, S.). The corrected mean temperature was 67·9°. The mean dry bulb temperature at 9 a.m. and 9 p.m. was 65·8°. On Tuesday, the shade thermometers rose to 79·5°; on Saturday they fell to 58·1°. The rainfall was ·698 inch on two days, ·616 inch falling in heavy showers on Friday, when some hail also fell. The prevailing wind was S.S.W. A good deal of fog hung about the coast on Sunday and Monday. The rainfall at Greystones, County Wicklow, was 1·033 inches on two days. The mean temperature of this week was 73·1° in London, 71·8° at Cambridge, 71·5° at Oxford and Loughborough, 70·6° at Southampton, 70·3° in Manchester, and 70·1° even at Scarborough on the sea.

Opening with typical cyclonic conditions and rough, rainy weather, the week ended Saturday, the 26th, closed with equally well-marked anticyclonic conditions and fine, quiet weather. On Sunday morning a large depression was found off the N.W. of Scotland. This system had caused a heavy rainfall during the previous night in most parts of Ireland and in some parts of Scotland. A few hours later a much more serious disturbance advanced towards the N.W. of Ireland from the S.W., causing a renewed and still heavier rainfall and moderate to fresh gales from S., S.W., and W. at several exposed stations. By 8 a.m. of Monday the barometer was down to 28·[illegible] inches in Donegal, and by 6 p.m. a minimal reading of [illegible] inches was reached at Wick, in Caithness-shire. During the next three days the arrival of several shallow secondary depressions kept the weather in an unsettled, showery state. On Thursday, however, an area of high pressure began to spread over our south-western districts and the N.W. of France, and this brought cool, dry N.W. winds and finer and brighter weather. Towards the close of the period the nights became very sharp, the thermometer in the screen falling on Friday night to 47·3° in Dublin; 46·0 in London, as well as at Wick, Belmullet, and Oxford; and 41·0° at Parsonstown. In Dublin the grass minimum was 41·7°. In Dublin the mean height of the barometer was 29·687 inches, pressure ranging from 29·290 inches at 9 a.m. of Monday (wind, W.S.W.) to 30·343 inches at 9 a.m. of Saturday (wind, N.W.). The corrected mean temperature was 59·6°. The mean dry bulb readings at 9 a.m. and 9 p.m. were 57·9°. On Sunday the thermometer rose to 68·6°; on Saturday it fell to 47·3°. The mean temperature was 8·3° lower than that of the previous week. Rain was measured on four days to the amount of ·718 inch, ·290 inch being entered on Sunday. The prevailing winds were first S.W., then N.W.

The last five days of the month were uneventful but favourable. An anticyclone of considerable intensity for the time of year lay throughout over Ireland and the Atlantic to the westward of this country. The weather was at first bright and cool, with northerly winds; but the sky afterwards became densely clouded, and on Thursday, the 31st, some rain fell with a N.W. wind. Temperature showed some recovery on this the closing day of the month.

The rainfall in Dublin during the eight months ending August 31st amounted to 14·378 inches on 108 days compared with 9·411 inches on 89 days during the same period in 1887, 17·204 inches on 121 days in 1888, 16·583 inches on 124 days in 1889, 15·386 inches on 137 days in 1890, 15·088 inches on 117 days in 1891, 17·779 inches on 131 days in 1892, and a 25 years' average of 17·348 inches on 122·1 days.

At Knockdolian, Greystones, Co. Wicklow, the rainfall in August, 1893, was 3·275 inches, distributed over 16 days. Of this quantity ·690 inch fell on the 19th. The total fall since January 1 amounts to 16·341 inches on 106 days, compared with 21·386 inches on 108 days in 1892.

SEPTEMBER.—September, 1893, was favourable throughout. It was a month of average temperature, with fresh westerly and north-westerly winds, and frequent showers, but no heavy rains near Dublin. At times the nights were very sharp, and even frosty, but, on the other hand, much bright sunshine was enjoyed by day. Towards the close the autumnal tints in the foliage were lovely beyond compare.

In Dublin the arithmetical mean temperature (55·9°) was as nearly as possible equal to the average (55·8°); the mean dry bulb readings at 9 a.m. and 9 p.m. were 54·8°. In the twenty-eight years ending with 1892, September was coldest in 1886 and in 1882 (M. T. = 53·0°), and warmest in 1865 (M. T. = 61·4°). In 1880, the M. T. was as high as 58·6°; in 1879 (the "cold year"), it was 54·3°; in 1887, 54·0°; in 1888, 54·4°; in 1889, 55·8°, or exactly the average; in 1890, it was as high as 59·6°; in 1891, it was 57·6°, and in 1892, 54·5°. So warm a September as that of 1890 had not occurred for a quarter of a century.

The mean height of the barometer was 29·848 inches, or 0·062 inch below the corrected average value for September—namely, 29·910 inches. The mercury rose to 30·345 inches at 9 a.m. of the 13th, and fell to 29·052 inches at 9 a.m. of the 29th. The observed range of atmospherical pressure was, therefore, 1·293 inches—that is, a little more than one inch and a quarter.

The mean temperature deduced from daily readings of the dry bulb thermometer at 9 a.m. and 9 p.m. was 54·8°, or as much as 6·5° below the value for August, 1893. Using the formula, *Mean Temp.* = *min.* + (*max.* − *min.* × ·476), the mean temperature was 55·5°, or exactly equal to the average mean temperature for September, calculated in the same way, in the twenty-five years, 1865–89, inclusive (55·5°). The arithmetical mean of the maximal and minimal readings was 55·9°, compared with a twenty-five years' average of 55·8°. On the 5th, the thermometer in the screen rose to 72·0°—wind, S.S.W.; on the 21st the temperature fell to 38·2°—wind, N.W. The minimum on the grass was 31·7° on the 24th. On the 21st the grass minimum was 31·9°.

The rainfall was only ·729 inch, distributed over as many as 14 days—the rainfall was thus considerably below the average. The average rainfall for September in the twenty-five years, 1865–89, inclusive, was 2·176 inches, and the average number of rainy days was 14·7. In 1871, the rainfall in this month was very large—4·048 inches on, however, only 13 days. On the other hand, in 1865, only ·056 inch was measured on but 3 days. In 1888, the rainfall was only ·728 inch on 10 days; in 1889, 1·048 inches fell on 13 days; in 1890, 2·469 inches on 14 days; in 1891, 2·163 inches on 18 days; and in 1892, 2·681 inches on 19 days.

High winds were noted on as many as 14 days, but attained the force of a gale on no occasion in Dublin. An aurora appeared on the 1st. Lightning was seen on the 5th and 21st. Thunder was heard on the 21st. The atmosphere was foggy on the 3rd, 4th, and 12th.

The month opened with an anticyclone forming over Ireland, where the weather during the first two days was mild and fine, although rather cloudy. In England rain had fallen, and the weather was taking up. In Scotland conditions were still unsettled and rainy. North-westerly winds were prevalent in nearly all parts of the United Kingdom.

During the week ended Saturday, the 9th, the weather, which was at first fair and warm, afterwards became cloudy, showery, squally, and finally cold for the time of year. On Sunday morning an anticyclone lay right over the British Islands, in all parts of which the barometer was high and remarkably uniform, the morning readings varying not one-tenth of an inch, from 30·20 inches at Loughborough, in Leicestershire, to 30·28 inches at Belmullet, in Mayo, and 30·31 inches at Valentia Island in Kerry. The weather was fair and bright after a calm, dewy and (in places) foggy morning. During the following two days the anticyclone retreated in a south-easterly direction to the Continent, and the barometer fell steadily. The wind meanwhile became S.W. in the North, and E. or S.E. in the South, temperature rising considerably on Tuesday—to 72° in Dublin and at Leith, 74° at York and Hurst Castle, 75° at Oxford, and 77° in London, at Loughborough and Cambridge. Wednesday was still hotter in the midlands and south of England, the thermometer reaching 80° at Cambridge and 81° in London; but already a decided fall of temperature had begun in Scotland and Ireland, and was spreading south-eastwards with clouds, rain, and high westerly winds. On Friday a V-shaped thunderstorm depression travelled south-eastwards across Great Britain, and in its rear temperature gave way still more rapidly, so that Saturday was quite a cool day. In Dublin the mean atmospheric pressure was 29·914 inches, pressure ranging between 30·275 inches at 9 a.m. of Sunday (wind, E.N.E.), and 29·570 inches at 9 p.m. of Wednesday (wind, W.S.W.). The corrected mean temperature was 58·7°. The mean dry bulb temperature at 9 a.m. and 9 p.m. was 57·3°. On Tuesday the screened thermometers rose to 72·0°, on Saturday they fell to 44·0°. Rain was registered on three days, the total measurement being ·252 inch, of which ·174 inch was recorded on Wednesday. Sheet lightning was seen on the eastern horizon on Friday evening. The prevalent winds were S.W. and N.N.W.

The two most striking features in the weather of the week ended Saturday, 16th, are the low night temperatures at the beginning and the continuous drought, except in the north and the extreme south of the British Islands. During Sunday and Monday a depression was passing south-eastwards from the mouth of St. George's Channel across the Bay of Biscay to the Peninsula. This disturbance caused heavy rains in the extreme S.W. of England, along the west coast of France, and finally in central Spain. Its presence was made evident from Dublin on Saturday, the 9th, as well as throughout Sunday, by a sheet of cirriform cloud which kept travelling in an upper current from W. to E. over the southern half of the sky. A strong easterly wind at the same time showed that an area of low barometer lay to the southward. As this breeze died down, the nights became very sharp in

England and Ireland. At Parsonstown the screened thermometer fell to 35° on Monday night and to 31° on Tuesday night. At Loughborough also the minimum on Monday night was 31°, or one degree below freezing-point. Large depressions now began to pass eastward across Northern Europe, so that for the rest of the week squally westerly (S.W. to N.W.) winds, high but variable temperatures, and cloudy skies—with heavy rain in the extreme north—were experienced. At Glencarron, in Ross-shire, the rainfall of this week was as much as 6 inches. In Dublin the mean height of the barometer was 30·140 inches, readings varying from 30·348 inches at 9 a.m. of Tuesday (wind calm), to 29·923 inches at 9 p.m. of Saturday (wind, N.W.). At 4 p.m. of this day a reading of 29·909 inches was recorded. The corrected mean temperature was 54·3°. The mean dry bulb readings in the screen at 9 a.m. and 9 p.m. were 57·1°. On Tuesday the minimum was 40·8°, on Friday the maximum was 70·6°. Light showers fell on Friday evening, yielding only ·009 inch of rain. The prevalent winds were E., W.S.W., and N.W.

All through the week ended Saturday, the 23rd, the atmosphere was in a disturbed state over north-western Europe, and cyclonic conditions prevailed generally. On Tuesday and the two following days a depression of the first magnitude lay between Scotland and Norway, while a series of secondary depressions travelled south-eastwards across the British Islands, keeping the weather in a changeable, squally, showery condition, especially on our northern and north-western coasts. The amount of atmospherical depression may be gauged by the fact that on Tuesday the barometer fell to 28·70 inches at Sumburgh Head, in the Shetlands. On Wednesday evening sheet lightning was seen from the shores of the Irish Sea, St. George's Channel, and the English Channel. At night sharp frost occurred over central Ireland and in some inland parts of England also. At 8 a.m. of Thursday a thunderstorm prevailed in the Scilly Isles, connected with a large secondary depression which at that time lay over Brittany. On the evening of this day massive cumuli and nimbi were seen from the east coast of Ireland passing southwards down the Irish Sea—vivid flashes of lightning shot from these clouds from time to time, and distant thunder was heard at intervals. On Friday night another secondary depression brought a considerable rainfall, followed by a renewed fall of temperature and fresh northerly winds on Saturday. On Friday and Saturday showers of snow and sleet fell in Scotland and over the north of England. In Dublin the mean height of the barometer was 29·612 inches, readings decreasing from 29·629 inches at 9 a.m. of Sunday (wind, W.N.W.) to 29·330 inches at 3 p.m. of Tuesday (wind also W.N.W.), but rising again intermittently to 29·877 inches at 9 p.m. of Saturday (wind, N.W.). The corrected mean temperature was 50·9°. The mean dry bulb readings at 9 a.m. and 9 p.m. were 50·7°. On Monday the thermometer rose to 63·6° in the shade; on Thursday it fell to 39·2° in the shade and to 31·9° on the grass. The rainfall was ·191 inch on four days—·112 inch being measured on Friday. The wind was generally N.W., varying only between W. and N.

A cyclonic distribution of atmospherical pressure over western and northern Europe caused the weather to be of a changeable, showery, and squally character throughout the week ended Saturday, the 30th. At the beginning, no doubt, an anticyclone was found over Ireland in the rear of a depression overlying the Skager Rack, but this high pressure area soon gave place to a new disturbance, which at 8 a.m. of Tuesday had its centre over Donegal, Derry, and Antrim. This system travelled eastwards, causing heavy rain, first in the north of Ireland, afterwards in the north of England. Indeed, on Wednesday thunderstorms occurred generally along the east coast of England and at the Helder, in connection with this depression. By 8 a.m. of Thursday a very decided reduction of pressure was in progress all over the British Islands and Scandinavia, and a large and deep depression was approaching the N.W. of Scotland. The showers now became heavier and more frequent in nearly all places, while the wind blew more and more gustily and strongly from S.W. or W. At 8 a.m. of Friday the barometer was down to 28·85 inches at Stornoway in the Hebrides, where a fresh southerly breeze was blowing. The reading was 30·30 inches at Nice and 30·06 inches at *Lisbon* at the same hour. Gales prevailed at many exposed stations—from S.E. in Norway, but from S.W. or W. in the English Channel, and at Pembroke. The showery weather continued to the close of the week; but fine, bright intervals were enjoyed. In Dublin the mean height of the barometer was 29·619 inches, the range of pressure being from 30·079 inches at 9 a.m. of Sunday (wind, W.N.W.) to 29·058 inches at 9 a.m. of Friday (wind, W.S.W.). The corrected mean temperature was 54·3°. The mean daily dry bulb reading at 9 a.m. and 9 p.m. was 53·1°. On Sunday the thermometer fell to 38·9° in the shade; on Thursday it rose to 63·5°. Rain fell in measurable quantity on six days, the total precipitation being ·379 inch, of which ·060 inch was referred to Thursday. The prevailing winds were westerly (W.N.W. to S.W.). Lunar rainbows were seen at Greystones, Co. Wicklow, on Thursday evening. Thunder and lightning occurred in many parts of Ireland in the course of the same night.

The rainfall in Dublin during the nine months ending September 30th amounted to 15·108 inches on 138 days, compared with 10·968 inches on 115 days during the same period in 1887, 17·992 inches on 131 days in 1888, 19·888 inches on 167 days in 1889, 20·688 inches on 151 days in 1890, 18·030 inches on 135 in 1891, 19·910 inches on 150 days in 1892, and a twenty-five years' average of 19·734 inches on 142·6 days.

At Knockdolian, Greystones, County Wicklow, the rainfall in September, 1893, was ·750 inch distributed over 12 days. Of this quantity ·150 inch fell on the 28th, and ·140 inch on the 5th. At that station the rainfall since January 1, 1893, has been 17·091 inches on 116 days, compared with 23·683 inches on 125 days in the same nine months of 1892.

At Cloneevin, Killiney, Co. Dublin, the rainfall in August, 1893, was 3·39 inches on 20 days (the maximal fall in 24 hours being ·37 inch on the 20th), compared with an eight years' average of 3·348 inches on 15·25 days. In September, 1893, only ·90 inch fell at Cloneevin on 11 days. The maximal fall in 24 hours was ·14 inch on the 5th. On an average of eight years the September rainfall at this station has been 1·707 inches on 13·8 days. Since January 1, 1893, 12·90 inches of rain have fallen at Cloneevin.

OCTOBER.—A favourable month, of average mean temperature and atmospheric pressure. There was an overwhelming prevalence of westerly and south-westerly winds, which kept the rainfall far below the average on the leeward side of the Dublin and Wicklow mountains—thus, it was only ·710 inch at both Greystones and Killiney; 1·032 inches in Dublin city; 1·110 inches at the Royal Botanic Gardens, Glasnevin; and 1·190 inches at the Ordnance Survey Office, Phoenix Park. West of the mountains inland, the rainfall was much heavier. Even in London, not less than 3·900 inches of rain fell during the month. On the 20th and 21st there was a remarkable wave of heat. On the 30th and 31st the cold was equally decided.

In Dublin the arithmetical mean temperature (50·0°) was slightly above the average (49·7°); the mean dry bulb readings at 9 a.m. and 9 p.m. were 48·8°. In the twenty-eight years ending with 1892, October was coldest in 1869 (M. T. = 46·8°), in 1880 (M. T. = 45·4°), and in 1883 (M. T. = 46·4°), and warmest in 1876 (M. T. = 53·1°). In 1886, the M. T. was as high as 52·0°; in 1879 (the "cold year"), it was 49·7°; in 1887, as low as 47·3°; in 1888, it was 46·1°; in 1889, it was only 48·1°; in 1890, it was 51·7°, and in 1891, it was 49·5°. October, 1892, bears the record for coldness, but October, 1893, has proved of normal warmth.

The mean height of the barometer was 29·855 inches, or 0·015 inch above the corrected average value for October—namely, 29·840 inches. The mercury rose to 30·507 inches at 9 a.m. of the 23rd, and fell to 29·061 inches at 9 a.m. of the 4th. The observed range of atmospherical pressure was, therefore, as much as 1·446 inches—that is, a little less than an inch and a half.

The mean temperature deduced from daily readings of the dry bulb thermometer at 9 a.m. and 9 p.m. was 48·8°, or 6·0° below the value for September. The arithmetical mean of the maximal and minimal readings was 50·0°, compared with a twenty-five years' average of 49·7°. Using the formula, *Mean Temp.* = *Min.* + (*max.* — *min.* × ·485), the value was 49·9°, or 0·3° above the average mean temperature for October, calculated in the same way, in the twenty-five years, 1865–89, inclusive, (49·6°). On the 21st, the thermometer in the screen rose to 67·7°—wind, S.W.; on the 31st the temperature fell to 31·7°—wind, N.W. The minimum on the grass was 24·0°, also on the 31st. On one night the thermometer sank below 32° in the screen, and on eight nights frost occurred on the grass. The corresponding figures in 1892 were 4 and 18 nights respectively.

The rainfall was only 1·032 inch, distributed over 16 days—the rainfall was considerably, while the rainy days were slightly, below the average. The average rainfall for October in the twenty-five years, 1865–89, inclusive, was 3·104 inches, and the average number of rainy days was 17·6. In 1880 the rainfall in October was very large—7·358 inches on 18 days. In 1875, also, 7·049 inches fell on 22 days. On the other hand, in 1890 only ·639 inch fell on but 11 days, in 1884 only ·834 inch on but 14 days, and in 1885 only ·836 inch on 13 days. In 1888, the rainfall was 1·227 inches on 16 days, and in 1889 no less than 4·633 inches fell on 22 days. In 1891, 3·690 inches fell on 16 days, and in 1892, 3·485 inches on 17 days. From these figures it will be seen that October, 1890, proved the driest on record for more than a quarter of a century at least, while the rainfall in October, 1893, was only one-third of the average.

A lunar corona was seen on the 24th. There was an aurora borealis on the evening of the 29th. High winds were noted on 10 days, and attained the force of a gale on two occasions—the 24th and 29th. The atmosphere was more or less foggy in Dublin on the 7th, 18th, and 20th. Lightning was seen on the evenings of the 3rd, 4th, 5th, and 30th. Hail fell on the 28th.

The week ended Saturday, the 7th, proved to be one of low atmospherical pressure, low temperature, and changeable showery weather, the showers being from time to time accompanied by thunder and lightning in many places. The most important reduction of pressure occurred on Tuesday and Wednesday—at 8 a.m. of the latter day the barometer was below 29 inches throughout a large triangular area covering two-thirds of Scotland, the north of England, and the north-eastern third of Ireland. Gradients were nowhere steep, and so the winds—although varying much in direction—were not strong except off the south of Ireland and in the English Channel. Connected with this large primary cyclonic system, were a number of shallow secondary depressions, which caused thunder and hail—as well as rain—showers as they passed across the country. Temperature was not so low in the S. and S.E. of England as in other parts of the kingdom, and on Sunday the thermometer rose to 67° at Loughborough and Cambridge, 66° in London and at Dungeness, and 65° at Hurst Castle. On the other hand, a minimum of 23° was registered at Nairn, in Scotland, on Wednesday morning. In Dublin the mean height of the barometer was 29·369 inches, pressure being observed to vary between 29·674 inches at 9 p.m. of Sunday (wind, W.), and 29·061 inches at 9 a.m. of Wednesday (wind also W.). The corrected mean temperature was 49·3°. The mean dry bulb temperature at 9 a.m. and 9 p.m. was 47·9°. On Sunday the thermometer rose to 59·3°, on Saturday it fell to 37·4° in the screen. The rainfall was ·155 inch on five days, ·051 inch being measured on Wednesday. Lightning was seen on the evenings of Tuesday, Wednesday, and Thursday. The prevailing wind was westerly. The weather was much more broken in England than in Ireland during the week.

Atmospherical pressure was unsteady during the week ended Saturday, the 14th, and therefore the weather was unsettled and changeable. Until Friday, when a very warm, moist south-westerly, or equatorial current began to pass over Ireland, the air was cold and rather dry in this country. In England, on the contrary, heavy falls of rain took place, accompanied by thunder and lightning and at times by strong and squally S.W. winds. In London, from one inch to an inch and a quarter of rain fell on Monday night, and the total fall for the three days ending 8 a.m. of Thursday was no less than 1·48 inches. These heavy rains were due to the passage up the English Channel of two depressions in quick succession—one on Monday, the other on Wednesday. At this time, although the barometer was rather low, bright, sharp weather prevailed in Ireland, showers occurring at intervals. On Thursday an area of high pressure passed over this country. The weather turned colder and became fine and dry in England, while in Ireland a warm S.W. wind arrived on Friday, causing dull, rainy weather, and an increase of temperature amounting to from 20° to 25° Fahr. The result in Dublin was that on Saturday the interior of most houses became dripping wet, from the condensation as dew of the vapour of the warm air current upon the walls, ceilings, and floors, chilled by the previous cold weather and remaining below the point of saturation or the dew point. Rain fell heavily on Saturday afternoon. In Dublin the mean height of the barometer was 29·848 inches, pressure ranging between 29·693 inches at 9 a.m. of Sunday (wind, W.), and 30·160 inches at 9 p.m. of Thursday (wind, W.N.W.). The corrected mean temperature was [illegible]°. The mean dry bulb temperature at 9 a.m. and 9 p.m. was also [illegible]°. On Tuesday the thermometers in the screen fell to 37·1°, on Saturday they rose to 65·0°. The rainfall was ·371 inch on three days, ·325 inch being measured on Saturday. The prevalent winds were W. and S.W.

Taken as a whole, the weather of the week ended Saturday, the 21st, was distinctly favourable and of a mild type—indeed, both at the beginning and at the end temperature was much above normal, although the minima were low on Tuesday night in Scotland and parts of both England and Ireland, and on Wednesday and Thursday nights in central England. On the other hand, Friday night proved abnormally warm in many places, and in Dublin the thermometer actually rose to 67·7° (nearly 68°) in the screen. Comparatively little rain fell, except in the south of Ireland and over the south and east of England as well as in parts of the English Midlands on Tuesday, when a shallow depression travelled in a direction from W.N.W. to E.S.E. from the mouth of St. George's Channel across the S.W. of England to the N.E. of France. This rain-system caused falls of 1·28 inches at Roche's Point, 1·57 inches at Hurst Castle, where a storm of thunder and lightning occurred at 1.30 a.m. of Wednesday, and ·73 inch in London. The rainfall was ·47 inch at Parsonstown, but only ·07 inch in Dublin. As this disturbance passed off, an anticyclone formed in the S., and the barometer rose to 30·40 inches or slightly more on Friday morning over the S. of England, N. of France, and centre of Germany. Along the north-western face of this anticyclone a very warm south-westerly current spread over Ireland on Friday, the temperature becoming singularly high at night. Saturday was first fine and warm, afterwards rainy and much cooler. In Dublin the mean height of the barometer was 30·029 inches, pressure ranging between a minimum of 29·752 inches at 9 p.m. of Sunday (wind, W.S.W.) and 30·370 inches at 9 a.m. of Thursday (wind, S.W.). The corrected mean temperature was 55·4°. The mean dry bulb reading at 9 a.m. and 9 p.m. was 54·5°. On Saturday the thermometers in the screen rose to 67·7°; on Wednesday they fell to 41·0°. The rainfall was ·238 inch on four days, ·120 inch being measured on Saturday. The prevailing winds were W. and S.W. A wet fog prevailed on Wednesday morning, and there was a smoke fog on Friday.

At first fine and dry, except in the S. and S.E. of England, where Sunday was dull and rainy, the weather afterwards became squally, showery, and generally changeable during the week ended Saturday the 28th. In the earlier period, an anticyclone lay over the S. of Ireland, the barometer rising on Monday morning to 30·35 inches at Valentia Island and Roche's Point, 30·38 inches at Parsonstown, and 30·31 inches in Dublin. This high pressure system soon moved away north-eastwards, and at the same time decreased in size. Simultaneously, a general reduction of atmospheric pressure took place in the N. and N.W., causing steeper gradients for westerly winds—that is, winds between S.W. and N.W., and showery, unsettled weather. On Tuesday and Wednesday rain fell heavily over the N. of Ireland and S. of Scotland, and in smaller quantities over the greater part of the kingdom. Hail fell in many places and lightning was seen at Scilly[illegible] on Wednesday night. On Thursday evening the moon shone with unusual lustre. A decided rise of temperature occurred on Friday, while Saturday was stormy with frequent showers, and, at times, rainbows. In Dublin the mean height of the barometer was 30·029 inches, pressure rising to 30·307 inches at 9 a.m. of Monday (wind, W.) and falling to 29·[illegible] inches at 4 p.m. of Saturday (wind, W.). The corrected mean temperature was 49·5°. The mean of the dry bulb readings at 9 a.m. and 9 p.m. was 49·[illegible]°. On Wednesday the thermometer rose to 59·8° in the screen; on Friday, it fell to 39·[illegible]°. The rainfall was ·184 inch on three days—·109 inch being registered on Wednesday and ·041 inch on Saturday. The prevailing wind was westerly.

The last three days were cool and fair in Ireland—an aurora borealis with auroral streamers was seen about 6 p.m. of Sunday, the 29th, and there was sheet lightning on the evening of the 30th. Sharp frost occurred on the 31st.

The rainfall in Dublin during the ten months ending October 31st amounted to 16·141 inches on 139 days, compared with 19·366 inches on 165 days during the same period in 1887, 19·219 inches on 167 days in 1888, 24·759 inches on 169 days in 1889, 21·494 inches on 163 days in 1890, 21·610 inches on 148 days in 1891, 22·445 inches on 167 days in 1892, and a twenty-five years' average of 22·540 inches on 160·4 days.

At Knockdolian, Greystones, Co. Wicklow, the rainfall in October amounted to only ·710 inch on 15 days. Of this quantity ·225 inch fell on the 17th. The rainfall at Greystones in October, 1889 was no less than 8·935 inches on 22 days, or more than 11 times as great as the fall in October, 1890, when only ·800 inch fell on 13 days. In 1891, 5·122 inches fell on 14 days, and in 1892, 3·310 inches on 13 days. From January 1st, 1893, up to October 31st, rain fell at Knockdolian on 122 days to the total amount of 17·601 inches. In 1892, the rainfall of the corresponding ten months was 27·223 inches on 140 days.

At Clonsvin, Killiney, Co. Dublin, the rainfall in October, was ·710 inch on 14 days, compared with 3·040 inches on 17 days in 1892, and an eight years' average of 3·201 inches on 16 days. Since January 1, 1893, 14·61 inches of rain have fallen at this station, compared with an average of 20·652 inches in the previous eight years.

NOVEMBER.—This was a generally favourable month. Its leading characteristics were—a prevalence of northerly winds, a tolerably low mean temperature, an absence of calm and fog, a moderate rainfall, but a high percentage of cloud.

The memorable storm of the period from the 16th to the 19th inclusive deserves special mention. The cyclonic depression which caused it was of great intensity, the barometer falling in its centre to about 28·7 inches on the morning of the 17th, and the system pursued a very erratic course, travelling in the first instance from S.S.W. to N.N.E., across Ireland and Scotland to the Moray Firth, and then "turning tail" and passing in a south-easterly direction down the east coast of Great Britain to the continent, over which it finally dispersed. The wind-velocity during the northerly gales of this depression was great everywhere, but it was altogether exceptional at Holyhead, where the anemometer registered 1,524 miles of wind in 24 hours, and in the hour 10.30 a.m. to 11.30 a.m. 89 miles were recorded.

A slight shock of earthquake was felt at Greystones, Co. Wicklow, at 5.35 p.m. of the 2nd.

In Dublin the arithmetical mean temperature (43·5°) was decidedly below the average (44·7°); the mean dry bulb readings at 9 a.m. and 9 p.m. were 43·3°. In the twenty-eight years ending with 1892, November was coldest in 1878 (M. T. = 39·2°), and in 1870 (M. T. = 45·2°), and warmest in 1881 (M. T. = 50·2°). In 1884, the M. T. was as high as 46·6°; in the year 1879 (the "cold year") it was 43·9°; in 1887, it was as low as 42·6°; in 1888, it was as high as 47·6°; in 1890, it was 46·4°; in 1890, 44·3°; in 1891, 43·4°; and in 1892, as high as 46·9°.

The mean height of the barometer was 30·058 inches, or 0·108 inch above the corrected average value for November—namely, 29·950 inches. The mercury rose to 30·594 inches at noon of the 21st, having fallen to 28·719 inches at midnight of the 16th. The observed range of atmospherical pressure was therefore, 1·875 inches—that is, slightly less than one inch and nine-tenths.

The mean temperature deduced from daily readings of the dry bulb thermometer at 9 a.m. and 9 p.m. was 43·3°, or 3·8° below the value for October, and 11·3° below that for September, 1893. The arithmetical mean of the maximal and minimal readings was 43·5°, compared with a twenty-five years' average of 44·7°. On the 3rd the thermometer in the screen rose to 57·6°—wind, W.S.W.; on the 7th the temperature fell to 30·6°—wind, calm. The minimum on the grass was 25·0°, also on the 7th.

The rainfall was 1·370 inches, distributed over 17 days—the rainfall was considerably below, while the rainy days were exactly equal to the average. The average rainfall for November in the twenty-five years, 1865–89, inclusive, was 2·431 inches, and the average number of rainy days was 17·0. In 1870 the rainfall in November was large—3·014 inches on 20 days; in 1872, also, 3·414 inches fell on 21 days; in 1887, 3·018 inches fell on 15 days; in 1888, 6·540 inches fell on 26 days; in 1890, 4·212 inches fell on no less than 27 days; in 1891, 2·911 inches fell on 16 days, and in 1892, 2·404 inches on 12 days. On the other hand, the rainfall in 1880 was only ·720 inch on 9 days; in 1870, only 1·315 inches were measured on but 11 days, and in 1879, only 1·251 inches on but 10 days.

High winds were noted on 15 days, but attained the force of a gale on only four occasions—the 16th, 17th, 18th, and 19th. The atmosphere was more or less *foggy* in Dublin on the 4th, 7th, 13th, 14th, and 30th.

A lunar halo was seen on the 21st. Snow or sleet fell on the 8th, 16th, 19th, and 22nd; hail on the 6th, 7th, 19th, 22nd, and 23rd.

With the coming of November, as in 1891, so in 1893, cold frosty weather gave place to comparative warmth and south-westerly winds. A severe frost had visited central England early on Tuesday evening, October 31, but in the course of the following night temperature rose with extreme rapidity, so that Parsonstown was 21° warmer at 8 a.m. on Wednesday, the 1st, than it had been 24 hours previously. On Thursday a secondary V-shaped depression crossed England from W. to E., causing a copious rainfall. Friday was a cloudy, mild, breezy day, but on Saturday a shift of wind to N.E. took place, and the air became drier and colder.

During the week ended Saturday, the 11th, showery, cloudy, and generally changeable weather, with north-easterly winds, prevailed. After Sunday an anticyclone was constantly found to the northwestward of the British Islands, while atmospherical pressure was relatively low both over the Baltic and over the Mediterranean Basin. At first areas of particularly sharp cold were found over the central districts of both England and Ireland—at 8 a.m. of Sunday the thermometer was as low as 23° at Loughborough and 25° at Cambridge and Parsonstown. At the first-named station it had been down to 18° during the previous night. In Dublin this day was fine, dry, and cold, but on Monday morning heavy showers of hail, sleet, and snow came up on a N.E. wind. In the neighbourhood of Stillorgan, Co. Dublin, some three inches of snow lay on the ground to an advanced hour in the forenoon. The frost continued inland, where also the weather remained dry. As usual in N.E. winds, the weather was most severe and broken in the extreme S.E. of England, where thunder and lightning accompanied sharp showers of cold rain and hail on Monday and Tuesday. After Wednesday temperature recovered, although the N.E. wind even freshened, and Saturday proved the coldest day of the whole week. In Dublin the mean height of the barometer was 30·364 inches, pressure ranging from 29·861 inches at 9 a.m. of Sunday (wind, W.N.W.) to 30·405 inches at 9 a.m. of Wednesday (wind, N.N.E.). The corrected mean temperature was 43·6°. The mean dry bulb temperature at 9 a.m. and 9 p.m. was 43·3°. On Tuesday the minimum was 30·8°, on Saturday the maximum was 50·7°. Rain fell on five days in frequent but not heavy showers, the maximal fall in 24 hours being ·040 inch on Wednesday, and the total fall amounting to ·163 inch. Hail, sleet, and snow fell on Monday morning.

The weather during the week ended Saturday, the 18th, was at first anticyclonic, quiet, and fair.

but it afterwards fell into a most unsettled stormy condition, severe gales from opposite quarters blowing on the last three days of the week. At the beginning an anticyclone lay over the British Islands, the North Sea, Holland, and North Germany—the barometer slightly exceeded 30·60 inches in the N.E. of Scotland. On Monday beautiful weather prevailed, but already a depression was advancing northwards across Spain and the Bay of Biscay. This system finally passed up the English Channel on Tuesday, and caused heavy rain both in France and in the S. and S.E. of England—·780 inch of rain fell in *London*, while Dublin got only ·020 inch in the form of a drizzle on Tuesday evening. Wednesday proved fine and dry, but at night the wind veered from E. to S.E., and freshened in front of a very deep depression, which on Thursday night passed directly over *Ireland*, travelling in a north-north-easterly direction. This disturbance brought a heavy rainfall to the Irish and Scotch stations—·631 inch fell in Dublin up to 9 a.m. of Friday, the heaviest fall in this city since July 11, when ·871 inch fell in two thunderstorms. About midnight on Thursday the barometer read 28·719 inches, the lowest reading recorded in Dublin since October 13, 1891, when the mercury fell to 28·361 inches. In front of the cyclonic centre a fresh S.E. gale and high temperature prevailed; in its rear came a violent N. storm and bitter cold on Saturday, when also the depression changed its course and travelled southwards down the North Sea. In Dublin the mean height of the barometer was 29·740 inches, pressure ranging between 30·369 inches at 9 a.m. of Sunday (wind, E.), and 28·719 inches at midnight of Thursday (wind, S.). The corrected mean temperature was 43·0°. The mean dry bulb readings at 9 a.m. and 9 p.m. were 42·3°. On Friday the thermometers in the screen rose to 55·1°, having fallen to 34·6° on Tuesday. The rainfall amounted to ·951 inch on three days—·631 inch being registered on Thursday. Snow showers fell on Saturday afternoon. The prevailing winds were E.S.E. and N.W. At Holyhead a gale from N. of hurricane force was reported on Saturday morning.

Changeable and unsettled weather held during the week ended Saturday, the 25th. At first, bitter northerly gales and showers of snow and hail prevailed in connection with the deep depression which had travelled northwards and then southwards across the British Islands in the closing days of the previous week. As the centre of this disturbance reached the Continent on Sunday morning, the barometer rose with great rapidity over the United Kingdom, so that gradients for northerly winds became excessively steep. The result was a disastrous northerly gale, which strewed the coasts of North-western Europe with wrecks and wreckage. The rise of the barometer continued until Tuesday morning, when the reading was 30·63 inches at Belmullet. Depressions then began to pass eastwards over Northern Europe, with their secondaries spreading south-eastwards over the British Islands, where showers of hail, sleet, or snow again fell plentifully at exposed stations. During Friday and Saturday a deep depression passed directly over our area, causing mild, damp, squally weather and a general fall of rain. The week closed with a finer and clearer state of the atmosphere. In Dublin the mean height of the barometer was 30·212 inches, pressure ranging from 30·594 inches at noon on Tuesday (wind, N.) to 29·457 inches at 9 p.m. of Saturday (wind, W.N.W.). The corrected mean temperature was 41·1°, which was also the value of the mean dry bulb readings at 9 a.m. and 9 p.m. On Thursday the screened thermometers fell to 31·7°, on Saturday they rose to 53·9°. Rain fell in registrable quantity on four days to the total amount of ·214 inch, ·188 inch being measured on Saturday. Snow and hail fell on Sunday and Thursday, hail on Wednesday also. The prevailing winds were N.E. and N.W.

The period from Sunday, the 26th, to Thursday, the 30th, inclusive, was chiefly remarkable for the sudden and extreme changes of temperature which occurred at its beginning and close. On the 26th, the thermometer stood low under the influence of a fresh northerly wind, forming part of the circulation round a depression whose centre had advanced from the N. of Scotland to Denmark by 8 a.m. Monday, the 27th, brought milder, damper weather and freshening westerly winds. The next two days were warm, but blustering, with a good deal of cloud, and squally W.S.W. winds. Rain fell at exposed stations, most heavily in Scotland. In the course of the night of the 29th–30th rain set in afresh, and the wind shifted to the northward, in the rear of a series of V-shaped depressions, which subsequently travelled towards S.E. across North-western Europe. A rapid fall of temperature followed beginning in the far N., and quickly extending southwards. In Dublin the mean height of the barometer during this closing period of the month was 30·034 inches, pressure varying from 30·229 inches at 9 a.m. of Monday (wind, W.) to 29·679 inches at 9 p.m. of Thursday (wind N.N.W.). The corrected mean temperature of the 5 days was 47·6°, the mean dry bulb temperature at 9 a.m. and 9 p.m. being 48·6°. On Sunday, the screened thermometer fell to 36·9°; on Tuesday it rose to 56·3°. Rain fell on the 29th to the amount of ·144 inch; on the 30th to the amount of ·123 inch; total precipitation, ·267 inch. The prevalent winds were N.N.W. and W.S.W.

The rainfall in Dublin during the eleven months ending November 30th amounted to 18·011 inches on 155 days, compared with 15·278 inches on 141 days during the same period in 1887, 25·783 inches on 173 days in 1888, 25·716 inches on 178 days in 1889, 25·703 inches on 183 days in 1890, 24·361 inches on 165 days in 1891, 24·649 inches on 188 days in 1892, and a twenty-five years' average of 25·293 inches on 177·4 days.

At Knockdolian, Greystones, Co. Wicklow, the rainfall in November, 1893, was 1·783 inches, distributed over 17 days. Of this quantity ·320 of an inch fell on the 17th, and ·310 of an inch on the 30th.

From January 1st, 1893, up to November 30th, rain fell at Knockdolian, Greystones, on 150 days, and to the total amount of 19·855 inches.

At Cloneevin, Killiney, Co. Dublin, 1·40 inches of rain fell on 17 days, compared with an eight years' average of 3·048 inches on 16·25 days. The maximal fall in 24 hours was ·31 inch on the 16th. Since January 1st, 1893, 16·01 inches of rain have fallen at this station, compared with an eight years' average of 23·461 inches.

DECEMBER.—A generally open, rainy, squally month. The prevailing trend of the atmospheric depressions was from S.W. to N.E. along the western shores of the British Isles and of Scandinavia. At the close of the month an anticyclone spread westwards from the Continent to the British Isles, and was accompanied by an abrupt fall of temperature, much cloud and fog. The rainfall of the whole month (2·482 inches) was above the average. Several serious gales were felt, but calms with fog prevailed during the closing days of the month.

In Dublin the arithmetical mean temperature (43·8°) was decidedly above the average (41·3°); the mean dry bulb readings at 9 a.m. and 9 p.m. were 43·6°. In the twenty-eight years ending with 1892, December was coldest in 1878 (M. T. = 32·8°), and in 1874 (M. T. = 36·6°), and warmest in 1865 (M. T. = 46·3°). In 1886 the M. T. was as low as 37·9°; in the year 1879 (the "cold year") it was also 37·9°. In 1887 the M. T. was 39·0°; in 1888, 43·6°; in 1889 43·4°; in 1890 39·5°; in 1891, 43·6°; and in 1892 39·6°.

The mean height of the barometer was 29·658 inches, or 0·013 inch below the corrected average value for December—namely, 29·675 inches. The mercury rose to 30·706 inches at 9 a.m. of the 30th, and fell to 28·530 inches at noon of the 10th. The observed range of atmospheric pressure was, therefore, no less than 2·176 inches—that is, a little less than two inches and two-tenths.

The mean temperature deduced from daily readings of the dry bulb thermometer at 9 a.m. and 9 p.m. was 42·8°, or only 0·5° below the value for November, and 6·0° below that for October, 1893. Using the formula, *Mean Temp.* = *Min.* + (*max.*—*min.* × ·52), the value was 43·7°, or 2·2° above the average mean temperature for December, calculated in the same way, in the twenty-five years 1865-89, inclusive (41·5°). The arithmetical mean of the maximal and minimal readings was 43·8°, compared with a twenty-five years' average of 41·3°. On the 15th the thermometer in the screen rose to 56·7°—wind, S.W.; on the 2nd the temperature fell to 29·3°—wind, W.N.W. The minimum on the grass was 23·0° also on the 2nd. There were only 8 days of frost in the screen and 16 days of frost on the grass.

The rainfall was 2·482 inches, distributed over as many as 19 days. The average rainfall for December in the twenty-five years, 1865-89, was 2·404 inches, and the average number of rainy days was 16·2. The rainfall, therefore, and the rainy days were above the average. In 1876 the rainfall in December was very large—7·165 inches on 22 days. In 1872, 4·239 inches fell on as many as 24 days; and in 1868 (which was otherwise a fine and dry year) 4·749 inches fell on as many as 27 days. On the other hand, in 1867, only ·771 inch was measured on 18 days; and in 1871 the December rainfall was only ·797 inch on 16 days. In 1885, only ·752 inch of rain was measured on but 16 days, but in 1886 the rainfall was 3·246 inches, distributed over as many as 21 days. In 1887 (the "dry year") the rainfall was 1·912 inches on 19 days; in 1888, 2·011 inches on 17 days; in 1889, 1·354 inches on 15 days; in 1890, 1·030 inches on 11 days, in 1891, 3·428 inches on 21 days; and in 1892, only ·798 inch on 10 days.

Lunar halos appeared on the 14th and 18th. High winds were noted on 17 days, and attained the force of a gale on five occasions—the 6th, 8th, 10th, 14th, and the 19th. The atmosphere was more or less foggy in Dublin on the 2nd, 17th, 27th, 28th, 29th, 30th, and 31st. Neither snow nor sleet fell in Dublin, although the mountains were covered with snow on the 18th and 20th. Hail fell on the 18th. Thunder and lightning occurred on the 8th.

Cold, bright weather prevailed during the two days of the month, especially in Ireland, where an anticyclone of considerable intensity formed on Friday, the 1st, in the wake of two depressions which had passed south-eastwards across Western Europe immediately before. The frost in Scotland was very sharp on the morning of the 1st, and the wave of cold travelled southwards, so that at 8 a.m. of the 2nd the thermometer read only 17° at Loughborough.

As regards the week ended Saturday, the 9th, at first the weather was mild and damp in Ireland, rainy in Scotland, very frosty in the E. and S.E. of England. Thus at 8 a.m. of Sunday the thermometer registered 49° at Belmullet, 45° at Stornoway, in the Hebrides, where 1·2 inches of rain had fallen in the previous 24 hours; but only 21 in London. An anticyclone in which the barometer exceeded 30·4 inches, lay over the S.W. of Ireland; but a cyclonic system was skirting the north coast of Scotland. On Tuesday the barometer gave way quickly as a series of large and deep atmospheric depressions began to encroach on the shores of the North-west of Europe from the Atlantic. These, as usual, brought unsettled weather, high but unsteady temperatures, gales and rains, to the greater part of the British Isles. On Thursday night a depression of exceptional magnitude rapidly passed northeastwards outside the north-west and north coasts of Ireland. The barometer fell to 28·17 inches at Malin Head on Friday morning, and to 27·97 inches at Stornoway at 4 p.m. of the same day. During the preceding night strong S.W. and W.S.W. gales and thunder and hail showers prevailed at many stations, and these were renewed in the course of Friday afternoon. At Navan, Co. Meath, lumps of ice fell in a thunder-shower towards evening. At night lightning was seen on the N.W. horizon from Dublin. Saturday was a bright, cold day and the week closed with a promise of frost, which, however, was not fulfilled. In Dublin the mean height of the barometer was 29·317 inches. Pressure varied from 30·398 inches at 9 a.m. of Sunday (wind, W.), to 28·637 inches at 7.30 a.m. of Friday (wind, W.S.W.). The corrected mean temperature was 44·9°. The mean dry bulb temperature at 9 a.m. and 9 p.m. was 44·1°. On Sunday the screened thermometers sank to 35·7°, on Wednesday they rose to 56·1°. The rainfall amounted to ·333 inch on three days. The maximal fall in 24 hours was ·179 inch on Thursday. The prevalent winds were W.N.W., W., and W.S.W.

Atmospheric pressure and temperature were in a most unstable condition throughout the N. and W. of Europe and over the adjoining parts of the North Atlantic during the week ended Saturday, the 16th. Consequently, the weather was extremely unsettled, strong southerly and south-westerly gales prevailed, and heavy rainfalls occurred on all exposed coasts. On Sunday a very deep depression advanced northeastwards over Ireland. Strong S.E. to S.W. gales blew and heavy rain fell on the S. and E. coasts and over the Irish Sea during the forenoon. In Dublin the barometer fell to

29·430 inches about midday. During the next two days a number of subsidiary depressions crossed England, keeping the weather unsettled and showery. A thunderstorm occurred at Valentia Island on Monday night, and lightning was seen over the North Channel at the same time. Early on Wednesday morning a new and very deep depression was found over Central Ireland, where the barometer scarcely exceeded 29·1 inches (29·03 inches at Parsonstown, King's Co.). As pressure was at this time everywhere low, no serious gales followed, but rain fell abundantly in nearly all parts of the United Kingdom. A singularly rapid recovery of atmospheric pressure ensued, so that the Thursday morning readings exceeded those of Wednesday morning by 1·31 inches at Parsonstown, 1·29 inches in Dublin and at Valentia, and 1·23 inches at Roche's Point, Co. Cork. An anticyclone now formed over France, where temperature fell fast; but strong S.W. winds and gales, and high readings of the thermometer were reported from Ireland, Scotland, and many parts of England on both Friday and Saturday. In Dublin the mean atmospheric pressure was 29·[illegible] inches, the barometer ranging between 29·[illegible] inches at 9 a.m. of Wednesday (wind, S.S.W.) and 30·[illegible] inches at 1 a.m. of Saturday (wind, S.W.). The corrected mean temperature was 49·3°; the mean dry bulb readings at 9 a.m. and 9 p.m. were 48·1°. On Friday the screened thermometers rose to 56·7°, having fallen to 33·[illegible]° the previous day. The rainfall was ·[illegible] inch on five days, ·[illegible] inch being measured on Tuesday and ·211 inch on Sunday. The prevalent wind was S.W. Gales occurred from S.E. on Sunday, and from S.W. on Friday.

Throughout the week ended Saturday, the 23rd, atmospheric pressure remained in a very disturbed condition, rain fell frequently—in Ireland and Scotland in particular—and blustering S.W. and W. winds or gales were very prevalent, especially from Tuesday to Friday inclusive. The barometer stood highest for the most part over the Peninsula and Central Europe, lowest off our extreme W. and N.W. coasts. Hence, the winds were strong from S.W. and W. Sunday was fine, bright and mild, but rain fell at night. Monday was colder, and snow lay on the higher ranges of the Dublin Mountains. The barometer fell fast during the ensuing night, and the wind rose to a gale from S. At 8 a.m. of Tuesday the barometer was down to 28·[illegible] inches at Belmullet, in Mayo. In the course of Tuesday night a still deeper secondary depression advanced to St. George's Channel from the S.W., the barometer reading only 28·80 inches at Pembroke and 28·64 inches at Roche's Point at 8 a.m. of Wednesday. This low pressure system brought with it gales and heavy rains—a strong S.W. gale being felt in the S. of England and a violent N.W. gale over the western parts of the English Channel. Hail fell in the W. and N. of Ireland and thunder occurred at Ardrossan. Thursday was a fine, bright day, but on Friday forenoon another rainfall occurred in Ireland. This was followed by a beautiful day, with which the week closed. In Dublin the mean height of the barometer was only 29·[illegible] inches, pressure ranging between 30·166 inches at 9 a.m. of Sunday (wind, S. by W.), and 28·784 inches at 9 a.m. of Wednesday (wind, N.N.E.). The corrected mean temperature was 44·0°. The mean dry bulb readings at 9 a.m. and 9 p.m. were 43·0°. On Thursday the thermometers sank to 34·[illegible]°; on Friday they rose to 52·6°, in the screen. The prevailing direction of the wind was S.W. Rain fell on each day of the week to the total amount of ·[illegible] inch, ·[illegible] inch being measured on Tuesday.

The week ended Saturday, the 30th, witnessed the gradual substitution of anticyclonic for cyclonic conditions over the extreme West of Europe, and the consequent dying out of the strong, squally S.W. winds which had so long been blowing. It also saw the establishment of calms and fogs, as well as a general and decided fall of temperature towards the close of the period. At the beginning, depressions skirted the west coasts of Ireland and Scotland, and rain fell heavily in those countries and in smaller quantities over England. On Sunday a warm, bright morning was followed by a downpour of rain in Dublin, where the measurement was just half an inch. Christmas Day (Monday) was finer and cooler, but sharp showers fell shortly after midday in this city. A succession of mild, dull, damp days followed, and in London dense dark fogs prevailed on Wednesday and the next two days. By Saturday, however, an anticyclone of great size and intensity had been fully established over central and western Europe and the weather brightened and became much colder. At 8 a.m. of Friday the barometer stood at 30·79 inches over the North of Germany, and the thermometer was as low as 3° F. at Munich, having fallen there 23° in the previous twenty-four hours. On Friday evening barometer rose to 30·[illegible] inches in Berlin. Sharp frost held in Germany, France, and the centre of England on Saturday. In Dublin the mean height of the barometer was 30·319 inches, pressure ranging between 29·841 inches at 9 p.m. of Sunday (wind, W.S.W.) and 30·708 inches at 9 a.m. of Saturday (wind, S.). The corrected mean temperature was 46·4°. The mean dry bulb readings at 9 a.m. and 9 p.m. were 45·6°. On Sunday the maximum in the shade was 55·8°; on Saturday the minimum was 33·9°. Rain fell on four days to the total amount of ·[illegible] inch; ·[illegible] inch being measured on Sunday. The prevailing winds were southwesterly.

Sunday, the 31st, was a raw, damp, very cold day in Dublin. In the morning a dense vapour fog prevailed, and as the thermometer stood below freezing point thick rime was deposited on trees and shrubs. On this day the distribution of both atmospheric pressure and temperature over Western Europe was peculiar. An anticyclone had its centre over the southern half of Ireland, the barometer reading 30·[illegible] inches at 8 a.m. at Parsonstown. A deep depression was at the same moment travelling eastwards across the north of Russia, the barometer being as low as 28·00 inches at Archangel. The thermometer at the hour named read 46° at Malin Head, but only 31° at Valentia Island in Kerry and 27° at Parsonstown. Dublin was 11° colder than Holyhead. At Nairn, in the N.E. of Scotland, the temperature was 48°, in Paris it was 18°, or 31° lower. On the Christiania Fjord it was 43°, at Biarritz 25°, and at Munich 1°. Scilly was [illegible]° warmer than London (44° compared with [illegible]°), and Stockholm was 8° warmer than Nice (37° against 29°).

The rainfall in Dublin during the year ending December 31st amounted to only 20·[illegible] inches on 174 days, compared with 23·344 inches on 1[illegible] days in 1892, 27·[illegible] inches on 184 days in 1891, 27·[illegible] inches on 200 days in 1890, 27·[illegible] inches on 1[illegible] days in 1889, [illegible] inches on 190 days in 1888, 16·601 inches on 160 days in 1887, and a 25 years' average of 27·696 inches on 194·3 days.

At Knockdolian, Greystones, Co. Wicklow, the rainfall in December, 1893, was 2·940 inches, distributed over 20 days. Of this quantity ·440 inch fell on the 12th and ·420 inch on the 18th.

From January 1st to December 31st, 1893, rain fell at Knockdolian, Greystones, on 170 days, and to the total amount of 23·586 inches.

At Clonsevin, Killiney, Co. Dublin, 3·04 inches of rain fell during December on 20 days. The maximal fall in 24 hours being ·29 inch on the 19th. The average rainfall for December at this station is 2·117 inches on 15 days.

From January 1st to December 31st, 1893, rain fell at Clonsevin, Killiney, on 176 days to the total amount of 19·03 inches.

RAINFALL IN 1893,

At 40 Fitzwilliam-square, West, Dublin.

Rain Gauge:—Diameter of funnel, 8 in. Height of top—Above ground, 3 ft. 8 in.; above sea level, 50 ft.

Month.	Total Depth.	Greatest Fall in 24 hours.		Number of Days on which ·01 or more fell.	Month.	Total Depth.	Greatest Fall in 24 hours.		Number of Days on which ·01 or more fell.
	Inches.	Depth.	Date.			Inches.	Depth.	Date.	
January,	[illegible]	[illegible]	[illegible]	[illegible]	August,	[illegible]	[illegible]	[illegible]	[illegible]
February,	[illegible]	·440	[illegible]	[illegible]	September,	[illegible]	·174	[illegible]	[illegible]
March,	[illegible]	[illegible]	[illegible]	[illegible]	October,	[illegible]	·371	[illegible]	[illegible]
April,	[illegible]	·100	[illegible]	[illegible]	November,	[illegible]	·831	[illegible]	17
May,	[illegible]	·720	[illegible]	[illegible]	December,	[illegible]	[illegible]	[illegible]	19
June,	[illegible]	[illegible]	[illegible]	[illegible]					
July,	[illegible]	·871	12th	[illegible]	Total,	[illegible]	–	–	174

The rainfall was 7·203 inches in defect of the average annual measurement of the twenty-five years, 1865–89, inclusive—viz., 27·696 inches.

It will be remembered that the rainfall in 1887 was very exceptionally small—16·601 inches, the only approach to this measurement in Dublin being in 1870, when only 20·859 inches fell, in 1884, when the measurement was 20·467 inches, and in 1893 with its rainfall of 20·493 inches. In seven of the twenty-five years in question the rainfall was less than 25 inches, and in 1885 it was 20·614 inches.

The scanty rainfall in 1887 was in marked contrast to the abundant downpour in 1886, when 32·954 inches—or as nearly as possible double the fall of 1887—fell on 220 days. Only twice since these records commenced has the rainfall in Dublin exceeded that of 1886—namely, in 1872, when 35·566 inches fell on 233 days, and in 1880, when 34·512 inches were measured on, however, only 183 days.

In 1893, there were 174 rainy days, or days upon which not less than ·01 inch of rain (one hundredth of an inch) was measured. This was considerably in defect of the average number of rainy days, which was 194·3 in the twenty-five years, 1865–89, inclusive. In 1868—the warm dry year of recent times—as well as in 1887, the rainy days were only 160, and in 1870 they were only 145. In 1868, however, the rainfall amounted to 24·935 inches, or more than 8 inches above the measurement in 1887, and even in 1870, 20·859 inches were recorded.

The rainfall in 24 hours from 9 a.m. to 9 a.m. exceeded one inch on two occasions in 1892—viz., May 25th (2·056 inches), and August 12th (1·310 inches). On no occasion in 1893 did one inch of rain fall on a given day in Dublin, the maximal daily measurements were ·871 inch on July 12th, and ·831 inch on November 18th.

Included in the 174 rainy days in 1893 are 17 on which snow or sleet fell, and 21 on which there was hail. In January hail was observed on 4 days, in February on 6 days, in March on 2 days, in April, August, and October on 1 day, in November on 5 days, and on one day in December. Snow or sleet fell on 4 days in January, on 7 days in February, on 2 days in March, on 4 days in November, and on but one occasion in December. Thunder occurred on ten occasions during the year—three times in May, twice in July and August, and once in June, September, and December. Lightning was also seen on four occasions in October, twice in August and September, and once in February and December.

The rainfall was distributed as follows:—5·198 inches fell on 49 days in the first quarter, 4·428 inches on 39 days in the second, 5·484 inches on 44 days in the third, and 5·384 inches on 43 days in the fourth and last quarter.

The rainfall in the first six months was 9·624 inches, on 78 days—that is, not one-half of the year's record. In February the rainfall was 2·668 inches on 23 days, in August 2·713 inches fell on 16 days, and in December 2·452 inches on 19 days.

Of the 5·251 inches which fell in the fourth quarter of the year, only 1·033 inches were measured in October on 18 days, and 1·670 inches in November on 17 days. In December the rainfall was both considerable and frequent.

Aurora borealis was observed on three occasions—namely, on February 16th, September 1st, and October 29th. More or less fog prevailed on 32 occasions—4 in January, 3 in February, 8 in March, 3 in April, 5 in August, September, and October, respectively; 3 in November, and 7 in December. The March fogs were very dry. High winds were noted on 130 days—16 in January, 11 in February and March, respectively; 6 in April and May, respectively; 7 in June, 9 in July, 10 in August, 14 in September, 10 in October, 13 in November, and 17 in December. The high winds amounted to gales (force 7 or upwards according to the Beaufort scale) on 24 occasions—4 in January and February, respectively; 1 in March and June, respectively; 3 in August, 3 in October, 4 in November, and 5 in December.

Abstract of Meteorological Observations taken at Dublin (89 Fitzwilliam-square, West), during the Year 1893.

Month.	Abs. Max.	Date.	Abs. Min.	Date.	Mean Dry Bulb Max.	Mean Dry Bulb Min.	Rainfall.	Rainy Days.	Max. fall in 24 hours.	Highest Pressure.	Date.	Lowest Pressure.	Date.	Prevalent Winds.
	°		°		°	°	Ins.		Ins.	Ins.		Ins.		
January,	[illegible]	[illegible]	[illegible]	[illegible]	[illegible]	[illegible]	[illegible]	[illegible]	[illegible]	[illegible]	[illegible]	[illegible]	[illegible]	W., N.W.
February,	[illegible]	[illegible]	[illegible]	[illegible]	[illegible]	[illegible]	[illegible]	[illegible]	[illegible]	[illegible]	[illegible]	[illegible]	[illegible]	[illegible]
March,	[illegible]	[illegible]	[illegible]	[illegible]	[illegible]	[illegible]	[illegible]	[illegible]	[illegible]	[illegible]	[illegible]	[illegible]	[illegible]	[illegible]
April,	[illegible]	[illegible]	[illegible]	[illegible]	[illegible]	[illegible]	[illegible]	[illegible]	[illegible]	[illegible]	[illegible]	[illegible]	[illegible]	[illegible]
May,	[illegible]	[illegible]	[illegible]	[illegible]	[illegible]	[illegible]	[illegible]	[illegible]	[illegible]	[illegible]	[illegible]	[illegible]	[illegible]	[illegible]
June,	[illegible]	[illegible]	[illegible]	[illegible]	[illegible]	[illegible]	[illegible]	[illegible]	[illegible]	[illegible]	[illegible]	[illegible]	[illegible]	[illegible]
July,	[illegible]	[illegible]	[illegible]	[illegible]	[illegible]	[illegible]	[illegible]	[illegible]	[illegible]	[illegible]	[illegible]	[illegible]	[illegible]	[illegible]
August,	[illegible]	[illegible]	[illegible]	[illegible]	[illegible]	[illegible]	[illegible]	[illegible]	[illegible]	[illegible]	[illegible]	[illegible]	[illegible]	[illegible]
September,	[illegible]	[illegible]	[illegible]	[illegible]	[illegible]	[illegible]	[illegible]	[illegible]	[illegible]	[illegible]	[illegible]	[illegible]	[illegible]	[illegible]
October,	[illegible]	[illegible]	[illegible]	[illegible]	[illegible]	[illegible]	[illegible]	[illegible]	[illegible]	[illegible]	[illegible]	[illegible]	[illegible]	[illegible]
November,	[illegible]	[illegible]	[illegible]	[illegible]	[illegible]	[illegible]	[illegible]	[illegible]	[illegible]	[illegible]	[illegible]	[illegible]	[illegible]	[illegible]
December,	[illegible]	[illegible]	[illegible]	[illegible]	[illegible]	[illegible]	[illegible]	[illegible]	[illegible]	[illegible]	[illegible]	[illegible]	[illegible]	[illegible]
Averages, Totals, and Extremes	[illegible]	Aug. [illegible]	[illegible]	[illegible]	[illegible]	[illegible]	Ins. [illegible]	Days [illegible]	Ins. [illegible]	Ins. [illegible]	[illegible]	Ins. [illegible]	[illegible]	[illegible]

RAINFALL AT KILLINEY, CO. DUBLIN, IN 1893.

Mr. Robert O'Brien Furlong, M.A., Univ. Dubl., reports that rain fell in 1893, at his residence, Clonmevin, Killiney, Co. Dublin, on 176 days to the total amount of 18·03 inches. The average figures for eight years were 25·118 inches on 174·25 days. In 1887—the Jubilee year—the rainfall at this station was only 17·44 inches on but 148 days. In that year 1·65 inches fell on one day. The maximal fall on any one day in 1893 was only ·63 inch on April 16. Periods of absolute drought—14 days without rain—occurred from April 1 to 14 and from June 7 to 21. From March 19 to April 14 only ·07 inch fell.

TABLE showing the Monthly and Yearly Rainfall at Dublin during the Twenty-one Years 1873 to 1893, inclusive; with the Means for the Twenty Years 1873 to 1892.

Year.	January.	February.	March.	April.	May.	June.	July.	August.	September.	October.	November.	December.	Total Rainfall.
	Inches.	Inches.	Inches.	Inches.	Inches.	Inches.	Inches.	Inches.	Inches.	Inches.	Inches.	Inches.	Inches.
1873,	[illegible]	[illegible]	[illegible]	[illegible]	[illegible]	[illegible]	[illegible]	[illegible]	[illegible]	[illegible]	[illegible]	[illegible]	[illegible]
1874,	[illegible]	[illegible]	[illegible]	[illegible]	[illegible]	[illegible]	[illegible]	[illegible]	[illegible]	[illegible]	[illegible]	[illegible]	[illegible]
1875,	[illegible]	[illegible]	[illegible]	[illegible]	[illegible]	[illegible]	[illegible]	[illegible]	[illegible]	[illegible]	[illegible]	[illegible]	[illegible]
1876,	[illegible]	[illegible]	[illegible]	[illegible]	[illegible]	[illegible]	[illegible]	[illegible]	[illegible]	[illegible]	[illegible]	[illegible]	[illegible]
1877,	[illegible]	[illegible]	[illegible]	[illegible]	[illegible]	[illegible]	[illegible]	[illegible]	[illegible]	[illegible]	[illegible]	[illegible]	[illegible]
1878,	[illegible]	[illegible]	[illegible]	[illegible]	[illegible]	[illegible]	[illegible]	[illegible]	[illegible]	[illegible]	[illegible]	[illegible]	[illegible]
1879,	[illegible]	[illegible]	[illegible]	[illegible]	[illegible]	[illegible]	[illegible]	[illegible]	[illegible]	[illegible]	[illegible]	[illegible]	[illegible]
1880,	[illegible]	[illegible]	[illegible]	[illegible]	[illegible]	[illegible]	[illegible]	[illegible]	[illegible]	[illegible]	[illegible]	[illegible]	[illegible]
1881,	[illegible]	[illegible]	[illegible]	[illegible]	[illegible]	[illegible]	[illegible]	[illegible]	[illegible]	[illegible]	[illegible]	[illegible]	[illegible]
1882,	[illegible]	[illegible]	[illegible]	[illegible]	[illegible]	[illegible]	[illegible]	[illegible]	[illegible]	[illegible]	[illegible]	[illegible]	[illegible]
1883,	[illegible]	[illegible]	[illegible]	[illegible]	[illegible]	[illegible]	[illegible]	[illegible]	[illegible]	[illegible]	[illegible]	[illegible]	[illegible]
1884,	[illegible]	[illegible]	[illegible]	[illegible]	[illegible]	[illegible]	[illegible]	[illegible]	[illegible]	[illegible]	[illegible]	[illegible]	[illegible]
1885,	[illegible]	[illegible]	[illegible]	[illegible]	[illegible]	[illegible]	[illegible]	[illegible]	[illegible]	[illegible]	[illegible]	[illegible]	[illegible]
1886,	[illegible]	[illegible]	[illegible]	[illegible]	[illegible]	[illegible]	[illegible]	[illegible]	[illegible]	[illegible]	[illegible]	[illegible]	[illegible]
1887,	[illegible]	[illegible]	[illegible]	[illegible]	[illegible]	[illegible]	[illegible]	[illegible]	[illegible]	[illegible]	[illegible]	[illegible]	[illegible]
1888,	[illegible]	[illegible]	[illegible]	[illegible]	[illegible]	[illegible]	[illegible]	[illegible]	[illegible]	[illegible]	[illegible]	[illegible]	[illegible]
1889,	[illegible]	[illegible]	[illegible]	[illegible]	[illegible]	[illegible]	[illegible]	[illegible]	[illegible]	[illegible]	[illegible]	[illegible]	[illegible]
1890,	[illegible]	[illegible]	[illegible]	[illegible]	[illegible]	[illegible]	[illegible]	[illegible]	[illegible]	[illegible]	[illegible]	[illegible]	[illegible]
1891,	[illegible]	[illegible]	[illegible]	[illegible]	[illegible]	[illegible]	[illegible]	[illegible]	[illegible]	[illegible]	[illegible]	[illegible]	[illegible]
1892,	[illegible]	[illegible]	[illegible]	[illegible]	[illegible]	[illegible]	[illegible]	[illegible]	[illegible]	[illegible]	[illegible]	[illegible]	[illegible]
Means,	[illegible]	[illegible]	[illegible]	[illegible]	[illegible]	[illegible]	[illegible]	[illegible]	[illegible]	[illegible]	[illegible]	[illegible]	[illegible]
1893,	[illegible]	[illegible]	[illegible]	[illegible]	[illegible]	[illegible]	[illegible]	[illegible]	[illegible]	[illegible]	[illegible]	[illegible]	[illegible]

* February, 18[illegible], was the driest month of the [illegible] years. † December, 18[illegible], was the month of the [illegible] rainfall.
‡ [illegible], was the wettest month of the [illegible] years. § [illegible] rainfall in 24 hours [illegible] inches, on October [illegible], [illegible].

TABLE showing the Monthly and Yearly Number of Rainy Days* at Dublin during the Twenty-one Years 1873 to 1893, inclusive; with the Means for the Twenty Years 1873 to 1892.

Year.	January.	February.	March.	April.	May.	June.	July.	August.	September.	October.	November.	December.	Total Rainy Days.
1873,	[illegible]	[illegible]	[illegible]	[illegible]	[illegible]	[illegible]	[illegible]	[illegible]	[illegible]	[illegible]	[illegible]	[illegible]	[illegible]
1874,	[illegible]	[illegible]	[illegible]	[illegible]	[illegible]	[illegible]	[illegible]	[illegible]	[illegible]	[illegible]	[illegible]	[illegible]	[illegible]
1875,	[illegible]	[illegible]	[illegible]	[illegible]	[illegible]	[illegible]	[illegible]	[illegible]	[illegible]	[illegible]	[illegible]	[illegible]	[illegible]
1876,	[illegible]	[illegible]	[illegible]	[illegible]	[illegible]	[illegible]	[illegible]	[illegible]	[illegible]	[illegible]	[illegible]	[illegible]	[illegible]
1877,	[illegible]	[illegible]	[illegible]	[illegible]	[illegible]	[illegible]	[illegible]	[illegible]	[illegible]	[illegible]	[illegible]	[illegible]	[illegible]
1878,	[illegible]	[illegible]	[illegible]	[illegible]	[illegible]	[illegible]	[illegible]	[illegible]	[illegible]	[illegible]	[illegible]	[illegible]	[illegible]
1879,	[illegible]	[illegible]	[illegible]	[illegible]	[illegible]	[illegible]	[illegible]	[illegible]	[illegible]	[illegible]	[illegible]	[illegible]	[illegible]
1880,	[illegible]	[illegible]	[illegible]	[illegible]	[illegible]	[illegible]	[illegible]	[illegible]	[illegible]	[illegible]	[illegible]	[illegible]	[illegible]
1881,	[illegible]	[illegible]	[illegible]	[illegible]	[illegible]	[illegible]	[illegible]	[illegible]	[illegible]	[illegible]	[illegible]	[illegible]	[illegible]
1882,	[illegible]	[illegible]	[illegible]	[illegible]	[illegible]	[illegible]	[illegible]	[illegible]	[illegible]	[illegible]	[illegible]	[illegible]	[illegible]
1883,	[illegible]	[illegible]	[illegible]	[illegible]	[illegible]	[illegible]	[illegible]	[illegible]	[illegible]	[illegible]	[illegible]	[illegible]	[illegible]
1884,	[illegible]	[illegible]	[illegible]	[illegible]	[illegible]	[illegible]	[illegible]	[illegible]	[illegible]	[illegible]	[illegible]	[illegible]	[illegible]
1885,	[illegible]	[illegible]	[illegible]	[illegible]	[illegible]	[illegible]	[illegible]	[illegible]	[illegible]	[illegible]	[illegible]	[illegible]	[illegible]
1886,	[illegible]	[illegible]	[illegible]	[illegible]	[illegible]	[illegible]	[illegible]	[illegible]	[illegible]	[illegible]	[illegible]	[illegible]	[illegible]
1887,	[illegible]	[illegible]	[illegible]	[illegible]	[illegible]	[illegible]	[illegible]	[illegible]	[illegible]	[illegible]	[illegible]	[illegible]	[illegible]
1888,	[illegible]	[illegible]	[illegible]	[illegible]	[illegible]	[illegible]	[illegible]	[illegible]	[illegible]	[illegible]	[illegible]	[illegible]	[illegible]
1889,	[illegible]	[illegible]	[illegible]	[illegible]	[illegible]	[illegible]	[illegible]	[illegible]	[illegible]	[illegible]	[illegible]	[illegible]	[illegible]
1890,	[illegible]	[illegible]	[illegible]	[illegible]	[illegible]	[illegible]	[illegible]	[illegible]	[illegible]	[illegible]	[illegible]	[illegible]	[illegible]
1891,	[illegible]	[illegible]	[illegible]	[illegible]	[illegible]	[illegible]	[illegible]	[illegible]	[illegible]	[illegible]	[illegible]	[illegible]	[illegible]
1892,	[illegible]	[illegible]	[illegible]	[illegible]	[illegible]	[illegible]	[illegible]	[illegible]	[illegible]	[illegible]	[illegible]	[illegible]	[illegible]
Means,	[illegible]	[illegible]	[illegible]	[illegible]	[illegible]	[illegible]	[illegible]	[illegible]	[illegible]	[illegible]	[illegible]	[illegible]	[illegible]
1893,	[illegible]	[illegible]	[illegible]	[illegible]	[illegible]	[illegible]	[illegible]	[illegible]	[illegible]	[illegible]	[illegible]	[illegible]	[illegible]

* i.e. days on which [illegible] of rain [illegible] in 24 hours. † [illegible] month of the twenty-one years. [illegible]
‡ [illegible] month of the twenty-one years. [illegible] § [illegible]

TABLE showing the Temperature of the Air in Dublin in the Twenty-one Years 1873–1893, and the Average Temperature for the Twenty Years 1873 to 1892, inclusive, as recorded by Dr. J. W. Moore.

Years.	January.	February.	March.	April.	May.	June.	July.	August.	September.	October.	November.	December.	Year.
1873,	[illegible]	[illegible]	[illegible]	[illegible]	[illegible]	[illegible]	[illegible]	[illegible]	[illegible]	[illegible]	[illegible]	[illegible]	[illegible]
1874,	[illegible]	[illegible]	[illegible]	[illegible]	[illegible]	[illegible]	[illegible]	[illegible]	[illegible]	[illegible]	[illegible]	[illegible]	[illegible]
1875,	[illegible]	[illegible]	[illegible]	[illegible]	[illegible]	[illegible]	[illegible]	[illegible]	[illegible]	[illegible]	[illegible]	[illegible]	[illegible]
1876,	[illegible]	[illegible]	[illegible]	[illegible]	[illegible]	[illegible]	[illegible]	[illegible]	[illegible]	[illegible]	[illegible]	[illegible]	[illegible]
1877,	[illegible]	[illegible]	[illegible]	[illegible]	[illegible]	[illegible]	[illegible]	[illegible]	[illegible]	[illegible]	[illegible]	[illegible]	[illegible]
1878,	[illegible]	[illegible]	[illegible]	[illegible]	[illegible]	[illegible]	[illegible]	[illegible]	[illegible]	[illegible]	[illegible]	[illegible]	[illegible]
1879,	[illegible]	[illegible]	[illegible]	[illegible]	[illegible]	[illegible]	[illegible]	[illegible]	[illegible]	[illegible]	[illegible]	[illegible]	[illegible]
1880,	[illegible]	[illegible]	[illegible]	[illegible]	[illegible]	[illegible]	[illegible]	[illegible]	[illegible]	[illegible]	[illegible]	[illegible]	[illegible]
1881,	[illegible]	[illegible]	[illegible]	[illegible]	[illegible]	[illegible]	[illegible]	[illegible]	[illegible]	[illegible]	[illegible]	[illegible]	[illegible]
1882,	[illegible]	[illegible]	[illegible]	[illegible]	[illegible]	[illegible]	[illegible]	[illegible]	[illegible]	[illegible]	[illegible]	[illegible]	[illegible]
1883,	[illegible]	[illegible]	[illegible]	[illegible]	[illegible]	[illegible]	[illegible]	[illegible]	[illegible]	[illegible]	[illegible]	[illegible]	[illegible]
1884,	[illegible]	[illegible]	[illegible]	[illegible]	[illegible]	[illegible]	[illegible]	[illegible]	[illegible]	[illegible]	[illegible]	[illegible]	[illegible]
1885,	[illegible]	[illegible]	[illegible]	[illegible]	[illegible]	[illegible]	[illegible]	[illegible]	[illegible]	[illegible]	[illegible]	[illegible]	[illegible]
1886,	[illegible]	[illegible]	[illegible]	[illegible]	[illegible]	[illegible]	[illegible]	[illegible]	[illegible]	[illegible]	[illegible]	[illegible]	[illegible]
1887,	[illegible]	[illegible]	[illegible]	[illegible]	[illegible]	[illegible]	[illegible]	[illegible]	[illegible]	[illegible]	[illegible]	[illegible]	[illegible]
1888,	[illegible]	[illegible]	[illegible]	[illegible]	[illegible]	[illegible]	[illegible]	[illegible]	[illegible]	[illegible]	[illegible]	[illegible]	[illegible]
1889,	[illegible]	[illegible]	[illegible]	[illegible]	[illegible]	[illegible]	[illegible]	[illegible]	[illegible]	[illegible]	[illegible]	[illegible]	[illegible]
1890,	[illegible]	[illegible]	[illegible]	[illegible]	[illegible]	[illegible]	[illegible]	[illegible]	[illegible]	[illegible]	[illegible]	[illegible]	[illegible]
1891,	[illegible]	[illegible]	[illegible]	[illegible]	[illegible]	[illegible]	[illegible]	[illegible]	[illegible]	[illegible]	[illegible]	[illegible]	[illegible]
1892,	[illegible]	[illegible]	[illegible]	[illegible]	[illegible]	[illegible]	[illegible]	[illegible]	[illegible]	[illegible]	[illegible]	[illegible]	[illegible]
Average,	[illegible]	[illegible]	[illegible]	[illegible]	[illegible]	[illegible]	[illegible]	[illegible]	[illegible]	[illegible]	[illegible]	[illegible]	[illegible]
1893,	[illegible]	[illegible]	[illegible]	[illegible]	[illegible]	[illegible]	[illegible]	[illegible]	[illegible]	[illegible]	[illegible]	[illegible]	[illegible]

DUBLIN CASTLE,

25th *August*, 1894.

SIR,

I have to acknowledge the receipt of your letter of the 24th instant, forwarding, for submission to His Excellency the Lord Lieutenant, a copy of the Agricultural Statistics of Ireland for the Year 1893.

I am, Sir,

Your obedient servant,

D. HARREL.

The Registrar-General,

Charlemont House,

Rutland Square.

www.ingramcontent.com/pod-product-compliance
Lightning Source LLC
Chambersburg PA
CBHW030558270326
41927CB00007B/972

9783742810496